Actology

Actology

Action, Change, and Diversity in the Western Philosophical Tradition

MALCOLM TORRY

RESOURCE *Publications* · Eugene, Oregon

ACTOLOGY

Action, Change, and Diversity in the Western Philosophical Tradition

Copyright © 2020 Malcolm Torry. All rights reserved. Except for brief quotations in critical publications or reviews, no part of this book may be reproduced in any manner without prior written permission from the publisher. Write: Permissions, Wipf and Stock Publishers, 199 W. 8th Ave., Suite 3, Eugene, OR 97401.

All Scriptural quotations are taken from the New Revised Standard Version of the Bible, copyright 1989, 1995 by the Division of Christian Education of the National Council of the Churches of Christ in the United States of America. Used by permission. All rights reserved.

Resource Publications
An Imprint of Wipf and Stock Publishers
199 W. 8th Ave., Suite 3
Eugene, OR 97401

www.wipfandstock.com

PAPERBACK ISBN: 978-1-7252-6674-2
HARDCOVER ISBN: 978-1-7252-6675-9
EBOOK ISBN: 978-1-7252-6676-6

Manufactured in the U.S.A.   07/07/20

Contents

Background and Acknowledgments		vii
Introduction: A meditation		xi
1	Actions in patterns: Definitions, relationships, and difficulties	1
2	Change and the unchanging among the ancient Greeks, Part 1: Parmenides and Heraclitus	20
3	Change and the unchanging among the ancient Greeks, Part 2: Plato and Aristotle	37
4	Hegel's dialectic	80
5	Maurice Blondel: "Action"	102
6	Henri Bergson: Time, Space, and Action	114
7	A Single Fire: Pierre Teilhard de Chardin's Search for Synthesis	131
8	Process Philosophy and Theology: Towards a suffering God	150
9	Geoffrey Studdert Kennedy's suffering God	176
10	Ludwig Wittgenstein and John Boys Smith: Changing language in the midst of changing action	189
11	Towards an actology	210
Bibliography		219
Index		237

Background and Acknowledgments

In 1974 I attended lectures in the philosophy of religion where I experienced Plato for the first time. The following year I studied systematic theology, and was reading works by the early theologians Justin Martyr and Origen—and found myself reading about what looked very like Plato's unchanging Forms of The One and The Good. It all felt rather arid. And by the mid-1980s that, and much else in the theology that I had learnt, felt particularly arid after two significant bereavements.

In 1985, a Church of England commission published *Faith in the City*,[1] and in its theological chapter (which I was not surprised to discover had been an afterthought) I found a God "infinitely transcendent," with no suggestion that God suffered in and with a suffering urban world, or with suffering human beings: and I was again reminded of Plato.[2] At the same time I was attending a theological society convened by the Very Rev'd David Edwards, Provost of Southwark Cathedral: so I prepared for it a short paper that suggested that because our society was increasingly characterised by change and diversity, and decreasingly by sameness and the unchanging, the church's theology needed to be expressed in terms of change and diversity. Life was busy, and further exploration of the idea had to wait until a period of sabbatical leave in 1994. The outcome was an essay, on which both Professor Robin Gill and David Atkinson (then Canon Missioner in the Diocese of Southwark, and subsequently Archdeacon of Lewisham and Bishop of Thetford) offered valuable comment; and the essay subsequently became a series of articles which the Ven. Bill Jacob, then Archdeacon of

---

1. Archbishop of Canterbury's Commission on Urban Priority Areas, *Faith in the City*.
2. Archbishop of Canterbury's Commission on Urban Priority Areas, *Faith in the City*, 70.

Charing Cross and Editor of *Theology*, published in *Theology*. I am most grateful to all of those who contributed in various ways to the writing and publication of those articles.

The first article, "On Completing the Apologetic Spectrum,"[3] suggested that in a context in which the changing and the diverse are becoming more important categories than the unchanging and the unitary, the Church's apologetics, and therefore the metaphysic (in the sense of a "system of metaphysics"[4]) underlying its theology, needed to reflect that trend. The Western philosophical tradition has for two thousand years given priority to the unchanging, to the static, to rest (as opposed to movement), to the unitary, to being, and to Being—being itself—and Christian theology has largely followed suit. Now a different conceptual structure—or perhaps, better, an additional conceptual structure—might be required if we are to express the Christian Faith in today's world: a metaphysic, or foundational conceptual framework, that prioritises change, the dynamic, movement, diversity, action, and Action: action itself.

A further article followed: "Action, Patterns and Religious Pluralism."[5] Just as a Being metaphysic has always needed some way to express the change that we experience, so an Action metaphysic will need to express the continuities that we experience. In this second article I suggested that "patterns of action" or "actions in patterns" might be a useful way to do this.

I have always been most grateful to St. John's College, Cambridge, for the hospitality that it has extended to me over many years. Each year for forty years I have spent three nights at the college to enable me to immerse myself in the Cambridge libraries; and the college has also offered occasional longer periods of residence. On one of my annual visits, the Dean of Chapel, the Rev'd Andrew Macintosh, asked whether I might like to visit a former Master of the College who had moved into a care home in South London near to where I was Vicar of St. Catherine's, Hatcham, at New Cross. At the age of ninety, John Boys Smith still had a lively mind, and we held an interesting discussion about process theology. He died soon after. On my next visit to Cambridge I discovered that the only theological or philosophical publication listed in the University Library catalogue under his name was a booklet that he had written in 1930, *Christian Doctrine and the Idea of Evolution*.[6] The booklet's contents were in many ways ahead of their time. Further research revealed that Boys Smith's son, Stephen Boys Smith, still

3. Torry, "On Completing the Apologetic Spectrum."
4. *Oxford English Dictionary*
5. Torry, "Action, Patterns and Religious Pluralism."
6. Boys Smith, *Christian Doctrine and the Idea of Evolution*.

possessed a holdall containing many of his father's sermons: so I edited and published the sermons with an introduction, and had the 1930 booklet reprinted as an appendix.[7] The third *Theology* article was an abridged version of the introduction to the edited sermons.[8]

In 2004 Keith Trivasse employed what he called "Torry's model", in a somewhat too adulatory fashion, to discuss the relationship between Muhammad and the Christian Faith.[9] This inspired further thought on my part, which led to my next article, "Testing Torry's Model,"[10] which distinguished my "actions in patterns" conceptual framework from the conceptual framework underlying process theology, and also related my framework to recent scientific developments. A final article, "'Logic' and 'Action': two new readings of the New Testament,"[11] asked how the conceptual framework might work as a lens through which to interpret passages from the fourth Gospel.

That last article was written in 2006 and published in 2008, and for nearly ten years after that I hardly thought about metaphysics. Being Team Rector of the Parish of East Greenwich, Co-ordinator of the Greenwich Peninsula Chaplaincy, Director of the Citizen's Income Trust, and a Visiting Senior Fellow at the London School of Economics (researching and writing on reform options for the benefits system, and on the management of religious and faith-based organisations) was quite enough. For over thirty years I have been involved in the debate about Citizen's Basic Income—an unconditional income for every individual—and in 2014 the debate began to demand rather a lot of my time. I was doing too much, so I retired early from the Church of England's stipendiary ministry in order to concentrate on the research and writing that the Citizen's Basic Income debate was demanding of me, and also to make time to revisit the subject-matter of the *Theology* articles. Those articles contained the sketchiest of surveys of the Western philosophical tradition, so to explore that tradition in more depth seemed like the obvious place to start. I was therefore pleased to be accepted as a candidate for the Archbishop's Examination in Theology. I was initially intending to complete a PhD thesis, but the demands that the Citizen's Basic Income debate were making on me made it necessary to rein in my ambition and to submit a thesis for the degree of Master of Philosophy, "Action, change and diversity in the Western philosophical tradition: Towards an 'action' metaphysic as a basis for Christian apologetics." In relation to the

7. Boys Smith, *The Sermons of John Boys Smith*.
8. Torry, "A Neglected Theologian: John Sandwith Boys Smith."
9. Trivasse, "May the Prophet Muhammad Be a Prophet to Christianity?."
10. Torry, "Testing Torry's Model."
11. Torry, "'Logic' and 'Action.'"

thesis I am most grateful to the board of studies and the administrators of the Archbishop's Examination in Theology, Cambridge University Library, the library of St. John's College, Cambridge, the library of King's College, London, and Gladstone's Library, for hospitality, and to my two supervisors, Professors George Newlands and Simon Oliver.

Completing two books on Citizen's Basic Income (*The Palgrave International Handbook of Basic Income*, and *A Modern Guide to Citizen's Basic Income: A multidisciplinary approach*) has required a two year delay in doing any further work on theological metaphysics, but now that those projects are complete I have been able to write a book based on the MPhil thesis. The examiners of the thesis, Professor Mike Higton and Dr David Cheetham, did not require any changes to be made before the degree was awarded, for which I was most grateful, but they did offer some useful advice as to how the thesis might be developed for publication, as did Professor Simon Oliver: advice that I have of course followed. Any remaining mistakes and infelicities in the book are of course entirely my responsibility.

As well as those individuals mentioned above, numerous individuals have contributed to the development of the ideas to be found in this book by their willingness to discuss them with me. There are too many to mention, and I cannot remember all of them: but particularly significant contributions have been made at various stages by the Rev'd John Byrom, Professor Stephen Sykes, the Rev'd James Bogle, Mr. Renford Bambrough, the Rev'd Jed Davis, chaplains of the South London Industrial Mission, members of the congregations of St. Catherine's, Hatcham, St. George's, Westcombe Park, and Holy Trinity, Greenwich Peninsula, and participants in seminars held in relation to the Archbishop's Examination in Theology. I am more than grateful to those who made possible several periods of study leave of varying lengths: staff members and officers of the parishes that I have served for their willingness to shoulder additional burdens; Bishops of Woolwich for permissions to take sabbaticals; St. John's College for appointing me a Fellow Commoner for a term; and particularly my wife Rebecca and children Christopher, Nicholas, and Jonathan, for putting up with me being away.

I am still most grateful to all of the people mentioned above for their encouragement and help along the way.

Introduction

A meditation

You are standing in a field. Imagine yourself getting smaller, and smaller, and smaller. The world around you changes. You are now among the grass stems, and the insects are the size that you are. Fortunately they don't notice you.

You continue to become smaller, and eventually you are the size of a molecule. And now you have to imagine the so-called particles, because you can see nothing. There are no things, not even fast-moving things. There is action. So imagine it as things moving, just so that you can think about it. There are protons, and neutrons, and electrons, and those are made up of other particles, all in constant motion, all relating to each other, with their actions in patterns.

And now concentrate on their action so that you cease to think about the things that your mind is seeing. The things dissolve, and there is only action, action in patterns. Don't think of the action as in layers, because if you do then you will again be thinking of things moving rather than of actions in patterns. All there is is action: chaotic action, actions in patterns, every action affecting every other, every pattern affecting every other, and all action.

Now cease to think of yourself as an object in amongst the action, watching it. You, too, are actions in patterns. That's what you are. Let the thing which you think you are dissolve. You can no longer see the action in the sense of having eyes which are things, and which therefore see. The seeing is now the action that you are, and the seeing is being caressed and buffeted by the actions that constitute the world around you. You no longer have a boundary. You are action, and you are particular patterns of action: but you are no longer isolated, defended, by being an object among other objects. All action changes the action that you are, and the action that you are changes the action around you.

You now begin to grow, and you see new patterns of actions, layer upon layer of patterns—or better, configuration upon configuration, patterns of patterns, and all action. No longer do you experience things: you are actions in patterns, and you are chaotic actions that appear to be patternless, and you are actions in complex patterns of patterns.

You are now at your natural size, and you know that action is all that there is: chaotic action, actions in patterns—in patterns that themselves change. You see things around you because that's how the actions in patterns that constitute our brains experience the actions in patterns around us. But there is no thing. There is no solid, unchanging stuff. The most solid-looking mountain is a ferment of actions in patterns at micro- and macro-levels.

Reality is action, and action is the real. The things that we see are illusions: they are how the actions in patterns that constitute light relate different sets of actions in patterns to each other. So let your mind see past the illusion to the world as it is: a ferment of action, some of it in interrelated and changing patterns; and let your mind see past the illusion to an understanding of ourselves as ferments of action, some of it in interrelated and changing patterns, and thus as members of the real world.

1

Actions in patterns

Definitions, relationships, and difficulties

A. INTRODUCTION

I am writing this in Switzerland after walking from Meiringen to the top of the Reichenbach Falls and looking down at the water falling on and wearing away the rock. Having returned from the walk there is now a violent thunderstorm rolling around the sky above me. The reality is the movement, the change, the action, the dynamic, the diversity. We might speak of these events by using nouns—"waterfall," "thunderstorm"—but the reality is better described by verbs: falling, wearing, rolling, thundering, flashing. Lightning is not a thing. It is pure action, in somewhat unpredictable patterns. A waterfall is not a thing: it is actions in patterns; and those patterns change constantly. Everything is action, at many levels—including the mountainside down which the water is falling. "Waterfall" is a verb.

Everything is of this character. There are no things. There are actions in changing patterns. And the same is true of myself.

When you look at a waterfall for any length of time, and then turn your eyes to the rock face next to it, the rock face rises. We only call this an optical illusion because we regard the rock face as static, at rest, unchangeable. It is not. It is whirling through the universe, around the sun, and around the earth's axis, along with everything else. There is no still point, no vantage point, no fixed standpoint. There are changing patterns of actions.

B. DEFINITIONS[1]

a. Definition by usage

What is the meaning of "definition"? That is, what are we doing when we "define" something? (How should we define "define"? Take care, reader, that you do not disappear down an infinite regress.)

Ludwig Wittgenstein suggested that we discover the meaning of language by studying how language is used, and, as the same word might be used in different ways in a multitude of different contexts, he offered the image of "family resemblances" to describe the relationship between one use of a word and another.[2]

By "definition" we generally mean a set of words that indicates the "meaning" of a word or group of words. This immediately poses a problem. If we study a particular use of a word and then construct a set of words to express the meaning of that use, then the use of the new set of words, and of each of its component words, will be specific to a particular context: so even if we employ the same definition (in the sense of the same set of words in the same order), it will have different meanings in different contexts. However, there really will be a family *resemblance*: and it is on this that dictionaries rely when they define a word or a group of words: so the Oxford English Dictionary not only offers a definition of each English word commonly in use, but it also lists the particular usages on which it has based its definition. Take, for example, definitions and examples given for the noun "action":

> I. Something that is done . . .
> Something done or performed, a deed, an act. . . .
> 1991   P. Barker *Regeneration* i. 8   The throwing away of the medal still struck him as odd. That surely had been the action of a man at the end of his tether. . .
> Chiefly with *the*. The event or series of events represented or described in a play, film, novel, or similar work. . . .

---

[1]. Some of this section appeared in a paper prepared for the Foundation for International Social Security Studies conference in Sigtuna, Sweden, in June 2017: "'Universal' and 'Unconditional': Definitions and applications."

[2]. Wittgenstein, *Philosophische Untersuchungen/Philosophical Investigations*, §§ 1, 66–67.

1994 *Guardian* (Nexis) 24 Mar. 8 I was invited to a meeting with Steven Spielberg in Cracow, which is where the action of the film takes place. . . .

II. The process or action of doing . . . .
The exertion of force or influence by one thing on another; influence, effect; agency ..
2007 *Brit. Archaeol.* Sept.–Oct. 9/1 Material churned up by former glacial action. . . .
With reference to a thing (material or abstract): the exertion of energy or influence; working, operation (as opposed to inaction or repose). . . .
1993 *Collins Compl. DIY Man.* (new ed.) xii. 516/2 Special "slots" . . . reject the tip of the screwdriver when the action is reversed in an attempt to remove the screw. . . .

What the definitions make clear is that even though "action" is here described as a noun, and functions grammatically as one, it always refers back to a verb or series of verbs. It is therefore no surprise to find "action" listed as a verb as well. The dictionary describes as "rare" the definition

To act upon physically; to move, manipulate. . .
1990 *Games Rev.* Jan. 7/2 It is difficult to move and action any pieces without creating mayhem with the rest. . . .

but as now common usage

Esp. in business jargon: to take action on, to deal with; to put into effect. . .
1985 *Rescue News* Summer 8/1 Concern has been expressed at the manner in which the whole operation has been put together and actioned. . . .

The related intransitive verb "to act" is given several definitions: for instance,

To perform actions, to do things; to take action. . . .
1997 W. F. Brundage *Under Sentence of Death* ii. 96 Shackleford claimed that Chase acted alone in promoting the peace warrant against him. . . .
To behave, to comport oneself. Frequently with adverbial complement. . . .
1947 G. Vidal *In Yellow Wood* ii. ix. 119 Mrs Stevanson didn't know their names but she acted as if they were her dearest friends. . . .

And as a transitive verb, the dictionary gives

> To perform an assumed role in a play, film, or other dramatic work; to be an actor. Also in extended use: to pretend, to put on an act. . . .
> 2002   *Courier Mail (Queensland)* (Nexis) 21 Sept. m4   Carroll is a man who loves to act, and is again enjoying the pace of rehearsing for the stage after his recent role on the big screen.

Whilst "action" is always a verb, or refers back to a verb or verbs, it normally relates closely to nouns, or to adjectives that imply nouns: "man," "film," "screwdriver," "pieces," "operation," "Chase," "Mrs Stevanson," "Carroll." These are not verbs and they do not refer back to verbs. The interesting exception is "glacial action." Here the action is the primary consideration, and "glacial" expresses a particular pattern of actions. This usage, and the first part of the related definition—"The process or action of doing . . ."—is close to the understanding of "action" that we are trying to develop in this book: that is, it sees "action" as expressing action abstracted from things, and things understood as actions in patterns.

The relevant definition of the noun "change" is

> Alteration . . .
> The action or process of making or becoming different; alteration, variation. Also: an instance of this; an alteration in the state or quality of something; a modification. . . .
> 1969   T. Alexander *Children & Adolescents* iv. 99   Early childhood . . . is increasingly seen as a period of rapid change and significant accomplishment.

And the relevant definitions of the verb "to change" are

> Senses relating to alteration, variation, or mutability. . . .
> *transitive,* To alter, modify, or transform (a thing); to make or render different. . . .
> 2014   T. McCulloch *Stillman* 121   The next night he brought me a book . . . "It'll change your life Helen, I swear to God." . . .
> *intransitive,* To undergo alteration; to become different or modified. . . .
> 1972   H. Arendt *Crises of Republic* 116   It is no secret that things have changed since then. . . .
> *intransitive,* To turn *into* (also *to*) something else. Also: to turn *from* something *into* (also *to*) something else. . . .
> 2008   A. Adiga *White Tiger* 292   I changed from a hunted criminal into a solid pillar of Bangalorean society. . . .

> *transitive*, To turn (a thing) *into* (also *to*) something else; to convert *into* . . . .
> 2005 E. Mordden *Sing for your Supper* v. 110 A garden set was changed into a ballroom with the addition of ten colossal columns. . . .

"Change," when used as a verb, always relates to a noun: "book," "things," "I," "set." However, the fourth of those examples is of interest, because although the change left the garden set in place, it might not have done. The change might have been complete. "A garden set was changed into a ballroom by clearing away the garden furniture and bringing in ten colossal columns." Equally interesting is the example that accompanies the definition of "change" used as a noun. "Childhood" is not what changes: it is the period during which change occurs. We have therefore found a similar spectrum of usage for "change" as we have for "action." The verb "to change" generally implies things that change, and some uses of the noun imply that as well, so that the changing is secondary to the primary things: but we also find the noun "change" implying that the change is primary rather than any things being the primary consideration; and we have found a use of the verb with the potential to express something similar.

The relevant dictionary definition of "movement" is

> A change of place or position; a progress, change, development, etc.
> A change of physical location. . . .
> The action or process of moving; change of position or posture; passage from place to place, or from one situation to another. Also: an instance or kind of this; a particular act or manner of moving.
> 1992 G. M. Fraser *Quartered Safe out Here* 151 There were no Japs to be seen, no movement at all.

We might understand the "Japs" to be doing the moving, but it is also possible to understand the movement as abstracted from things that are moving.

The related verb "to move" is defined as

> To go from one place, position, state, etc., to another. . . .
> *intransitive,* Of a person or thing: to go, advance, proceed, pass from one place to another.
> 1992 B. Unsworth *Sacred Hunger* xxviii. 282 Deakin saw figures moving like dark flames to encircle him. . . .
> *transitive,* Of a person or animal: to change the position or posture of (the body or a part of the body). . . .

> 1987 *Grimsby Evening Tel.* 8 Dec. 18 Keep your head still while all about you are moving theirs.
> *transitive,* To change the place or position of (a thing; occasionally a person); to cause to change from one place, position, or situation to another; to shift, remove; to dislodge or displace (something fixed). . . .
> 1987 E. Rhode *Birth & Madness* vii. 205 The removal men complained about having to move the piano. It was too heavy.

Here the moving is always of something in particular.

The similar noun "motion" is defined as

> the action or process of moving or being moved, with respect to place or position; . . .
> 1883 *Encycl. Brit.* XV. 687/1 We must now consider the composition of simple harmonic motions in directions at right angles to each other. . . .
> 1931 A. Uttley *Country Child* iv. 63 She could feel the earth moving, a great majestic motion. . . .

Again we find diversity. In one example, the motion is firmly connected to a particular thing, "the earth," but, in the other, motion is abstracted from any consideration of things in motion. So in relation to both "movement/move" and "motion," we have found the same as we have with "change": the nouns "movement" and "motion" can be understood in relation to things that move or that are in motion, or they can be understood as abstracted from any particular things that are moving or in motion.

Two questions arise: What should we make of the connections between "action," "change," and "movement/motion"? And which of the words can we use to build a metaphysic based on action rather than being? As we shall see, the questions and their answers are connected.

First of all: according to the definitions, "motion" is defined in relation to "movement," and "movement" is defined in terms of "change," so a hierarchy of meanings is indicated, with "motion" dependent on "movement," and "movement" dependent on "change." Change clearly implies action of some kind, and action implies change, which might suggest that the words can be used interchangeably. However, there is an important difference of emphasis. "Change" implies two states and the transition from one to the other. Even if change is continuous, the word still suggests a series of successive states. "Action" does not assume anything static: in fact, rather the opposite. Once there is a static situation there is no more action. I shall therefore take "action" to be the foundational word to suggest the metaphysic that I have in mind; I shall take "change" to be a word that implies both a diversity of static points (see below on "diversity") and the action that occurs between them; and I shall take "movement" and "motion" to connote change of location, and thus again static points and action between them.

A further question arises: How should we understand the dualities "action/being," "movement/rest," and "change/the unchanging"? "Action" and "being" are different and incommensurable ways of understanding reality; "change" and "unchanging" are opposites; and "movement/motion" and "rest" are opposites. We might therefore term the relationship between "action" and "being" a "distinction," and the other two relationships as "opposites."

The relevant definitions of "dynamic" are

> Active, potent, energetic, effective, forceful.
> 1878 W. E. H. Lecky *Hist. Eng. 18th Cent.* I. i. 14 It [Greek intellect] has been the great dynamic agency in European civilisation.
> Opposed to *static*.
> 1876 C. P. Mason *Eng. Gram.* (ed. 21) 117 (To borrow a metaphor from mechanics) the adjective is a *static attribute*, the verb is a *dynamic attribute*.

Action, change and movement are dynamic; being, the unchanging, and rest, are static; and "dynamic" and "static" are opposites. "Dynamic" is therefore a category into which we can locate action, change, and movement/motion; and "static" is a category into which we can locate being, the unchanging, and rest. Both change and movement imply action, and the dynamic implies action, so "action" remains the primary factor in our understanding of reality, as well as belonging within the category that it defines. The situation is somewhat different with the other members of the pairs described above. The word "being" allows both change and the unchanging, both movement and rest, both the static and the dynamic. It is when we ask about "Being," being itself, that we might find more of a parallel with "Action," that is, action itself. "Being" tends to imply rest, the unchanging, and the static: but it might not do so. This suggests that we ought to call the "Action/Being" relationship a distinction, in much the same way as the "action/being" relationship is one. They are not opposites.

The definitions given for "diverse" are

> Different in character or quality; not of the same kind; not alike in nature or qualities. . . .
> 1841   T. R. Jones *Gen. Outl. Animal Kingdom* xxx. 633   With habits so diverse, we may well expect corresponding diversity in their forms. . . .
> Differing from itself under different circumstances at different times, or in different parts; multiform, varied, diversified. . . .
> 1875   B. Jowett in tr. Plato *Dialogues* (ed. 2) IV. 19   Enlarging on the diverse and multiform nature of pleasure.

Throughout this book, the meanings of all of the words that we have discussed—"action," "change," "movement," "move," "motion," "dynamic" and "diversity"—will change constantly, because each new usage will be in a different context. This is not a problem: after all, the book is about action, change, movement, the dynamic, and diversity. The reader will have to judge whether there remain sufficient family resemblances between the different meanings of each word for comprehension to be achieved.

b. Definition by characteristics

What is sometimes called the "classical" way of defining a definition is to envisage a category defined by a list of characteristics, with the category name being defined by the names of the characteristics. Thus a rectangle is a four-sided figure with opposite sides parallel and all four of its angles right angles: so a square is a rectangle because it has four sides, opposite sides are parallel, and the angles are right angles, whereas neither a triangle nor a circle are rectangles. Those entities that possess the characteristics are in the category, and those entities that do not possess them are not. But for anything other than simple cases of definition this strategy quickly breaks down because there are frequently cases where we cannot determine whether the entity concerned is in the category or not. If the category "table" is defined by the characteristics "horizontal surface" and "supported on legs," then a folded drop-leaf table is not a table, whereas a stool is a table.

Eleanor Rosch has suggested that categories are not the clear-cut things that we often think that they are, and that it is often not the case that entities are either in the category or not in it; and neither is it the case that entities belong equally. Thus a robin is more a bird than an ostrich is, and a bat is on the boundary of the category. Rosch points out that in the real world we define categories in terms of prototypes and then decide whether something is in the category by asking how similar it is to the prototype. For the category "bird" the prototype might be "robin."[3] Mark Johnson has successfully used this means of definition to give a coherent account of how we categorize actions as moral or otherwise: we have in our minds a prototype lie, and we then ask whether other actions are more or less like it.[4]

So the question to ask is this: Is there a set of characteristics by which we might be able to decide whether something belongs in the category labelled "action"? There are a number of ways to approach this:

1. Each user of the term "action" could select their own preferred characteristics. The individual's autonomy would thus be honoured, but at the risk of losing mutual comprehension.
2. We could study a wide variety of actual usages of the term and then work out the list of characteristics either stated or assumed by users of the term. If we could find characteristics employed in *all* actual usages, then we would have discovered the "family likeness," and we would be able to list a definitive set of characteristics. However, that does not mean that everyone would agree with the list. It would only take one user of the term "action" to insist that they understood a characteristic not in the list to be essential to the definition of the category for the definition to become problematic in relation to attempts at mutual comprehension.
3. An authority of some kind could decide on the list of characteristics that would qualify something as belonging to the category "action."

c. A recognised authority

If a field of interest has related to it an organisation that those involved in the field believe to have some standing or authority, then participants might look to that organisation to supply definitions of terms. This will be by way of something like a social contract. In order to avoid the chaos of multiple definitions, participants might be willing to forego their autonomy and to grant authority to the recognised organisation.

There are a number of ways in which the organisation might construct the expected definitions. It might construct a list of characteristics that something has to have in order to be included in the named category; or it might collect examples of the use of the term and on that basis decide on a

---

3. Rosch, *Cognition and Categorization*; "Reclaiming Concepts," 61–77.
4. Johnson, *Moral Imagination*.

definition; or it might employ a mixture of those methods, constructing a list of characteristics and testing the list against current usage.

We have chosen to employ the Oxford English Dictionary as our recognised authority. The dictionary compilers have collected and ordered various uses of the words that we have chosen to use, and out of each ordered set of usages they have created a category within which we might be able to locate the subject-matter of a discussion. So, for instance, if we are discussing something that is "differing from itself under different circumstances at different times, or in different parts; multiform, varied, diversified," then we can locate it in the category named "diversity." If our subject of discussion is "acting upon [something] physically," or if it is "moving" or "manipulating" something, then we can locate it in the "action" category. If it is "the action or process of moving" or is "changing the place or position of a thing," then it is in the "movement/move" category, and we also find that it belongs in the "action" category.

The problem that we have to solve is that the use to which we need to put the word "action" in this book does not fit neatly into the category that the dictionary compilers have constructed out of uses of the word "action." We have found uses in which "action," "change," and "movement" are abstracted from particular things, but the uses still assume that someone or something is doing the acting, the changing, or the moving. I might therefore need to function as my own authority and create my own working definitions, at the same time as recognising that they need to exhibit family resemblances with the definitions listed above if uses of the same words are to be legitimate.

d. Working definitions

As a working definition I shall define "action" as in the Oxford English Dictionary definition

> II. The process or action of doing. . . .
> The exertion of force or influence by one thing on another; influence, effect; agency. . . .
> 2007   *Brit. Archaeol.* Sept.–Oct. 9/1   Material churned up by former glacial action. . . .

with the caveat that the definition does not require that a "thing" is exerting the force or influence, and that it does not require that there is "another" on which force or influence is being exercised: so the definition becomes simply "the exertion of force or influence." It is somewhat counterintuitive to attempt to extract our understanding of action from any sense that things are acting and that things are acted upon, but that is what we are attempting to achieve. I hope that by the end of the book the counterintuitive will have become a little more intuitive.

But having said that, a complexity arises. The reader will often find the word "action" used in a more normal sense, as "the exertion of force or influence by one thing on another," or "something done or performed; a deed, an act," both of which assume someone or some thing exerting the force or influence, or doing the thing that is done, or doing the deed or the act. The reader will need to judge from the context whether any particular use assumes that the action is an example of the more normal variant, or whether the use is an example of the less intuitive variant: that is, abstracted from any connection with things acting or being acted upon.

For "change," "movement," "motion," "dynamic," and "diversity," I shall assume the definitions provided by the Oxford English Dictionary.

C. RELATIONSHIPS BETWEEN THE WORDS

We have already discovered that "motion" and "movement" imply "change," and that "change" implies "action," so that "action" is a foundational term with meanings that underlie the meanings of change, movement, and motion. We found that "dynamic" can be regarded as a category that includes action, change, movement, and motion, and that "dynamic" is itself defined by "action." We can now add that "change" and "movement" imply "diversity." One continuous action might not imply it, but it might, and actions in the plural certainly do.

The conclusion that we must draw is that none of the words that we have discussed are redundant, so we need all of them; and that because words change their meanings as their contexts change, we shall find the connections between the words shifting as the contexts in which we use them change. We might find family resemblances between the diverse meanings of words in different contexts, and we might find family resemblances between the different relationships between the words as those relationships change, but we can still conclude, on the basis of our discussion, that "action" is a primary term in relation to such secondary terms as movement, motion, and change; that "dynamic" is a category into which all of them can be put; that "dynamic" is itself defined by action, suggesting that by "dynamic" we simply mean "action and its subcategories." We might also conclude that "change" and "the unchanging" are opposites, that "movement/motion" and "rest" are opposites, that "dynamic" and "static" are opposites, and that "diversity" and "the unitary" are opposites ("diversity" can imply "unity," but not "the unitary"):[5] but that "being" and "action" are different and incommensurable foundational terms and so are not to be regarded as opposites, and that the same appears to be true for "Being" and "Action."

Just as in a "being" metaphysic we might define "Being" as the category of all beings, and perhaps as the origin of all beings, so in an "action" metaphysic we might define "Action" as the category of all actions, and perhaps as the origin of all actions: which suggests that actions are diverse, but that Action is unitary, in the sense that there is one of it—although of course it might still be internally diverse.

By saying that "action" and "being" are "incommensurable" I mean that we cannot understand the meaning of "action" on the basis of the meaning of "being," and that we cannot understand the meaning of "being" on the basis of the meaning of "action." They are not opposites. However, we have understood Action as the category of all actions, and perhaps as their origin, in a way similar to the way in which we might understand Being as the category of all beings, and perhaps as their origin. We might also understand Action as expressing "action itself": that is, that in which all actions participate in some way, just as we might understand Being as expressing "being itself": that is, that in which all actions participate in some way. The similar structural relationships between "being" and "Being," and between "action" and "Action," do not imply that we can formulate relationships between "being" and "action" or between "Action" and "Being": although it is of course legitimate for a philosopher to argue for doing so, as we shall find Blondel doing.[6]

The fact that we have termed "movement" and "rest" as "opposites," and "diversity" and "the unitary" as "opposites," does not of course mean that we cannot discover relationships between terms in the "static" group ("being," "the unchanging," "rest," "the static," and "the unitary") and terms in the "dynamic" group. Just as we might find a range of relationships *within* each group, it is perfectly possible that in a particular case we might find relationships between members of the different categories: for instance, between rest and diversity.

Just as we shall find the meanings of all of these words changing constantly, so we shall find the relationships between them changing. Just as the reader will have to judge whether there remain sufficient family resemblances between the different meanings of each word for comprehension

---

5. If I use "unity" in distinction from "diversity" then I shall mean by it "the one" as opposed to "the many," and in the sense of a single being with no parts. "The unitary" is a somewhat clumsy expression, but I shall sometimes use it.

6. See chapter 5.

to be achieved, so the reader will need to decide whether there remain sufficient family resemblances between the relationships between the different words for some kind of consistency to be maintained.

While "change" and "the unchanging" might describe a distinction, we shall often find ourselves treating them as spectrums,[7] both because we shall find philosophers constructing metaphysics in the ground between the two, and also because we can define change and the unchanging in terms of each other. The other oppositions—the static and the dynamic, rest and movement, diversity and unity—will also be treated as spectrums for the same reason; and we shall also find that in some ways we can treat Action and Being as defining a spectrum, and action and being as doing so as well.

I am grateful to David Goodbourn[8] for questioning the use of the notion of the spectrum in relation to the conceptual framework that I have developed. He asks whether a diagram with two axes might be more appropriate:

> One axis would be between the poles of "being" and "acting," and the other axis between "changing" and "unchanging." You and Plato would then be in opposite corners of the diagram: you opting for "acting" and "changing," Plato for "being" and "unchanging."

Goodbourn rightly suggests that a "being and change" model would thus become possible, and thinks that this might be a good description of Whitehead's framework.[9] This is a helpful complexification of the framework: and if we were to allow ourselves any number of dimensions, then a framework could be built with axes in many dimensions, each axis relating to a spectrum strung between two poles. This would allow us to value even more diversity than ever.

D. ACTIONS IN PATTERNS

If in our minds we attempt to abstract actions from the things or people performing actions (for instance, if we abstract running from a person running), then we shall have in our minds a particular pattern of actions: a pattern that will itself be changing. If we then try to abstract the very notion of action from all particular actions, we might begin to grasp the meaning

---

7. I shall employ the Anglicised plural "spectrums" rather than the Latin "spectra."

8. In private correspondence. David Goodbourn was General Secretary of Churches Together in Britain and Ireland.

9. See chapter 8.

of "action," of "action itself," and of the totality of action, and thus of what I term "Action." This is much the same process as abstracting particular beings from any temporary characteristics that they might possess, and then abstracting the very notion of being from all particular beings, and finally grasping the meaning of "being," of "being itself," and of the totality of being, and thus of "Being." But actions are never experienced as entirely chaotic, with no order to them or connections between them. Whether our minds create order in them, or we experience an order that already exists, is not at issue here. What is at issue is that we experience stabilities as well as change, beings as well as actions. We therefore need a way of expressing the stabilities, the ordering. Whilst the word "pattern" can mean an ordering of *things*:

> Something shaped or designed to serve as a model from which a thing is to be made; a design, an outline; an original. . . .
> 1994 *Guardian* 6 Aug. (Weekend Suppl.) 22/2 They build to traditional patterns using local limestone and yellow bricks of coquina. . . .

it can also refer to any ordering:

> A regular and intelligible form or sequence discernible in certain actions or situations; esp. one on which the prediction of successive or future events may be based. . . .
> 1951 J. M. Fraser *Psychol.* iii. xx. 236 Different patterns of relationships will develop according to what kind of task the group happens to be engaged in. . . .
> 1968 P. B. Weiz *Elem. Zool.* viii. 123/2 A given external stimulus usually leads to the completion of several or many simultaneous reflex responses, all occurring as a single, integrated pattern of activity.[10]

"Patterns" therefore seems to be an entirely legitimate way to express the order of action that we experience as objects, events, and other aspects of reality.

We can either conceptualize what we experience as "things that change/move/act" or as "actions in patterns," "actions in configurations," and so on. We thus have two ways in which we can understand the universe and everything else: as "things that change" and as "actions in patterns."

As I developed the "actions in patterns" conceptual structure through an essay written in 1994 and subsequent articles in *Theology*,[11] I found it

---

10. Oxford English Dictionary.

11. Torry, "On Completing the Apologetic Spectrum"; "Action, Patterns and Religious Pluralism"; "A Neglected Theologian: John Sandwith Boys Smith"; "Testing

helpful to make a clear distinction between a Being metaphysic and an Action metaphysic: the former characterized by the unchanging, and resulting in an understanding that reality is beings or objects that might or might not change; and the latter characterized by action, and resulting in an understanding that reality is actions that might or might not exhibit continuities: "actions in patterns,"[12] with the patterns themselves changing. It is this latter metaphysic that this book is all about.

"Action" is the primary concept, and change is brought about by action: so if a pattern of action is changing, then it is actions that bring about the changing, and action remains the primary concept. Movement is a pattern of actions that brings about a change of position: but this assumes an understanding of space, and, as we shall see, space is itself a function of actions in patterns. We shall discover that every aspect of reality can be understood in terms of actions in patterns—except for action itself, which remains a foundational concept.

E. LINGUISTIC DIFFICULTIES

In relation to the various distinctions and spectrums, it is not unproblematic that the way in which we use language favours the "being" option: that is, it favours seeing reality as things that change rather than as actions in patterns. "Change" and "action" are nouns, whereas we ought to be using verbs. This linguistic difficulty is no doubt to some extent a function of the fact that we find it difficult to abstract action from things that act, both in practice and conceptually. Take the example of a waterfall. We can either view the water as primary, and the fact that the water is falling as secondary to the fact that it is water that is falling, or we can regard the falling as primary, and the fact that it is water that is falling as secondary. We employ a noun, "waterfall," which suggests that a waterfall is a thing. We do not use a qualified verb: "falling waterly." Similarly, if we wish to prioritize the walking rather than the woman who is doing the walking, then replacing "The woman is walking" with "Walking womanly" doesn't really work, and I'm not sure what would.

Not only is it difficult to express particular realities as actions in patterns rather than as things that change: it is equally difficult to express in general a conceptual structure based on "action" rather than "being," and in this respect I might sometimes struggle to express my meaning, and the reader might struggle to understand parts of the book.

Torry's Model"; "'Logic' and 'Action'" (in date order).
    12. Torry, "Action, Patterns and Religious Pluralism," 108–109.

Might coining a new word help us? Or some way of denoting the fact that by "action" we mean action abstracted from things, and only in a secondary manner forming what we call "things" through its patternings? Maybe "!action!"? I shall not go down that road: instead, I shall occasionally remind myself and my readers that where nouns are used for "Action," "action," "change," and "movement," we might have used verb forms such as "to act," "acting," "to change," "changing," "to move," or "moving," if there had been no problems related to doing so.

We call by the name "ontology" "the science or study of being; that branch of metaphysics concerned with the nature or essence of being or existence"; and we call "a theory or conception relating to the nature of being" "an ontology."[13] But what should one call "a theory or conception relating to the nature of action"? "Ontology" is too closely connected with the primacy of being, and "metaphysic," while not inaccurate, is perhaps too general. Heraclitus uses the Greek verb *metabállō*[14] to refer to change; Aristotle also uses *metabállō* to refer to change, and *enérgeia*[15] to speak of activity and actuality (and also the verb form, *energéō*, "to be in action"[16]); and both Plato and Aristotle employ *kínēsis* to speak of movement, sometimes with a somewhat broader meaning suggesting change more generally.[17] The fact that the dative case of *enérgeia*[18] can mean "actually," or "in actuality," is not a problem, because those uses indicate the act of becoming and the act of holding in existence, so "an energology" might still be an option; and "a metaballology," or "a metabology," might also be a candidate: but those are all clumsy words. Although *kínēsis* sometimes has a meaning restricted to movement, in the sense of change of location, it can also be used with a broader meaning, so "kinology" might have been a useful way of denoting "a theory or conception relating to the nature of action." However, "kinology" already means "that branch of physics that treats of motion,"[19] so to use it for something else could be confusing. We are left with "actology," which fortunately does not

---

13. Oxford English Dictionary.

14. Heraclitus, *Fragments*, fragment 84.

15. Aristotle, *Nicomachean Ethics*, in Aristotle, *Aristotle's Ethica Nicomachea*, 1178b. English translation from Aristotle, *Aristotle in 23 Volumes*, Vol. 19, 1178b.

16. Liddell and Scott, *An Intermediate Greek-English Lexicon*.

17. Plato, *Timaeus*, 37e6–38a8. Here *kínēsis* is related to "becoming," and in *Timaeus* 37a–b it is the mechanism whereby the World Soul's knowledge of the Forms gives birth to the cosmos. In Aristotle's *Metaphysics*, book II, 994b26, *kinouménō* is translated "changing," which seems to be what the sense of the passage demands. See Oliver, *Philosophy, God and Motion*, 15.

18. Aristotle, *Metaphysics*, book XI, 1065b.

19. *Oxford English Dictionary*.

appear in the Oxford English Dictionary. It suffers from having a mixture of Latin and Greek roots, but it is preferable to "ontology" as a term for "a theory or conception relating to the nature of action," so we shall use it.

New ideas need new language,[20] so we should expect to reshape language as we discuss a new way of thinking about reality, and we should expect to struggle over finding the right language to use. In that last sentence, "reality" is a noun. A verb would be better: ". . . thinking about how becoming works"? The noun-based character of English is not an inevitable characteristic of language. Hebrew is generally more verb-based than European languages. Many nouns are still verbs that have simply added the letter *mem*, pronounced *m*, to the root; and the verb *ehye*[21] means "I happen," or "I become," or "I occur,"[22] and is generally translated "I am" or "I will be." Being is something that happens.[23] Perhaps one day English will be experienced as a language in which verbs are the primary consideration, and in which nouns are understood as expressing patterns of action.

We have discovered that language is an imperfect vehicle for the explication of such new conceptual frameworks as the one that we are trying to construct. But at least we can now be clear that what we need is a language constituted by verbs that express actions in patterns, and nouns that express patterns of actions. Such a language would reflect in its own construction the fact that language itself changes constantly in relation to the wider linguistic context. What we need is a primacy of verbs, and nouns as secondary linkages. But "action" is a noun, so we cannot escape patterns of actions' yearnings to become objects, thus making action into the action of subjects and itself into an object. Within the context of the language that we use today, action is frozen into a thing, and until we can evolve a new verb-based language we shall have to remind ourselves that action is prior to patterns, and that our language constantly subverts our intentions.

F. CONCLUSION

We are rapidly turning nouns into verbs: "to weekend," "to mail," "to exit." This is symptomatic of a slow shift away from nouns and towards verbs, away from "being" and towards "doing." "What do you do?" is often the first question that we ask of someone (although it is unfortunate that what we usually mean is "What is your paid employment?" rather than what are the

---

20. Floridi, *The Fourth Revolution*, x.
21. אֶהְיֶה, Exodus 3:14.
22. Elliger and Rudolph, *Biblica Hebraica*, 1751.
23. Rocine, *Learning Biblical Hebrew*, 289, 51–52.

many actions that constitute who you are). Marxism might be comatose as practical politics and economics, but as a view of history as something that is propelled onwards by continuous and diverse conflict it still determines how we see the world: as a series of activities rather than as a collection of states of affairs.

The reality that we experience is constituted by a ferment of action: of multiple connected actions. There is nothing underlying action. As Rowan Williams puts it when discussing energy:

> All energy we encounter is involved in energy exchanges; but are we not then pushed to ask about the character of energy as such (pure act, in an older terminology), energy that is simply what or as it is, not as the result of a process of exchange? If we move in that direction, then in order to make sense of all specific cases of talking about energy or action we do not seek for another object to explore. It cannot be another instance of anything. . . .[24]

Action is the datum, the axiom, the fundamental presupposition. But at the same time, we experience continuities as well, so we must understand reality as "actions in patterns," with patterns understood as informational and relational. These patterns of action are not immutably fixed. Because everything changes, the patterns themselves change: so a better description of reality might be "actions in changing patterns." There is no suggestion here that this formulation captures ultimate reality in any sense. It is a narrative that draws our attention to experienced characteristics of reality, and that enables us to speak about those characteristics, and to draw connections between different aspects of reality. "Things that change" is how we normally think about reality. I am proposing an alternative: "actions in changing patterns." Both the "actions in changing patterns" and the "things that change" narratives are perfectly legitimate: but there are at least three reasons for emphasizing the "actions in changing patterns" narrative. 1. The "things that change" narrative has dominated our understanding of reality for more than two thousand years, so perhaps it is time to explore the usefulness of an alternative; 2. The world is changing faster than ever, so it might be useful to understand the primary reality as the changing rather than as the unchanging, as actions rather than beings, and as movement rather than rest; and 3. We now understand the world around us in dynamic categories rather than in static ones. It is not insignificant that the French philosopher Henri Bergson, whom we shall encounter in chapter 6, was working at the same time as Albert Einstein was developing his relativity theories.

24. Williams, *The Edge of Words*, 10.

Just as in the "being" narrative we can understand "Being" as being itself, as the source of all being, and as the totality of beings, so in the "action" narrative we shall understand "Action" as action itself, as the source of all action, and as the totality of all actions: which suggests that we might understand God as Action as well as as Being: a possibility to which we shall return throughout the book.

This book might be said to be a brave and perhaps foolish attempt to return to a Medieval tradition: to encompass the whole of reality in a single conception, and thus to unite the many different disciplines in a single whole, with theology at its heart. Perhaps the nearest equivalent is Aquinas's attempt to draw the whole of theology and everything else into a conceptual structure based on Aristotle's thought-forms: but here we go further, not only because we now know so much more about the universe in which we live, but also because we are employing a highly restricted set of concepts, primarily "action" and "pattern," and in a secondary fashion "change," "movement," "dynamic," and "diversity," to shape the conceptual structure within which we shall be working: and, in the end, a single concept: actions in changing patterns.

Whether this book has achieved consistency and coherence in relation to these concepts I shall leave the reader to judge. All I shall say here is that I have found consistency and coherence difficult to achieve. This is partly because our default categories are Being, being, rest, the unchanging, the static, and the unitary, and we normally understand the dynamic, Action, action, change, movement, and diversity, within those, so we find treating the other member of each pair as fundamental a somewhat difficult task; and it is also no doubt due to my lack of philosophical ability. I hope that in the years ahead writers more skilled than I will be able to repair the gaps and mistakes.

2

Change and the unchanging among the ancient Greeks, Part 1

Parmenides and Heraclitus

A. INTRODUCTION

Whatever someone's interest in constructing and employing a metaphysic—for instance, scientific, philosophical, or theological[1]—to quarry the Greek philosophies from two and a half thousand years ago will often be a fruitful place to begin. This chapter begins that process: not this time on behalf of a Being ontology, but on behalf of an Action actology. We shall return to the same quarry that has nurtured a dominant Being metaphysic for two and a half millennia, and we shall find there some conceptual structures based on action, change, and diversity.

Change, action, and diversity are of course ideal end-points, in the sense that no philosophy is purely about change (because there must be some continuity in order for us to be able to discuss change), and no philosophy is purely about the unchanging (because the speaker or writer changes, so language changes its meaning, and "the unchanging" alters its relationships and therefore changes): but we shall attempt to locate philosophers and

---

1. For instance: Justin Martyr, "First and Second Apologies" and "Hortatory Address to the Greeks."

philosophies along spectrums defined by these ideal end-points in order to discover the kind of philosophy that might be helpful to us as we construct an actology. At the two ends of one spectrum lie "being" and "action," and at the two ends of a related spectrum lie Action and Being—action itself, and being itself—both of which are genuinely difficult to envisage: and whether it is possible to envisage positions between action and being, and between Action and Being, is a question to which we shall return. At the two ends of another spectrum we find "change" and "the unchanging." In terms of the change/unchanging spectrum, we live in the middle ground, experiencing things that change, and actions in patterns: so we shall conceptualize positions along our "unchanging/change" spectrum as representing different relative priorities. Nearer to the "unchanging" end will be an understanding of reality as things that change; nearer to the "changing" end will be actions in patterns; and in the middle will be a conception that balances the two perspectives. At the "unchanging" end, change might be more difficult to envisage, and diversity might be difficult as well. At the "changing" end there is no stability, the unchanging is difficult to envisage, and the unitary looks more difficult than diversity. We might term the far "changing" end "chaos," and the far "unchanging" end "solid."

In relation to the philosophical works that we shall study in this chapter I shall mainly be employing a "change/unchanging" spectrum in order to give some semblance of order to our discoveries. This is because, as we shall see, Parmenides' use of *estin*, "it is," might not be as clearly at the "being" end of the "being/action" spectrum as might at first appear, making the "being/action" distinction somewhat complex to employ in this context.

Philosophical debate about the relationship between the changing and the unchanging, and about the underlying relationship between action and being, was at the heart of the ancient Greek philosophers' interests: so this is where we shall begin our quest for a deeper understanding of these interesting and important relationships. We shall begin by reading from the surviving fragments of the writings of Parmenides and Heraclitus, both of whom lived about five hundred years before the common era; and we shall ask how they might have seen the relationship between action and being, and between the changing and the unchanging.

B. PARMENIDES

Parmenides worked in what is now Italy about two and a half thousand years ago, and although only fragments of his writings have come down to us, and all of them in other authors' books, they reveal a fertile and agile mind. There are many ways of reading these fragments, and here I shall concentrate on two of those ways: as a description of reality as one unchanging Being in which no diversity or change can occur; and as a description of reality in which diversity and change *can* occur.

a. One unchanging Being

Xenophanes (who might have been Parmenides' teacher) suggested that there is a being that "ever abides in one place and never moves."[2] Parmenides radicalizes this position in the first of his two "ways of search":

> The only two ways of search that can be thought of.
> The first, namely, that It is,[3] and that it is impossible for anything not to be,
> is the way of conviction, for truth is its companion.
> The other, namely, that It is not, and that something must needs not be,
> —that, I tell you, is a wholly untrustworthy path.
> For you cannot know what is not—that is impossible
> —nor utter it; . . .
> for it is the same thing that can be thought and that can be.[4]
>
> It needs must be that what can be thought and spoken of is;
> for it is possible for it to be, and it is not possible for what is nothing to be.[5]

Parmenides' source for truth is reason rather than the evidence of his senses, and we can rearrange his statements into the following logical argument: that something exists or it does not exist; that what is thought can exist; that nothing cannot exist; so what can be thought must exist (because if something can be thought then it is not nothing and so must be something).[6] Parmenides draws the conclusion that something cannot cease to exist or come to be (for then we would have to say "it is not," which would be a contradiction), so temporal distinctions become impossible; and similarly, if there is a place in which "it is not" is true, then again we have a contradiction, and we have to say that "it" is "alone": that is, that there is only one thing. If there

---

2. Xenophanes, *Elegy and Iambus*, fragment CURFRAG.tlg-0267.25; Barnes, *Early Greek Philosophy*, 97.
3. *estin*
4. Parmenides, *Fragments*, fragments 2 and 3.
5. Parmenides, *Fragments*, fragment 6.1–2.
6. Hamlyn, *A History of Western Philosophy*, 40.

was space that "it" did not fill, then again we would have to say "it is not," so we have to conclude that it fills all space and therefore cannot move.

> One path only is left for us to
> speak of, namely, that It is.[7] In it are very many tokens that
> what is, is uncreated and indestructible,
> alone, complete, immovable and without end.
> Nor was it ever, nor will it be; for now it is,[8] all at once,
> a continuous one.[9]

One problem with translating and then understanding all of the passages above is that *estin*, "it is," is the third person singular present active of the verb "to be," and it can mean either "is" or "it is," because, in the Greek, a pronoun subject does not need to be stated. So it is perfectly possible that in some of the passages Parmenides means simply "is" rather than "it is": but in the passage just quoted, definite characteristics are given to the subject of *estin*, so to translate *estin* as "it is" throughout seems to be quite reasonable. But that does not mean that we can be sure what Parmenides understood as the subject of *estin*.

If Parmenides means "the one Being, which is all that there is" by "it" in "It is,"[10] and if he means "exists" by "is," then he means that a single unitary Being exists, and that it cannot not exist, so it exists necessarily. The past and the future are irrelevant because in relation to "It is" they are the same as the present.[11] As Tarán concludes, the fragments suggest that Parmenides ought to be located at the extreme "Being" and "unchanging" end of the spectrum:

> From the necessity of existence and the impossibility of conceiving non-Being, Parmenides inferred that no difference can be real, for difference would imply the assertion that non-Being exists. The denial of difference makes all process impossible.[12]

b. Change and diversity

However, there are other possibilities for "it" in "It is." Perhaps Parmenides means everything that is, in the sense of "all the many things that are"; or

---

7. *estin*
8. *estin*
9. Parmenides, *Fragments*, fragment 8.1–6.
10. Parmenides, *Fragments*, fragment 2.2.
11. Sedley, "Parmenides and Melissus," 118.
12. Tarán, *Parmenides*, 175.

perhaps he means to draw attention to a single typical thing that is.[13] By "is" he might mean "exists," or he might mean "is" in the sense that "x is F,"[14] where F is some characteristic of x.[15] If "It is" means "something has this characteristic," then he would appear to be on the "way of opinion" rather than on the "way of conviction": and it is not entirely clear that the "way of opinion" is where Parmenides wishes to be:

> Thus, according to men's opinions, did things come into being, and thus they are now.
> In time (they think) they will grow up and pass away.
> To each of these things men have assigned a fixed name.[16]

Parmenides would also be allowing that something might "not be" some characteristic, because if something is green then it is not blue, and if it is fire then it is not water.[17] But something that coheres with Parmenides' fragments is still being said. As Curd suggests:

> What we know in knowing what-is is the real or genuine character of a thing . . . . Each thing that is can be only one thing; it can hold on to the one predicate which indicates what it is . . . . to be a genuine entity, a thing must be a predicational unity, with a simple account of what it is: but it need not be the case that there exists only one such thing.[18]

And as Bredlow argues: "The predicate belongs to its subject essentially, constitutively, and inseparably."[19]

But here again the questions begin. Does Parmenides mean by "It is" "Everything exists eternally" or "Everything exists for now and might cease to exist at some other time"?: in which case we are now some distance from the extreme "unchanging" end of the spectrum. Further support for this latter understanding of Parmenides' fragments, whether or not he would have argued in this way himself, comes from the fact that "it is the same thing

---

13. Wedin, *Parmenides' Grand Deduction*, 79.

14. *hópōs éstin* could mean "that it is" or "how it is"; and *hōs ouk ésti* could mean "that it is not" or "how it is not." Mourelatos, *The Route of Parmenides*, 70.

15. Wedin, *Parmenides' Grand Deduction*, 7; Brown, "The verb 'to be' in Greek philosophy."

16. Parmenides, *Fragments*, fragment 19.

17. Wedin, *Parmenides' Grand Deduction*, 159. See also Curd, *The Legacy of Parmenides*, xxii: If something is fire then it is not water.

18. Curd, *The Legacy of Parmenides*, 39, 66.

19. Luis Andrés Bredlow, "Parmenides and the Grammar of Being," 289.

that can be thought and that can be."[20] Our thought changes, which suggests that the "it that exists is also changing."[21] Our thought is also diverse, and requires that beings should be determined in some way if they are to be thought. As Perl puts it: "Denied all determination, internal or external, being loses its intelligibility and thus ceases to be anything. . . . being must somehow include determination, and therefore otherness as well as sameness, in order to be intelligible and so to be being."[22]

c. Unifying the diverse understandings

In relation to this present moment, any particular thing will always be as it is in this moment, so it will necessarily be unchanging. Once we start to move through time, we are constantly in a different present, and new reality becomes possible. Might Parmenides have entertained this possibility? His

> Nor was it ever, nor will it be; for now it is,[23] all at once,
> a continuous one[24]

is rather ambiguous. He could either mean that the past and the future are not different from the present, or he could mean that the single and continuous "it" did come to be and will cease to be, because we can only experience it in the present moment, and things might have been different before and after that moment.

We could of course add "at the same time"[25] after "It is and cannot not be,"[26] thus keeping Parmenides' original wording and at the same time allowing a diversity of changing beings.

A further mediating possibility is that Parmenides is saying that the many particular and different things are all made of the same substance. This substance "is" and "cannot not be": but any particular things can move in and out of existence and can change their characteristics.[27] However, there is no suggestion in the fragments of the kind of two-tier understanding of things that Aristotle later developed, so this is unlikely to be Parmenides' meaning.

20. Parmenides, *Fragments*, fragments 2 and 3.
21. Gallop, *Parmenides of Elea*, 11, 28.
22. Perl, *Thinking Being*, 17.
23. *estin*
24. Parmenides, *Fragments*, fragment 8.5–6.
25. Adluri, *Parmenides, Plato and Moral Philosophy*, 72.
26. Parmenides, *Fragments*, fragment 2.
27. Curd, *The Legacy of Parmenides*, xviii.

Année suggests another route towards the inclusion of all of reality in the "it" of "It is." The meaning of *estin* is revealed by the word's use in the poem as a whole, so it might be of diverse meaning: "is" as "exists"; "is" as in "x is F"; and "is" as in "is there" (*être là*):[28] so perhaps it is to the verb *estin*, rather than to its subject, that Parmenides is drawing attention.[29]

> Thus, according to men's opinions, did things come into being,
> and thus they are[30] now.
> In time (they think) they will grow up and pass away.
> To each of these things men have assigned a fixed name.[31]

Here we find Parmenides including in the things that are—*éasi*—things that are born, grow up, and pass away. This fragment therefore joins together the two parts of the poem, the "way of truth" and the "way of opinion," into a single whole, and thus joins all things into a single global entity.[32] Both the verb "to be" and the cosmos are continuities, and they imply each other.[33] In Année's words, *esti* is the "substrate" of a single, continuous discourse, and it represents a cosmic *koinōnía*, "community." Everything is included: continuities, diversity, action, and change—everything which at any point in time "is" and "cannot not be."[34]

Gustavo Romero arrives at a similarly comprehensive solution by suggesting that Parmenides might be working with a remarkably modern conceptual framework that regards time as a fourth dimension. The situation at any particular set of space-time co-ordinates will never change; and the situations at all possible space-time co-ordinates constitute the whole of reality, which Romero terms "the ontological sum of all events of all things";[35] so the whole of reality can be represented by a four-dimensional object that never changes:[36] "Change appears only when we consider 3-dimensional slices of 4-dimensional objects. . . . Time does not flow. It cannot flow

---

28. Année, *Énoncer le Verbe* être, 33, 41–49, 57–58.
29. Année, *Énoncer le Verbe* être, 91–92.
30. *éasi*
31. Parmenides, *Fragments*, fragment 19.
32. Année, *Énoncer le Verbe* être, 104.
33. Année, *Énoncer le Verbe* être, 105.
34. Année, *Énoncer le Verbe* être, 129, 132, 135; Cherubin, Review of *Parménide*.
35. Romero, "Parmenides Reloaded," 292.
36. Romero, "Parmenides Reloaded," 292. Romero uses a "manifold" to represent this idea: a mathematical concept, which understands every event as represented by a point of the manifold. But we don't need to use the mathematical concept to grasp this four-dimensional "block" understanding of the universe.

because it is not a thing. Time does not go by. We do."[37] And as Herman Weyl puts it:

> The objective world simply is, it does not happen. Only to the gaze of my consciousness, crawling upward along the life line of my body, does a section of this world come to life as a fleeting image in space which continuously changes in time.[38]

So yes, "space-time emerges from things that change": but once formed in a particular moment, that slice of space-time cannot change,[39] so, once formed, the whole of space-time cannot change.

We cannot interrogate Parmenides on his intentions, but it rather looks as if he was saying that reality is single and unchanging—even if it incorporates the changing and the diverse—and that particular things that come into being and cease to be are a form of "not being" if viewed in isolation.[40] We can therefore legitimately locate Parmenides' writings close to the "unchanging" end of our spectrum. In relation to something's characteristics, and in relation to the present moment, "It is [those characteristics]," and in this respect it does not change; and in relation to the totality of everything that is, "It is," and it does not change. But we can also recognise that Parmenides leaves open the possibilities of diversity and change. The non-existent *can* be thought or spoken, so it can exist; change and plurality *can* be thought and spoken, so they too can exist;[41] and change and diversity can belong to the unchanging "it" if "it" means "everything." If "is" means existence, then non-existence is excluded:[42] but if "is" connects things with their characteristics, then those things might come to be, they might cease to be, and they might change; and if "is" relates to the entire manifold of events and things, then the changing "is." We can therefore interpret Parmenides' philosophy as a philosophy of a unified, unchanging reality, and in a secondary manner as a philosophy of things that change. As Bredlow concludes:

> The mere indeterminate mass of what-there-is, without any further qualification, turns out to be the only real entity that truly meets the formal requirements for a perfect definition: it is what it is, and cannot ever be anything else but what it is . . . . This is

37. Romero, "Parmenides Reloaded," 294, 296.
38. Weyl, *Philosophy of Mathematics and Natural Science*, 116.
39. Romero, "Parmenides Reloaded," 295.
40. Pellikan-Engel, *Hesiod and Parmenides*, 98.
41. Parmenides, *Fragments*, fragment 3; Wedin, *Parmenides' Grand Deduction*, 194.
42. Wedin, *Parmenides' Grand Deduction*, 159.

why, according to Parmenides, we end up at the starting point. "x is x."[43]

Romero and Bredlow have between them provided us with a way of being true both to our experience of reality and to the possibility that Parmenides really was, in the words of John Anderson, "a proponent of strict monism, the metaphysical position that exactly one thing exists, and he held this unique entity to be both spatially and temporally undifferentiated."[44] However much there is both change and the unchanging, there is a primary unchangingness underlying the "It is." Melissus, a disciple of Parmenides, argued for what came to be called "Eleatic monism": What exists must last forever (as things cannot cease to be), reality is one single thing, there is no motion, and no alteration (because motion assumes that there is an emptiness to go into: but that would be nothing; so there is no motion—a position reached by Spinoza two thousand years later).[45] Scepticism eventually set in after Zeno took such arguments to an extreme and argued that an arrow is always at rest because it is always in a place equal to itself;[46] and Georgias suggested that "nothing is" is just as consistent as "it is." But Parmenides himself seems to have been a more subtle thinker than this. As Mourelatos points out, Parmenides was a poet.[47] Aristotle accused him of not understanding that "being is spoken of in many senses":[48] but perhaps he did understand that. "It is," but the complexity of Parmenides' language leaves a number of options open: and one particular option, perhaps a little surprisingly, is that Being is necessarily active. After all, Parmenides expresses the "isness" of "it" with a verb, *estin*, "it is," rather than with Aristotle's noun, *tò ón*, "the being."[49] Being is therefore something that does something: it endures in the midst of a changing cosmos—and it is in this sense that we are human beings, and in which all other beings are beings.[50] The conclusion to draw is that Being is perfectly capable of including movement, change, and diversity, and that Being and Action might in fact be inseparable. We still cannot help locating Parmenides at the extreme "unchanging" end of one of our spectrums, but at the same time he might be no stranger to much of the

---

43. Bredlow, "Parmenides and the Grammar of Being," 91, 294.
44. Anderson, *Parmenides and Presocratic Philosophy*, 17.
45. Barnes, *Early Greek Philosophy*, 145.
46. Barnes, *Early Greek Philosophy*, 157.
47. Mourelatos, *The Route of Parmenides*, 260.
48. Aristotle, *Physics*, I, 185b20–30, and *Metaphysics*, XIV, 1089a1–15, quoted in Mourelatos, *The Route of Parmenides*, 262.
49. Adluri, *Parmenides, Plato and Moral Philosophy*, 74.
50. Adluri, *Parmenides, Plato and Moral Philosophy*, 77.

rest of the spectrum: and if he understood Being as including change and diversity, then his writings warn against any easy identification of a Being/Action distinction with an unchanging/changing one.

C. HERACLITUS

Heraclitus worked in Ephesus, also around 500 BCE. Of his writings we again possess only fragments that are not necessarily accurate quotations (as is the case for many early philosophers). The purposely authoritative and somewhat prophetic literary style is full of imagery, and is characterized by both diversity and unity, and so reflects the character of the philosophy expressed within it.[51] Like Xenophanes and Parmenides, Heraclitus believed that there is a unity underlying opposites: "The way up and [the way] down is one and the same";[52] and underlying any diversity "it is wise, listening not to me but to the report, to agree that all things are one."[53]

Heraclitus's predecessors found in the actions of divine beings the reasons for action and change, but for Heraclitus there is a largely autonomous *lógos*, a shared "account" or "reasoning":[54] "Although the account is shared, most men live as though their thinking were a private possession."[55] There is a *kósmos*, an "ordering"—and here is the difference from Parmenides: this ordering is constituted by radical change, for which Heraclitus uses the image of *pūr*, "fire": a fire that is action or change without any fixed substance, and that both goes in and out of existence, and changes in intensity: "The ordering,[56] the same for all, no god nor man has made, but it ever was and is and will be: fire everliving, kindled in measures and in measures going out."[57] It is always fire, but always changing, and the changing has a pattern, or an order;[58] and, similarly, the same river is always different: "As they step into the same rivers, other and still other waters flow upon them."[59] When Plato refers to this passage we rather lose the identity or sameness

---

51. Jordan, "Heraclitus' Discursive Authority."
52. Heraclitus, *Fragments*, fragment 60. This fragment might be making a metaphysical point about the unity of opposites, or a point about the relativity of knowledge of the same thing, or both: Williams, *Hegel, Heraclitus and Marx's Dialectic*, 12.
53. Heraclitus, *Fragments*, fragment 35.
54. Granger, "Early Natural Theology," 171, 189.
55. Heraclitus, *Fragments*, fragment 2.
56. *kósmon*
57. Heraclitus, *Fragments*, fragment 30.
58. Irwin, *Classical Thought*, 25–26.
59. Heraclitus, *Fragments*, fragment 12.

of the river, so all we are left with is motion and change: "Heraclitus says, you know, that all things move and nothing remains still, and he likens the universe to the current of a river, saying that you cannot step twice into the same stream."[60] This is to misrepresent Heraclitus,[61] for whom the river is the *same* river, and is constantly a river because the water flows:[62] "It rests by changing."[63] It also misrepresents him because it ignores most of the fragment. As Robjant suggests,[64] the person stepping into the river matters, and so does *hétera kaì hétera*, "other and still other." The *kaì* might here represent a superlative rather than a conjunction, that is, "extremely different" rather than "different and different again." Robjant draws attention to a second fragment about rivers:[65] "Into the same rivers we step and do not step, we are and we are not."[66] "As they step into the same rivers" and "we are and we are not" suggest that these fragments are at least as much about the experiencing subject as they are about the object of the river,[67] and Robjant's theory is that Heraclitus is using the river as a metaphor for our personal experience. My experience is always my experience, but it is superlatively different from moment to moment, and the experiencing I of this moment is not the experiencing I of the next. It is my memory that identifies the river of one moment with the river of a previous moment, just as it identifies me with the same person at a previous time.[68]

The early Greek philosophers, finding themselves surrounded by a diversity of things with diverse characteristics, wondered whether the many different objects were made of a small number of different elements, or perhaps of just one. For Anaximenes, air was the foundational element out of which water, earth and stones were made;[69] Hippo thought that water was the first principle;[70] for Xenophanes, earth and water were the first principles;[71] but

---

60. Plato, *Cratylus*, 402a. See Panayides, "Heraclitus and the Theory of Flux," 265, on Aristotle's statement that Cratylus thought that we could not step twice into the same river.

61. Graham, "Once More into the Stream," 311, 314.

62. Romero, "Parmenides Reloaded," 296.

63. Heraclitus, *Fragments*, fragment 84.

64. Robjant, "Nauseating Flux," 641–42.

65. Robjant, "Nauseating Flux," 642–43.

66. Heraclitus, *Fragments*, fragment 49a.

67. Robjant, "Nauseating Flux," 644–45.

68. Robjant, "Nauseating Flux," 647–51; Panayides, "Heraclitus and the Theory of Flux," 268.

69. Barnes, *Early Greek Philosophy*, 77–79.

70. Barnes, *Early Greek Philosophy*, 224–25.

71. Barnes, *Early Greek Philosophy*, 97–98.

for Heraclitus, only fire underlies the universe: "All things are [exchanged] for fire,[72] and fire[73] for all things, as goods for gold and gold for goods."[74] Here Heraclitus seems to be joining in the discussion about which is the primary element: but Kahn suggests that that is not all that he is doing.[75] Heraclitus says of the Lord who speaks through the oracle at Delphi that he "neither utters nor hides his meaning, but shows it by a sign."[76] This suggests that his own discussion of *pûr*, fire, might be a "sign," and therefore a purposely ambiguous means of saying both that earth, water and air emerge from fire, and that there is something radically active and changing underlying the whole of reality: including, we can now suggest, our own experience. "Cold warms up, warm cools off, moist parches, dry dampens."[77]

Sometimes a careful balance between unity and diversity is expressed, with diversity and unity constantly emerging from each other: "Graspings: wholes and not wholes, convergent divergent, consonant dissonant, from all things one and from one thing all":[78] but Irwin might be correct when he says that "Heraclitus dissolves things into processes."[79] Heraclitus might have been the first to locate the ordering and unity of the diverse and changing world in a *lógos*,[80] a "reasoning," an "account,"[81] a "word," the rational aspect of reality:[82] but that *lógos* remained diverse,[83] with ambiguous and unstable meanings,[84] and ultimately incomprehensible.[85] When it comes to the *kósmos*, the "ordering," Heraclitus identifies it with *pûr*, fire: so however continuous it might be, it is also characterized by action and change.[86] Schindler points out that "light" and "fire" are ancient as well as modern metaphors for intelligibility: so *pûr*, fire, and *lógos*, reason, are one

72. *purós*
73. *pûr*
74. Heraclitus, *Fragments*, fragment 90. See Barnes, *Early Greek Philosophy*, 122–23.
75. Kahn, *The Art and Thought of Heraclitus*, 20; and see pp 132–38 on the view that Heraclitus's discussion of *pûr*, fire, is both a discussion of how different elements relate to each other, and an exploration of the fundamental nature of reality.
76. Heraclitus, *Fragments*, fragment 93.
77. Heraclitus, *Fragments*, fragment 126.
78. Heraclitus, *Fragments*, fragment 10.
79. Irwin, *Classical Thought*, 25.
80. Long, "Heraclitus on Measure and the Explicit Emergence of Rationality," 202.
81. Robinson, "Heraclitus and *Logos*."
82. Hülsz, "Heraclitus on *Logos*," 289.
83. On the multiple meanings of *lógos* see Hussey, "Heraclitus," 91–92.
84. Reames, "Heraclitus, Material Language, and Rhetoric."
85. Dilcher, "How not to conceive Heraclitean," 280.
86. Heraclitus, *Fragments*, fragment 30.

and the same; and Panayides suggests that the *lógos*, the account, *is* that everything is *pūr*, fire, and that everything changes.[87] This means that *lógos* and *pūr* are intimately related to each other. Schindler also points out that for Heraclitus *lógos*, intelligibility, is rooted in the combination of unity and diversity expressed in his lists of opposites.[88] The divine is located in the same combination:[89] "God: day night, winter summer, war peace, plenty famine; but it becomes of another kind, as [fire],[90] when it is mingled with incense, is named according to the savour of each."[91] As Braun puts it:

> the impersonal Logos, the general Fire, the fire-wielding God, the designing Wise, the Salient Common, and the kingly War, are all one and are finally one even with the Cosmos itself.[92]

And Barnes can sum up Heraclitus's view of the world:

> the world is an eternal and ever-changing modification of fire, its various contents each unified and held together by a dynamic tension of contrarieties. This truth is the account in accordance with which everything happens, and it underlies and explains the whole of nature.[93]

So there are no unchanging things, and there is no permanent experience, but there is "fire," which at the same time is action, change, and continuity, and constantly gives birth to changing diversities. It remains fire, but there is no aspect that does not change. Here we have a vision of reality that echoes Parmenides', in the sense that it encompasses both change and the unchanging, and both unity and diversity: but the unchanging and the unity are themselves *pūr*, fire: so they too are changing and diverse. The outcome is that, rather than prioritizing unity, being, and the unchanging, Heraclitus prioritizes diversity,[94] action, and change,[95] and is closer to "actions in pat-

---

87. Panayides, "Heraclitus and the Theory of Flux," 251–70, 258.
88. Schindler, "The Community of the One and the Many."
89. Owen, Review of *Heraclitus*, 19.
90. *pūr*
91. Heraclitus, *Fragments*, fragment 67. The subject has to be supplied. For a discussion of this fragment, see Kahn, *The Art and Thought of Heraclitus*, 101.
92. Braun, *The Logos of Heraclitus*, 67.
93. Barnes, *Early Greek Philosophy*, 39.
94. Beets, *The Coherence of Reality*, attempts to align Heraclitus with Parmenides and Plato by reducing Heraclitus's diversities to temporal and causal relationships. There is no suggestion in Heraclitus's fragments that this is what was intended.
95. Graham, "Once More into the Stream," 319.

terns" than to "things that change," as is his God. Heraclitus might not have been a poet, but he was just as much a metaphysician as Parmenides.[96]

D. RECONCILING DEVELOPMENTS

An early attempt to reconcile Parmenidean unchangeableness and a cosmos that changes was made by the "Atomists" Leucippus and Democritus. They posited a "nothingness" between objects, and they regarded stuff as not infinitely divisible, at least in practice. The distinct units or atoms are each solid and unchanging, but they move and entangle in different ways; so things can come into being and they can cease to be. The atoms provide an unchanging bedrock of reality, but what we experience is the equally real intermingling of atoms in the things and events around us. We are not told *how* the atoms relate to each other, so this attempt at reconciliation between the changing and the unchanging leaves unsolved the problem of the relationship between change and the unchanging: but the Atomists had constructed a genuine scientific theory, and so are understandably recognised as precursors of modern science, which still operates within the Atomists' basic framework.[97]

Similarly, Diogenes took up the earlier idea that air is the basic stuff, and that everything else comes from condensation and rarefaction. This conceptual construction had the same effect as Heraclitus's of giving order and unity to the universe at the same time as making change possible. For Diogenes, science was possible (and he successfully described blood vessels); and although modern science might not understand the connection between unchangeableness and change in quite the same way as Diogenes did, there are significant connections.[98]

The early Greek philosophers' achievements were enormous. They saw the world as ordered and understandable, sent the gods to the sidelines, developed elementary science (with internal explanations, economical methods, and systematic approaches), and invented the concepts of *lógos* (word, argument, or reason), *phúsis* (nature), and *kósmos* (ordering, or world). They were not dogmatic, but instead relied on arguments. They set in train a materialism (particularly the Atomists) from which the mental was expunged (although it returned), and thus set in motion the oscillations between unity and diversity, one and many, mind and matter, which we have now experienced for over two thousand years, with the Eastern

---

96. Hülsz, "Heraclitus on *Logos*," 282.
97. Barnes, *Early Greek Philosophy*, 247–50.
98. Barnes, *Early Greek Philosophy*, 289–94.

Ionians, such as Heraclitus, favouring the particular and the changing, and the Western Italians, such as Parmenides, the universal and the unchanging. Together, they grappled with the distinction between the changing and the unchanging, and tried to reconcile them in a coherent account of reality; and they left us with a variety of different positions that were already to some extent reconciliations between the changing and the unchanging: Parmenides' "It is" perhaps incorporating change and diversity; and Heraclitus ameliorating his *pūr*, fire, with his *lógos* (word, argument, reason, account) and his *kósmos* (ordering, or world). Both of these thinkers belong at different extreme points on the changing/unchanging spectrum, but neither of them belong purely at one end or the other. As Romero puts it:

> I offer the suggestion that the ontological antagonism between Parmenides and Heraclitus usually mentioned by so many authors is the result of a doxographic tradition that has its origin in Plato. There is not much in Parmenides' poem nor in Heraclitus's extant fragments to support a frontal opposition. The cosmos (or space-time in modern view) might be changeless and nonetheless formed by changing things, as Heraclitus's river.[99]

But having said that, there is a significant conclusion waiting to be drawn. At first sight, it might look as if Parmenides offers a balance: a position between Being and Action. Being and beings can be understood as active: they *are*, which is a verb; and action *is*, and so belongs within Being. However, that "is" is a verb, so what we are in fact saying is that action belongs within Action. We are on the Action side of the distinction. Parmenides can be understood as saying that diversity constitutes a unity across time, but we cannot argue that unity necessarily implies diversity. If change is ubiquitous, then a temporary unchangingness can always occur; but if the unchanging is ubiquitous, then change cannot occur. Contrary to the way in which Parmenides has generally been read, the logic of his poem is that only a metaphysic constructed on the basis of Action, and at the changing and diversity ends of the changing/unchanging and diversity/unity spectrums, can ensure that we can speak of both Action and Being, both actions and beings, both change and the unchanging, both diversity and unity. We can draw the same conclusion from Heraclitus's philosophy. There might be an unchanging fire, Being might be fire, and beings might be constituted by fire, making fire a unifying factor within the diversity: but that fire is itself changing, active, and diverse. Again we find ourselves on the Action and action sides of the Action/Being and action/being distinctions, and at the change and diversity ends of the changing/unchanging and diversity/unity

---

99. Romero, "Parmenides Reloaded," 296.

spectrums, if we wish to be able to converse about Action and Being, actions and beings, change and the unchanging, diversity and unity.

And according to Heraclitus, God is as much constituted by fire and by diversity as is anything else. Action, change, the dynamic, and diversity, are not only how reality is and how it works: it is also how God works and how God is.

E. A LOOK BACK AT HESIOD

From the seventh century before the common era—and so about two hundred years before Heraclitus and Parmenides—comes this remarkable myth:

> At the first Chaos[100] came to be, but next wide-bosomed Earth, the ever-sure foundations of all the deathless ones who hold the peaks of snowy Olympus, and dim Tartarus in the depth of the wide-pathed Earth, and Eros (Love), fairest among the deathless gods, who unnerves the limbs and overcomes the mind and wise counsels of all gods and all men within them. From Chaos came forth Erebus and black Night; but of Night were born Aether and Day, whom she conceived and bare from union in love with Erebus. And Earth first bare starry Heaven, equal to herself, to cover her on every side, and to be an ever-sure abiding-place for the blessed gods.[101]

Here is a cosmology very different from the one that Parmenides assumed, as *Kháos*, "chaos," appears to simply emerge out of nothing.[102] Hesiod's chaos is a long way from being

> ... uncreated and indestructible,
> alone, complete, immovable ... [103]

It is much closer to the *pûr*, "fire," from which Heraclitus thinks that the diverse and changing world emerges.[104]

Out of Hesiod's chaos comes a stable order of gods, landscape, and human society;[105] out of Heraclitus's fire comes an "ordering":[106] and even

---

100. *Cháos*
101. Hesiod, *The Theogony*, II, 116–28.
102. Pellikan-Engel, *Hesiod and Parmenides*, 48–49.
103. Parmenides, *Fragments*, fragment 8.1–6.
104. Heraclitus, *Fragments*, fragments 30, 90.
105. Hesiod, *The Theogony*, II, 116–28.
106. Heraclitus, *Fragments*, fragment 30.

though Parmenides' "way of conviction and truth" leads to an "it" that "is, cannot not be," and is "uncreated and indestructible, alone, complete, immovable and without end,"[107] there is still a "way of opinion" in which things "come into being . . . and pass away."[108] We experience both change and stability, and however much a thinker might prefer the one over the other, they both have to be expressed if we are to recognise the philosopher's language as connected with our own experience of reality.

F. BEING WITHIN ACTION

If we had been living two and a half thousand years ago, and had known the writings of Parmenides, Heraclitus, and Hesiod, then we might have recognised four possibilities for our future understanding of reality: 1. We could have followed Parmenides in prioritizing being over action, the unchanging over the changing, unity over diversity, and we could have got our experience of action, change and diversity to fit in as best we could; 2. we could have followed Heraclitus and Hesiod in prioritizing action over being, the changing over the unchanging, diversity over unity, and fitted in our experience of being, of the unchanging, and of unity, as best we could; 3. we could have maintained a perhaps rather untidy balance between these two possibilities, as Heraclitus appears to have done on occasion; or 4. we could have understood that both Parmenides and Heraclitus were offering us a metaphysic within which Being, beings, the unchanging, and unity, make sense within Action, actions, change, and diversity, and not necessarily vice versa.

We shall now study Plato, and we shall find him following the first option. We shall then study Aristotle, and we shall find him trying to pull the trajectory of Western philosophy back towards something like the balance of the third option. The second and fourth options will disappear from sight, and will only reappear when Hegel and then Marx discover in Heraclitus's unity of opposites a dialectic that in Hegel's case represents the nature of reality, and in Marx a route to knowledge; and when Hegel and Bergson discover in Heraclitus an understanding of reality characterized by the changing rather than the unchanging, and in Heraclitus's *lógos*, the *Geist*, "Spirit," and the *élan vital*, the "living trajectory," that represent the possibility of relatively stable patterns or trajectories within ubiquitous action and change.[109]

---

107. Parmenides, *Fragments*, fragments 2, 3, 8.3–4.
108. Parmenides, *Fragments*, fragment 19.
109. Williams, *Hegel, Heraclitus and Marx's Dialectic*, v, 4, 11–13, 26.

3

Change and the unchanging among the ancient Greeks, Part 2

Plato and Aristotle[1]

A. INTRODUCTION

Plato and Aristotle are arguably the two most significant philosophers for the Western philosophical tradition. Both of them had wide-ranging interests, and the numerous books that they wrote (or that their disciples wrote on the basis of their lectures) reflect the diversity of those interests. For Parmenides and Heraclitus, the question of whether fundamental reality was characterized by change or by the unchanging, by action or by being, by movement or by rest, by unity or by diversity, was at the heart of their work. This was not the case to the same extent for either Plato or Aristotle. We shall therefore have to be even more selective than we were in relation to Parmenides and Heraclitus, and equally selective in relation to the secondary literature.

The same will be true of our discussion of Thomas Aquinas, whom we shall study in relation to his "*in actu*": "in act," or "actually."

---

1. This chapter has benefited considerably from a reading of chapters 1, 2 and 4 of Simon Oliver's *Philosophy, God and Motion*.

In all three cases, we shall be looking for their thoughts on whether change or the unchanging is a fundamental characteristic of reality, on how motion and change might relate to each other, and on whether "action" or "being" might be the best way of expressing the nature of reality. We shall also ask how they understood unity and diversity to relate to reality.

All else we shall have to leave to one side.

B. PLATO

The Athens of Plato's lifetime was hardly a stable place. During his early years, Athens was at war. When Plato was fourteen, the city was defeated at Syracuse. When he was eighteen, democracy was overthrown, and was restored two years later. When he was twenty-three, Sparta besieged and took Athens, and imposed their own rulers, "the thirty," who included two members of Plato's family. When Plato was twenty-six, democracy was once again restored: and four years later it killed Plato's mentor Socrates.[2]

It is not surprising that Plato sought an unchanging world in order to find a sense of security; and it is not surprising that he came to see fundamental reality as unchanging and as something other than the world of experience, and change as less real than a set of foundations that stay the same.

a. The Forms

Plato's earlier works are written as Socratic dialogues, and might to some extent reflect discussions in which Socrates took part and to which Plato listened. The dialogue form is designed to explore an opponent's argument in order to uncover contradiction. For instance, in *Euthyphro*, Socrates explores the nature of piety: is an action pious because it pleases the gods, or do the gods approve the action because it is pious? No conclusion is reached.[3]

Plato's transition from Socratic method to working out his own programme occurs in the *Meno*, which poses the classic question about the search for knowledge: If we know what we seek, then the enquiry is not necessary; but if we do not know, then we cannot seek it, as we would not know what to look for and we would not know it if we found it. So Plato posits an immortal soul which recollects what it has seen in a life before the person's birth, and he proves his point by questioning Meno's young slave

2. Melling, *Understanding Plato*, 5–7.

3. Plato, *Euthyphro*, 5d1–16a4. The section and line numbers for quotations from Plato are taken from the Greek text as it is found in the Harvard University Press printed editions in the Loeb Classical Library.

about a geometrical problem, which the slave seems able to work out even though he has never done so before.[4]

> "Seeing then that the soul is immortal and has been born many times, and has beheld all things both in this world and in the nether realms, she has acquired knowledge of all and everything; so that it is no wonder that she should be able to recollect all that she knew before about virtue and other things."[5]

In the *Phaedo*, the metaphysics is elaborated. Socrates is in his death-cell explaining why he is willing to die, and again an immortal and pre-existing soul is central to the dialogue, the proof of its existence being the fact that we know about equality itself when all we ought to be aware of are particular things that are equal to each other.[6] Then comes a description (in dialogue form, and in the person of Socrates) of the Forms of Beauty, Goodness, and so on, in which everything that we experience participates:

> "Is the absolute essence, which we in our dialectic process of question and answer call true being, always the same or is it liable to change?[7] Absolute equality, absolute beauty, any absolute existence, true being—do they ever admit of any change[8] whatsoever? Or does each absolute essence, since it is uniform and exists by itself, remain the same and never in any way admit of any change[9]?"
> "It must," said Cebes, "necessarily remain the same, Socrates."
> "But how about the many things, for example, men, or horses, or cloaks, or any other such things, which bear the same names as the absolute essences and are called beautiful or equal or the like? Are they always the same? Or are they, in direct opposition to the essences, constantly changing[10] in themselves, unlike each other, and, so to speak, never the same?"
> "The latter," said Cebes; "they are never the same."
> "And you can see these and touch them and perceive them by the other senses, whereas the things which are always the same

---

4. Melling, *Understanding Plato*, 58. In the first part of the *Meno*, as in the earlier dialogues, bewilderment enables us to discard belief and to seek knowledge via questioning.

5. Plato, *Meno*, 81c6–10.

6. Plato, *Phaedo*, 74a8–d3.

7. *aeì ékhei katà tautà ḗ állot' állōs*; The wording suggests the translation: "Does it keep its characteristics, or does it become otherwise?"

8. *metabolḕn*

9. *alloíōsin*

10. *allḗlois*

> can be grasped only by the reason, and are invisible and not to be seen?"
> "Certainly," said he, "that is true."
> "Now," said he, "shall we assume two kinds of existences, one visible, the other invisible?"
> "Let us assume them," said Cebes.
> "And that the invisible is always the same and the visible constantly changing[11]?"
> "Let us assume that also," said he.[12]

The Forms of Goodness, Beauty, and so on, have no opposites (so tallness itself is not the opposite of shortness itself, and is not derived from it), and the soul, having the Form of Life, cannot admit its opposite, and so the whole discussion of Forms serves the purpose of providing an additional argument for the immortality of the soul (maybe something in which Plato needed to believe, following Socrates' death): but the important consequence for Western philosophy of this dialogue is that a number of related dualisms had been given birth: Forms and particulars, the invisible and the visible, the objects of knowledge and the objects of opinion, soul and body.

Plato's *Republic* elaborates on the Theory of Forms, and on the educational process that is constituted by systematic intellectual questioning, and leads the philosopher to an intellectual grasp of the Good and of the other Forms.[13] Plato begins with a discussion of "justice," of which every definition given in the dialogue is proved to be inadequate:[14] so he goes on to explore the notion of a just republic in order to describe a just man,[15] and then shifts attention to the education of the Philosopher King who is to rule the Republic.[16] At the pinnacle of this education lies acquaintance with the Forms, and particularly with the Form of the Good:

> "We predicate 'to be'[17] of many beautiful things and many good things, saying of them severally that they are, and so define them in our speech."
> "We do."

---

11. *mēdépote katà tautá*: This suggests the translation: "It never keeps its characteristics."
12. Plato, *Phaedo*, 78d–79a10.
13. Melling, *Understanding Plato*, 94.
14. Plato, *Republic*, book I.
15. Plato, *Republic*, book II.
16. Plato, *Republic*, books III, VI, VII.
17. *eînai*

"And again, we speak of a self-beautiful and of a good that is only and merely good, and so, in the case of all the things that we then posited as many, we turn about and posit each as a single idea [Form] or aspect, assuming it to be a unity[18] and call it that which each really is."

"It is so."

"And the one class of things we say can be seen but not thought, while the ideas [Forms] can be thought but not seen."[19]

We have been translating *idéas* as "Forms," and Tredennick suggests that that is the correct translation.

> The Forms are *not* mere concepts (hence the traditional alternative name "Ideas" is undesirable, as being misleading); they are ultimate facts, intelligible to our minds but quite independent of them. The things of our sensible world exist in a secondary sense, only in so far as they approximate to the corresponding Forms. They are effects of which the Forms are causes, although the precise relation is difficult to describe. It is generally expressed by one of two metaphors: "imitation," the relation of copy to pattern, and "participation," the relation of part to whole.[20]

The Forms might not be "mere concepts," but that does not answer the question as to whether they somehow exist separately from the things that participate in them. Plato describes them as "separate," *diairētai khōrìs*,[21] "set apart," but they are also described as *paradeígmati*, "patterns,"[22] existing in the soul,[23] which suggests that they are not a set of objects different from the objects that we experience. Perl suggests that they are "higher and lower ways in which reality may be apprehended."[24] The somewhat diverse ways in which Plato describes the relationship between the Forms and the world of experience suggests that he knew that he was trying to describe the indescribable: that he was at the edge of what we could comprehend, that precise description of the situation was not possible, and that only analogy

---

18. *miãs oúsēs*: "one essence." The "unity" of the Form is not simply a unity of kind: "one essence" might be a better translation.

19. Plato, *Republic*, VI, 507b1–c1.

20. Tredennick, "Introduction," 15. Plato uses both *eîdos* and *idéa* apparently interchangeably, and both are best translated "Form": see Saunders, "Introduction," 21.

21. Plato, *Parmenides*, 129d7–8.

22. Plato, *Euthyphro*, 6e3–6.

23. *en tē̃ psukhē̃ ékhontes parádeigma*: Plato, *Republic*, VI, 484c7.

24. Perl, *Thinking Being*, 37, 63.

could provide anything like an appropriate understanding.[25] For instance: the Good is like the sun:

> "The sun, I presume you will say, not only furnishes to visibles the power of visibility but it also provides for their generation and growth and nurture though it is not itself generation."
> "Of course not."
> "In like manner, then, you are to say that the objects of knowledge not only receive from the presence of the good their being known, but their very existence and essence[26] is derived to them from it, though the good itself is not essence but still transcends essence in dignity and surpassing power."[27]

The world of the visible is "the opinable," *tò doxastòn*, that is, that about which we have opinion; whereas the world of the intelligible is *tò gnōstón*, "the knowable," and the object of knowledge.[28] Plato asks us to consider a divided line, with the world of the visible at one end, and the world of the intelligible at the other. The line is divided in four, with the four associated "affections in the soul" described as "intellection or reason for the highest, understanding for the second; . . . belief to the third, and to the last picture-thinking or conjecture."[29]

In Plato's complex analogy of the cave,[30] prisoners see only shadows, until one of them can turn and see the puppets, and the fire behind them dazzles him. Outside the cave, he sees the real objects and the sun. The prisoner returns and appears foolish, as he is now less good at interpreting the shadows as a world. This analogy suggests that we cannot see objects clearly before we start out on the dialectical educational process that Plato prescribes. The divided line and the cave, when taken together, clearly distinguish between knowledge and opinion, and between the Forms (and particularly the Good) and the objects among which we live. The objects change; the Forms do not: and it is the Forms that matter, even though Plato's later *Parmenides* raises a number of problems with the theory. For instance: it is not clear what there are Forms of and what there are not Forms

---

25. Saunders, "Introduction," 33; Melling, *Understanding Plato*, 99.

26. *tò eînaí te kaì tền ousían*: the "to be" and the essence: terms that can only be used of the Forms. The things that participate in the Forms can both be and not be whatever it is that the Form imparts to them: for instance, they can either be or not be just, or a bed: see Brown, "The verb 'to be' in Greek philosophy," 227.

27. Plato, *Republic*, VI, 509b1–10.

28. Plato, *Republic*, VI, 510a9.

29. Plato, *Republic*, VI, 511d10–e2.

30. Plato, *Republic*, VII, 514a1–521b10.

of. Are there forms of mud? Or of hair?[31] Throughout the book, problems are raised about the "participation" that connects the Forms with the things that we experience, with the best-known problem being that of the "third man." The Form is not itself an example of the entities of which it is the Form, so in order to ascertain that the Form and an object of our sense perception are related to each other, the characteristics via which the object of sense perception participates in the Form will need to be specified: so another Form is generated, and potentially an infinite regress.[32]

As Hare suggests,[33] the root of the problem is the way in which the abstract Forms are constructed by the Greek habit of adding a definite article to an adjective to create a noun: "the Good," "the Just," "the True." The continuing adjectival content of the noun suggests that the Form possesses the characteristic of which it is the Form (an example of self-predication). It is this that creates of the Form, and of the object participating in it, two objects that share a characteristic, and thus need a third entity to represent the characteristic that they share.

Plato attempts to solve the "third man" problem by describing the Forms as *paradeígmata*, "patterns."[34] We now use the word "paradigm" to mean "a pattern or model, an exemplar; . . . a typical instance of something, an example," or "a conceptual or methodological model underlying the theories and practices of a science or discipline at a particular time; (hence) a generally accepted world view."[35] For Plato, the word *paradeígmata* characterizes a Form as a pattern to which the different things have to conform if they are to participate in it. This is not in fact a solution to the "third man" problem, but it usefully describes the Forms as patterns that characterize the events and objects that we experience.

Plato offers a further means of understanding the way in which particular visible things participate in the invisible Forms by employing the concept of "motion." In the *Timaeus* we find a Demiurge[36]—a Constructor or Craftsman, also described as "God"[37]—creating a cosmos, which Plato understands as being a mixture of things in motion and things at rest.[38]

---

31. Plato, *Parmenides*, 130c7–10.
32. Plato, *Parmenides*, 132d1–133a3.
33. Hare, "Plato," 143.
34. Plato, *Parmenides*, 132d1–133a3.
35. *Oxford English Dictionary*.
36. *Dēmiourgòs*: Plato, *Timaeus*, 29a1–9.
37. *theós*: Plato, *Timaeus*, 53b3.
38. *Akínēta kaì kekineména*: Plato, *Sophist*, 249a2. Perl, in *Thinking Being*, 68, suggests that this means that everything is in motion and at rest. This does not seem to be a better translation.

There is a "place"[39] in which God uses an "errant" or "wandering" cause[40] to persuade disorder into order,[41] and in this process the Craftsman's

> gaze was on the Eternal; for the Cosmos is the fairest of all that has come into existence, and He the best of all the Causes. So having in this wise come into existence, it has been constructed after the pattern of that which is apprehensible by reason and thought and is self-identical:[42]

that is, the Forms. The Demiurge is behaving rather like the craftsman discussed in *The Republic*, who "sees" and follows a form as he makes a bed.[43] The heavens that are created are characterized by orderly motion,[44] and the invisible world soul at the heart of the cosmos is *en hautę̄ strephoménē*, "revolving within itself,"[45] resulting in a cosmos that is "an ensouled living entity,"[46] and that is connected with the Forms via the harmonious heavens and the heavens' Constructor. The *Timaeus* myth recommends that we should seek the "congenial motions"[47] that are "the intellections and revolutions of the Universe," and that

> these each one of us should follow, rectifying the revolutions within our head, which were distorted at our birth, by learning the harmonies and revolutions of the Universe, and thereby making the part that thinks like unto the object of its thought, in accordance with its original nature, and having achieved this likeness attain finally to that goal of life which is set before men by the gods as the most good both for the present and for the time to come.[48]

Motion, variously described, is a thread running through Plato's cosmology, and Plato even understands "coming to be"[49] as "changing places,"[50] that is, as moving into a place; and he understands ceasing to be as moving

---

39. *khṓra*: Plato, *Timaeus*, 52a6.
40. Plato, *Timaeus*, 48a6. See Johansen, *Plato's Natural Philosophy*, 96–98.
41. Plato, *Timaeus*, 53a6–b6.
42. Plato, *Timaeus*, 29a5–9.
43. *pròs tḕn idéan blépōn*: Plato, *Republic*, X, 596b6–8.
44. Plato, *Timaeus*, 35b1–36d9.
45. Plato, *Timaeus*, 36e3.
46. Oliver, *Philosophy, God and Motion*, 13.
47. *kinḗseis*
48. Plato, *Timaeus*, 90c6–90d7.
49. *génesin*: Plato, *Timaeus*, 52b1.
50. *diameíbetai tàs khṓras hápanta*: Plato, *Timaeus*, 57c1.

elsewhere. This is a kind of motion that is not about location, so *kínēsis* is here broadly understood: but the "place" terminology suggests that something closer to "motion" than "change" might in fact be intended.[51]

We have already seen how Plato envisages motion mediating the Forms to the cosmos;[52] in the *Sophist*, we find *kínēsin*, motion or change, ascribed to "being";[53] and now we have discovered being itself being achieved by a kind of motion: but the duality remains, because the Forms do not change, whereas the objects of experience do; and although motion can be ascribed to every element of the hierarchy of the cosmos, it is not ascribed to the Forms themselves. Later "Neoplatonic" writers such as Proclus posited an "unmoved motion" of the Forms: a kind of motion distinguished from the motion that we experience by the fact that "unmoved motion" belongs to eternity whereas our motion belongs in time:[54] but as far as Plato was concerned, motion seems to have stopped at the heavenly spheres, just below the level of the Forms.

We ascribe "being" to the things that we experience,[55] but this is a derivative being that relies on its participation in the Forms. It is not clear whether the Form of the Good is also the Form of Existence, or whether the Form of the Good "transcends essence,"[56] which would imply a Form of Existence of a lesser dignity than the Form of the Good:[57] but either way, the Form of the Good is at or off the Being end of any Being/Action spectrum; and, because the Forms do not change,[58] it is also at or off the end of the unchanging end of the unchanging/changing spectrum: so what we have here is a philosophy that occupies extreme positions, whatever other positions it might also occupy. Similarly, although Plato's philosophy recognises a kind of reality for the objects of experience (we ascribe being to them[59]), meaning that reality is to some extent diverse, the reality that is diverse remains a derivative reality; and although there is a multiplicity of Forms, suggesting a diversity at the highest level of reality, that diversity is subsumed in the unity supplied by the Form of the Good, which binds together the many different Forms.

51. Johansen, *Plato's Natural Philosophy*, 112.
52. Oliver, *Philosophy, God and Motion*, 27–28.
53. Plato, *Sophist*, 248e1–249a2.
54. Opsomer, "Proclus on Demiurgy and Procession," 114.
55. Plato, *Republic*, VI, 507b1–c1.
56. Plato, *Republic*, VI, 509b9.
57. Melling, *Understanding Plato*, 103.
58. Plato, *Phaedo*, 78d–79a10.
59. Plato, *Republic*, VI, 507b1–c1.

But there is still more to be said about the relationship between being and change. Bostock finds in Plato's dialogues two contradictory positions in relation to the question as to how being and change are related to each other.[60] In the *Timaeus*, a strict division is maintained between the Forms—which do not change and which have existence—and things that are subject to change and that cannot be said to *be*. Writing of *tḕn aídion ousían*, "the eternal being," Plato says:

> For we say that it "is" or "was" or "will be," whereas, in truth of speech, "is" alone is the appropriate term; "was" and "will be," on the other hand, are terms properly applicable to the Becoming which proceeds in Time, since both of these are motions[61]; but it belongs not to that which is ever changeless in its uniformity to become either older or younger through time, nor ever to have become so, nor to be so now, nor to be about to be so hereafter, nor in general to be subject to any of the conditions which Becoming has attached to the things which move in the world of Sense.[62]

However, in the *Parmenides*, Plato writes this: "But were coming into being[63] and perishing anything else than receiving and losing existence[64]?"[65] Bostock suggests that the difference between change excluding being in the *Timaeus*, and change being intimately connected with being in the *Parmenides*, is not particularly significant. I beg to differ. The position in the *Parmenides* ascribes existence—*ousía*—to the objects of sense as well as to the Forms, and thus locates the objects of sense on the "being" side of a being/action distinction. The position in the *Timaeus* reserves "being" for the Forms, and leaves the objects of sense further along the spectrum, with their capacity for change firmly isolated from the Forms.[66]

A further factor confirms the spectrum position suggested by the passage in the *Parmenides*. The objects of sense participate in the Forms, and these Forms do not change. There is thus an element of changelessness related to each object that we experience, so each of the things that we experience belongs to some extent at the far "unchanging" end of the change/unchanging spectrum, even if they occupy other positions as well.

60. Bostock, "Plato on Change and Time in the Parmenides," 229–30.
61. *kinḗseis*
62. Plato, *Timaeus*, 37e6–38a8.
63. *gígnesthai*: "to become."
64. *ousían*
65. Plato, *Parmenides*, 163d2–4.
66. Prince, "Physical Change in Plato's Timaeus."

The passage from the *Timaeus* answers another question so far unexplored: that of the relationship between motion and change. Plato describes *génesin*, "becoming," as *kinéseis*, "motions," and distances "to become," *gígnesthai*, from "changelessness," *akinḗtōs*.[67] Motion and change belong together, as we would expect, with both of them relating to a variety of positions on the "being/action" and "change/unchanging" spectrums.

b. Plato's God

Where does Plato's God lie on the spectrums that we have constructed? As we have seen, the gods appear in the early dialogues as subjects for discussion: but it is not until we get to *The Republic* that we find Plato reflecting on the relationship between a creator God and the eternal Forms. In book X, there are three beds or couches:

> "one, that in nature, which, I take it, we would say that God produces, or who else?"
> "No one, I think."
> "And then there was one which the carpenter made."
> "Yes."
> "And one which the painter. Is not that so?"
> "So be it."
> "The painter, then, the cabinet-maker, and God, there are these three presiding over three kinds of couches."
> "Yes, three"[68]

—so here the Form of the bed, and presumably the Forms generally, are created by the god, or by a *dēmiourgós* who created the heavens,[69] and presumably created the world as well. However, this is the only instance in Plato's dialogues in which he envisages a creator God creating the Forms. It might be thought that Forms being eternal and the Forms being created constitute a contradiction,[70] which of course they do not, particularly if the Forms are internal to God in much the same way as the Forms are internal to the soul of the philosopher king:[71] but it remains true that throughout Plato's dialogues the Forms have a formative function that might make a creator God somewhat redundant: or would at least reduce a creator God to creating a

---

67. Plato, *Timaeus*, 37e6–38a8.
68. Plato, *Republic*, X, 597b4–10.
69. Plato, *Republic*, VII, 530a7.
70. Melling, *Understanding Plato*, 150–51.
71. Plato, *Republic*, VI, 484c7–d2. See Perl, *Thinking Being*, 63.

world in conformity with the existing Forms, which is what we find in the *Timaeus*, where the *dēmiourgós*, the creator God, who is coeternal with the Forms, creates an ensouled universe using the eternal Forms as a model.[72] The *psukhḗ*, "Soul," at the heart of the cosmos, is constituted by a combination of attributes that includes "being," suggesting an intimate connection with the Forms; but the Soul is also *kinouménē*, "moved."[73] It is through this Soul that movement is given to the cosmos, and through her that the cosmos experiences its connection with the Forms. Simon Oliver concludes his survey of material on the Forms, the cosmos, and the Soul:

> The motion which characterizes the realm of becoming . . . is both beautiful and symmetrical; it is a rational revolution which expresses the harmonic balance of the Good . . . motion as presented in the *Timaeus* is the perfect synthesis of the ideal "end" with the embodied means of fulfilment in that end.[74]

Plato employs *kínēsis*, "motion"—which, as we have seen, is a broader concept than movement through space—as mediated by the created *psukhḗ*, "Soul," to represent the method by which the cosmos participates in the Forms. Everything apart from the Forms themselves is on the "action" side of the being/action distinction, and at the "changing" end of the changing/unchanging spectrum: for however beautiful the pattern of action or change might be, it is action and change nevertheless. If Plato's God really does create the Forms, then they experience becoming: but the suggestion of this in the *Republic* is an outlier, and we have to assume that Plato's settled view is that any creative activity will model the created order on eternal and unchanging Forms. The Forms remain firmly at the Being end of the spectrum.

There is of course no reason in logic why the God who creates the universe in time should not also create the Forms eternally, even if that is not exactly what Plato envisaged: but perhaps there is another possibility as well.

c. Forms as verbs

A possibility that Plato does not appear to have considered is that the Forms could be verbs rather than adjectival nouns. We find the Forms of the Good and of Beauty,[75] but not forms of loving and of running. This is odd. It would

---

72. Plato, *Timaeus*, 29a1–9.
73. Plato, *Timaeus*, 37a2–b2.
74. Oliver, *Philosophy, God and Motion*, 28.
75. Plato, *Republic*, VI, 507b4.

be as rational to say that every instance of someone running participates in a Form of running as to say that every good thing participates in a Form of the Good. For Plato to have pursued the possibility of verb-based Forms, as well as the Forms based on adjectival nouns that he did discuss, would have located his philosophy as much on the "action" side of our distinction as at the "being" side of it. This would also have enabled a creator God, also defined in terms of action, constantly to give birth to the Forms, and at the same time to create a universe on the model of the Forms. But as things stand, Plato's Forms and everything else are at the "unchanging" end of the spectrum, even if particular things also occupy other positions on it: and a consequence is that a creator God, who by definition acts, is subject to the Forms, rather than the Forms being subject to God.

Plato's Theory of Forms has had a quite remarkable history. It has been the unchanging pattern in which every philosophy since Plato has participated in some way or other: so not only has this philosophy been a philosophy *of* the unchanging pattern: it has itself *been* an unchanging pattern. It has been a Form. And the Theory of Forms has been the unchanging pattern in which every theology constructed since Plato has participated in some way or other: the One, or the Good, controlling our notion of God, and thus locating God at the far "unchanging" end of the changing/unchanging spectrum.

C. ARISTOTLE

While there is little consistent order to the collection of books that we now know as Aristotle's *Metaphysics*, and no single and clear grand theory emerges, there is a fairly consistent set of questions underlying the explorations: Why are things as they are? What is the relationship between unity and diversity? What is the relationship between continuity and change? What are the causes of things?

a. Being and substance, diversity and unity

> ... "being"[76] is used in various senses, but always with reference to one principle. For some things are said to "be" because they are substances; others because they are modifications of substance; others because they are a process towards substance, or destructions or privations or qualities of substance, or productive or

76. *tò òn*

generative of substance or of terms relating to substance, or negations of certain of these terms or of substance. (Hence we even say that not-being is not-being.) And so, just as there is one science of all healthy things, so it is true of everything else. For it is not only in the case of terms which express one common notion that the investigation belongs to one science, but also in the case of terms which relate to one particular characteristic; for the latter too, in a sense, express one common notion. Clearly then the study of things which are[77], qua being, also belongs to one science. Now in every case knowledge is principally concerned with that which is primary, i.e. that upon which all other things depend, and from which they get their names. If, then, substance[78] is this primary thing, it is of substances[79] that the philosopher must grasp the first principles and causes.[80]

We are at the "being" end of the spectrum, but also in the realm of both unity and diversity. There are many "beings," *tà ónta*,[81] but Aristotle feels able to speak of "being," *tò òn*. This "being" is of a variety of substances— *Tōn ousiōn*—of which the philosopher must understand the principles and causes: but Aristotle can also write about "substance," *hē ousía*, in the singular, suggesting that there is a category of "substance" to which every substance belongs: and then he writes that the question "What is being?" simply *is* the question "What is substance?":[82] so perhaps "reality" might be a better translation of *ousía* than "substance."[83]

In book V we find two very different definitions being given to "substance": "the ultimate subject, which cannot be further predicated of something else; and whatever has an individual and separate existence"[84]—and

77. *tà ónta*
78. *hē ousía*
79. *tōn ousiōn*

80. Aristotle, *Metaphysics*, IV, 1003b5-20. The section and line numbers are taken from the Harvard University Press printed editions of the Loeb Classical Library. Line numbers are approximate because the marginal numbers in the printed edition give only an approximate indication of the numbering system.

81. Jonathan Barnes suggests that because *tò òn* refers to "the being" in the sense of a generalised being, rather than to Being, it should be translated as the plural "beings": Barnes, "Metaphysics," 69-70.

82. Aristotle, *Metaphysics*, VII, 1028b3-4: *tí tò ón, toũtó esti tís hē ousía*. The translation given is "'What is Being?' is in other words 'What is substance?'" The Greek suggests a stronger connection: "'What is Being?" is "What is substance?'"

83. Perl, *Thinking Being*, 83. Perl translates *tí tò ón, toũtó esti tís hē ousía* in *Metaphysics*, VII, 1028b3-4 as "What is that which is, that is, what is reality?"

84. Aristotle, *Metaphysics*, V, 1017b24-26; Barnes, "Metaphysics," 91.

then, in book VII, a single definition is offered: "We have now stated in outline the nature of substance—that it is not that which is predicated of a subject, but that of which the other things are predicated":[85] which suggests that the first of the definitions in book V means that, to be a substance, some being must be separable *and* not predicable of something else. The being must therefore be a separable *tóde ti*, a "separable this so-and-so."[86] Aristotle takes the example of a "snub nose." Here "nose" is the substance, because it is that of which "snub" is predicated, and a nose is separable.

> Now of things defined, i.e. of essences[87], some apply in the sense that "snub" does, and some in the sense that "concave" does. The difference is that "snub" is a combination of form with matter, because the "snub" is a concave nose, whereas concavity is independent of sensible matter.[88]

The connection between "essence" (*tí esti*, "what it is") and "substance" suggests a close relationship between substance and identity or definition: but Aristotle then has to recognise that "essence" is broader than "substance." "Substance" is generally a combination of form and matter—where "form," *eîdos*, is the particular characteristics of the particular substance under consideration—whereas "concave" is an example of an essence that might or might not be connected with matter.

> Now in one sense we call the matter[89] the substrate; in another, the shape; and in a third, the combination of the two. By matter I mean, for instance, bronze; by shape, the arrangement of the form; and by the combination of the two, the concrete thing: the statue. Thus if the form is prior to the matter and more truly existent, by the same argument it will also be prior to the combination.[90]

Here Aristotle recognises that there is a variety of ways of arranging *ousía*, "substance," *húlē*, "matter," *tí esti*, "essence" (*ousía* is often translated "essence" as well as "substance," which is rather confusing),[91] and *eîdos*, "form": but the tenor of the argument appears to be that the essence of something is

---

85. Aristotle, *Metaphysics*, VII, 1029a6–9.
86. Barnes, "Aristotle," 247.
87. *Tōn tí esti*
88. Aristotle, *Metaphysics*, VII, 1025b31–36.
89. *hē húlē*
90. Aristotle, *Metaphysics*, VII, 1029a2–8.
91. Aristotle, *Metaphysics*, I, 993a; IV, 1007a22.

its form,[92] or is its combination of matter and form, whereas the substance is more usually the combination of matter and form. Crucially, the "form," *eîdos*—which Aristotle also calls a "pattern," *parádeigma*, and sometimes *ousía prótē*, "primary or first substance"[93]—can be prior to the matter and therefore to the substance. The same Greek word that Aristotle uses for "form," *eîdos*, he also uses for "species," which is also referred to as "secondary substance" on the basis that species are not separable but also are not predicable of something else.[94] We can see the connection. All animals of the same species have the same form, and, because they are made of the same matter, they also have the same substance.

This all looks very sensible, and, if Plato's Forms are understood as "patterns," rather than as separate realities, then Aristotle and Plato differ only in relation to emphasis:[95] but, as Irwin suggests, "why should we prefer to follow common sense?"[96] There is in fact little consistency about what is a substance and what is not; and it is all rather arbitrary, particularly in relation to the "level" at which we find substances, and the level at which we find particulars that are not substances. (Barnes is harsher than this: "the argument is tortuous in the extreme . . . the *Metaphysics* is a farrago, a hotch-potch."[97])

When Aristotle turns to what kinds of item *are* substances, we find natural objects at the top of the list:

> Now some substances are agreed upon by all; but about others certain thinkers have stated individual theories. Those about which there is agreement are natural substances: e.g. fire, earth, water, air and all the other simple bodies; next, plants and their parts, and animals and the parts of animals; and finally the sensible universe and its parts; and certain thinkers individually include as substances the Forms and the objects of mathematics. And arguments show that there are yet other substances: the essence and the substrate. Again, from another point of view, the genus is more nearly substance than the species, and the universal than the particulars.[98]

---

92. Aristotle, *Metaphysics*, VII, 1032b1-2.
93. Aristotle, *Metaphysics*, VII, 1034a3; 1037a6.
94. Aristotle, *Categories*, I, 2a15-17; Lawson-Tancred, "Ancient Greek Philosophy II: Aristotle," 406-7.
95. Perl, *Thinking Being*, 86.
96. Irwin, *Classical Thought*, 126.
97. Barnes, "Metaphysics," 67-68.
98. Aristotle, *Metaphysics*, VIII, 1042a6-15.

But why *these* levels of reality? Why the genus rather than the species, or the species rather than the genus? And precisely which *mória*, "parts"? Why not atoms?—for each atom is a particular thing, with an essence. Aristotle assumes that the parts are less basic than the whole: but why regard the atom as part of a whole and thus less basic, and not the horse as part of the animal kingdom and thus less basic? Is there perhaps a system based on the use of words like "thing" at work here? With species, Aristotle has found a level at which thing and essence are identical, thus leading naturally to an identification between species and substance (when substance is identified with form), and of animal with substance (when particulars are in view); and at the same time he is able to define a "substance" as a particular thing: a *tóde ti*,[99] a something in particular. Language operates at the level of "horse," "man," and generally "thing," and not at the level of "atom": and so language-use has become the conceptual framework. After all, Aristotle often writes *légetai*, or *legoménōn*,[100] "as we say . . ."

But perhaps Aristotle cannot avoid adding conceptual and linguistic diversity to diversity of concepts. He compares his "forms," which never exist independently of particular beings, with Plato's Forms, which do:

> The thing in the sense of form or essence[101] is not generated, whereas the concrete whole[102] which is called after it is generated; and . . . in everything that is generated matter is present, and one part is matter and the other form.[103] Is there then some sphere besides the particular spheres, or some house besides the bricks? Surely no individual thing would ever have been generated if form had existed thus independently. Form means "of such a kind"[104]; it is not a definite individual, but we produce or generate from the individual something "of such a kind"; and when it is generated it is an individual "of such a kind." The whole individual, Callias or Socrates, corresponds to "this bronze sphere," but "man" and "animal" correspond to bronze sphere in general.[105]

---

99. Aristotle, *Metaphysics*, VII, 1017b18.

100. Aristotle, *Metaphysics*, IV, 1003b7, 9, 14, 15, 18.

101. *eĩdos è ousía*.

102. *súnolos*

103. *tò mèn tóde tò dè tóde*: It might be better to translate: "and it is both form and matter."

104. *tò toiónde*

105. Aristotle, *Metaphysics*, VII, 1033b17–27. See also I, 991a1–9.

Plato's Forms were always ideal, in the sense that no particular thing could perfectly embody a Form. This is necessarily the case with such Forms as Justice and the Good, but not with such forms as "horse."[106] For Aristotle, a bronze sphere is genuinely a sphere, and each man is genuinely a man, constituted by a soul combining with the matter of "body":

> Indeed there will be matter in some sense in everything which is not essence or form[107] considered independently, but a particular thing. . . . It is clear also that the soul is the primary substance,[108] and the body matter; and "man" or "animal" is the combination of both taken universally. And "Socrates" or "Coriscus" has a double sense, that is if the soul too can be called Socrates (for by Socrates some mean the soul and some the concrete person); but if Socrates means simply *this* soul and *this* body, the individual is composed similarly to the universal[109]

—that is, the individual man is soul and body, just as any man is. But however much the bronze sphere is genuinely a sphere, the lack of any transcendent world that can bind together the diverse things that we experience, and that we express using language that divides things into categories and levels, means that diversity will be untamable. There might be levels at which unity occurs (for instance, a substance is a unity, and any piece of matter is a unity): but still there are many different kinds of matter (bronze, the matter of a human being, and so on);[110] there are many different substances (both particular substances and species); and there are many forms, and many essences. Diversity is everywhere.

b. Motion and change

Things move, and Aristotle wants to understand how and why they do so: but things change in other ways, too, so we sometimes find "motion" treated as a particular example of a more general "change." Usually *kínēsis* implies movement, and *metabolé* (or the verb *metabállō*) mean change more generally: but sometimes *kínēsis* also seems to mean change in a more general sense, as when Aristotle discusses the fact that "natural" substances—that is, living beings—do not need to be moved by something or someone else

---

106. Chen, "Aristotle's Analysis of Change," 143.
107. *eînai kaì eîdos*
108. *psukhḕ ousía hē prṓ ousía hē prṓ tē.*
109. Aristotle, *Metaphysics*, VII, 1037a1–11.
110. Aristotle, *Metaphysics*, VII, 1029a5; VIII, 1045a23.

in order to produce movement, but must instead possess their own inner principle of motion:[111]

> Of things that exist, some exist by nature, some from other causes. "By nature" the animals and their parts exist, and the plants and the simple bodies (earth, fire, air, water)—for we say that these and the like exist "by nature." All the things mentioned present a feature in which they differ from things which are not constituted by nature. Each of them has within itself a principle of motion and of stationariness[112] (in respect of place, or of growth and decrease, or by way of alteration). On the other hand, a bed and a coat and anything else of that sort, qua receiving these designations, i.e. in so far as they are products of art—have no innate impulse to change.[113]

Here *arkhḕn kinḗseōs* is a "principle of motion," expressing change from within, with the change being as integral to a "thing that exists by nature" as is its form: and indeed, the ways in which the natural thing changes would appear to belong to its form.[114] As well as producing motion, the natural thing might produce change that we would not call "motion": "growth and decrease, or by way of alteration." *Kínēsis* is here change of place, of growth, and of alteration, so it possesses a more general meaning that is close to that of *metabolḗ*. Waterlow suggests that usually *metabolḗ* means change in a general sense, while *kínēsis* implies "process": but she also recognises that Aristotle can use *kínēsis* in a more general sense, as here.[115]

In the first chapter of the third book of the *Physics* we find an extended discussion of *kínēsis*:

> We may start by distinguishing (1) what exists in a state of fulfilment only, (2) what exists as potential, (3) what exists as potential and also in fulfilment.[116] ... Now each of these belongs to all its subjects in either of two ways: namely (1) substance—the one is positive form, the other privation; (2) in quality, white and black; (3) in quantity, complete and incomplete; (4) in respect of locomotion, upwards and downwards or light and heavy.

---

111. Waterlow, *Nature, Change, and Agency in Aristotle's* Physics, 1.
112. *hékaston en heautō̜ arkhḕn ékhei kinḗseōs kaì stáseōs*
113. *metabolḗs*: Aristotle, *Physics*, II, 192b8–21.
114. Lear, *Aristotle*, 19.
115. Waterlow, *Nature, Change, and Agency in Aristotle's* Physics, 94.
116. *ésti dḕ [ti] tò mèn entelekheía̜ mónon, tò dè dunámei kaì entelekheía̜*. "We may start by distinguishing (1) what exists in a state of fulfilment only, and (2) what as potential and also in fulfilment," would seem to be a more natural translation.

> Hence there are as many types of motion or change[117] as there are meanings of the word "is." ... Examples will elucidate this definition of motion.[118] When the buildable, in so far as it is just that, is fully real, it is being built, and this is building. Similarly, learning, doctoring, rolling, leaping, ripening, aging.[119]

Here *kínēsis* represents a variety of kinds of change, and in relation to all of them it means change or motion *towards* something. There is always an end or purpose, a *télos*, represented in the passage above by the process of building, and not the building being built.

Aristotle suggests that there are four different causes of things: the formal, material, efficient, and final causes:

> Of these we hold that one is the essence or essential nature of the thing (since the "reason why" of a thing is ultimately reducible to its formula, and the ultimate "reason why" is a cause and principle); another is the matter or substrate; the third is the source of motion[120]; and the fourth is the cause which is opposite to this, namely the purpose or "good"[121]; for this is the end[122] of every generative or motive process.[123]

"Cause" for Aristotle is not some event separate from the event that constitutes the change. The "cause" is the form, the matter, the "source of motion," and the "end." The "source of motion" might look like an event separate from the change caused, but it is not, as the example of building shows. The builder building is the "efficient cause": but there is no sense that the event of the builder building is different from the process of building.[124] If there is something antecedent to the event of the change, then that something is a thing: for instance, a builder, and not another event.[125]

As well as *télos*, Aristotle employs the word *entelékheia*, "actuality," "actualisation," or "fulfilment." Do the two words mean the same? "The fulfilment[126] of what exists potentially, in so far as it exists potentially, is

---

117. *kinéseōs kaì metabolḗs*
118. *kínēsis*
119. Aristotle, *Physics*, III, 1.
120. *kinéseōs*
121. *agathón*
122. *télos*
123. Aristotle, *Metaphysics*, I, 983a24–35.
124. Lear, *Aristotle*, 33.
125. Lear, *Aristotle*, 63.
126. *entelékheia*

kínēsis."[127] Does *entelékheia* mean the *télos* itself, or the *process* whereby the *télos* is reached, as Kosman proposes ("the actuality of the buildable *qua* buildable, that is, *the constitutive actuality of being buildable*, must be the process of building"[128]), and as Heinaman also suggests ("the potentiality whose actuality is change"[129])? While Aristotle identifies *télos* with *enérgeia*,[130] in the *Metaphysics* he prefers the more active term *enérgeia* to the more static *télos*:

> Now of these processes we should call the one type motions[131], and the other actualizations[132]. Every motion[133] is incomplete—the processes of thinning, learning, walking, building—these are motions, and incomplete at that. For it is not the same thing which at the same time is walking and has walked, or is building and has built, or is becoming and has become, or is being moved and has been moved, but two different things; and that which is causing motion is different from that which has caused motion. But the same thing at the same time is seeing and has seen, is thinking and has thought. The latter kind of process, then, is what I mean by actualization[134], and the former what I mean by motion[135].[136]

Ackrill has discovered a number of different distinctions between *kínēsis* and *enérgeia* in Aristotle's various treatises,[137] but in this passage *kínēsis* seems to apply where there is an end in view, and movement (understood as change) towards it, whereas *enérgeia*, actualization, expresses a situation that has been reached, but one that we might also describe as an ongoing situation or process.[138] *Enérgeia* is different from change because the doing of it and the having done it occur at the same time, whereas the changing

---

127. *Hē toũ dunámei óntos entelékheia, hē̦ toioũton, kínēsís estin*: Aristotle, *Physics*, III, 1, 201a10–11. See Lear, *Aristotle*, 60.

128. Kosman, "Aristotle's Definition of Motion," 54.

129. Heinaman, "Is Aristotle's Definition of Change Circular?" 36–37.

130. Aristotle, *Metaphysics*, IX, 1050a7–10: *télos d' hē enérgeia*

131. *kinēseis*

132. *energeías*

133. *kínēsis*

134. *enérgeian*

135. *kínēsin*

136. Aristotle, *Metaphysics*, IX, 1048b27–35.

137. Ackrill, "Aristotle's Distinction between *Energeia* and *Kinesis*."

138. Ackrill, "Aristotle's Distinction between *Energeia* and *Kinesis*," 122; Oliver, *Philosophy, God and Motion*, 42.

and having changed do not occur at the same time.[139] Activity or actuality is also different from change because an activity belongs to the being itself, whereas change is caused by some outside influence, or by something within a being that is not integral to the being itself.[140] The English "actualization" suggests a static final destination of a movement or other process, but this is not what *enérgeia* in fact suggests. *Enérgeia* is as active as is the movement that arrives at it: so "activity" might generally be the better translation:[141] suggesting that in the context of Aristotle's philosophy, "action" and "motion" need to be kept separate from each other, the former being the end towards which the latter moves, and the latter not being complete until the "action" is reached.[142] "Motion," *kínēsis*, is not an "end," whereas *enérgeia*, "action," "actuality," is.[143]

Dúnamis, "potentiality," can be "any principle of motion or of rest"[144],[145] a "capacity to change"[146] waiting for change to occur. Aristotle relates *dúnamis* to *enérgeia*, "potentiality" to "actuality": "A thing may exist only actually[147] or potentially[148], or actually and potentially"; and he also thought, that whereas in terms of a being's particular history potentiality precedes actuality, actuality in fact has to precede potentiality, because only something that actually possesses some characteristic can propel something from the potential for that characteristic towards its actuality: "the actual is prior to the potential with which it is formally identical, but not to that with which it is identical numerically."[149] [150] Aristotle's *dúnamis*, "potentiality," can also be translated "power" or "activity," which somewhat removes the sense that the potential might not be being realised, but does emphasize

---

139. Heinaman, "Alteration and Aristotle's Activity-Change Distinction," 227. Heineman shows that alteration in something's "quality" can be both change and activity, meaning that the boundary between activity and change is not a very clear one: Heineman, "Alteration and Aristotle's Activity-Change Distinction," 237, 243, 257.

140. Gill, "Aristotle's Distinction between Change and Activity," 11.

141. Perl, *Thinking Being*, 90.

142. Broadie has shown how both action and particular things are subject to the same fourfold causation, suggesting a point of connection between action and being: Broadie, "Aristotle on Rational Action," 80.

143. Aristotle, *Metaphysics*, IX, 1048b27–35.

144. *arkhēs kinētikēs è statikēs*

145. Aristotle, *Metaphysics*, IX, 1049b6–11.

146. Barnes, "Aristotle," 255–56.

147. *energeía*

148. *dunámei*

149. Aristotle, *Metaphysics*, IX, 1049b18.

150. This is an unnecessary presupposition: Barnes, "Metaphysics," 96.

the idea's close connection with movement, and also suggests that *dúnāmis* is an internal principle of motion that can itself propel a situation towards *enérgeia*.[151]

In the *Physics*,[152] Aristotle had used the term *entelekheía*, "actuality," "actualizing," "fulfilment," or perhaps "what is fully real," to express the actualizing of potential: but in the *Metaphysics* he prefers the more active word, *enérgeia*, "energy," "action," rather as Heraclitus did, to express something actualizing its potential. This gives a more active expression to the idea of change: so while there is a difference between the two ways of existing—*dunámei* and *energeíą*—both of them imply action or activity: and by identifying *télos* with *enérgeia*[153] Aristotle has identified the "end" of motion or change as an active driving force rather than a static end-point. Aristotle is of course aware that "rest"[154] occurs, but it is not insignificant that in the context of this discussion, *télos*, *enérgeia* and *dúnāmis* all connote action rather than something more static.

c. Being and substance, motion and change

How does the movement and change that we have discussed in the previous section relate to the matter, substance, and form, that we discussed in the section before that? For Aristotle, change is highly diverse in relation to the different categories of being:

> A thing may exist only actually[155] or potentially[156], or actually and potentially; it may be a substance or a quantity or one of the other categories. There is no motion[157] apart from things, for change[158] is always in accordance with the categories of Being; and there is nothing which is common to these and in no one category. Each category belongs to all its members in two ways—e.g. substance[159], for this is sometimes the form of the thing and sometimes its privation; and as regards quality there is white and black; and as regards quantity, complete and

151. Aristotle, *Physics*, II, 192b8–21.
152. Aristotle, *Physics*, III, 201a10–12.
153. Aristotle, *Metaphysics*, IX, 1050a7–10. See Perl, *Thinking Being*, 91.
154. *stasis*
155. *energeíą*
156. *dunámei*
157. *kínēsis*
158. *metabállei*
159. *tò tóde*: "what it is"; not *ousía*

incomplete; and as regards spatial motion there is up and down or light and heavy—so that there are as many forms of motion[160] and change[161] as there are of Being.[162]

If the matter were to change then the substance would change. If the matter in question is purely one of the elements, and if one element changes into another element, then the matter will change.[163] Change can also occur when the matter is not purely one of the elements:

> The actual matter of the living body becomes by degeneration the potentiality and matter of the dead body, and water the matter of vinegar; for the one becomes the other just as day becomes night. All things which change reciprocally[164] in this way must return into the matter; e.g., if a living thing is generated from a dead one, it must first become the matter, and then a living thing; and vinegar must first become water, and then wine.[165]

However, the matter does not need to change for the substance to change. At the beginning of this section we discussed Aristotle's use of *kínēsis* in the context of living beings possessing their own principles of motion or change. Non-natural substances do not possess their own principles of change: but they can be changed by external agents,[166] as when a sculptor makes a statue:[167] an example of a substance changing by a concrete whole[168] coming into existence.[169] The matter does not change (bronze remains bronze), and the form does not change (a sphere remains a sphere), and species do not change: but the substance of the bronze sphere (a substance because separable and not predicable of something else) comes into existence, so change occurs.

---

160. *kinḗseōs*

161. *metabolḗs*

162. Aristotle, *Metaphysics*, XI, 1065b1–14.

163. Krizan, "Substantial Change and the Limiting Case of Aristotelian Matter," 297, 307.

164. *metabállei eis állēla*

165. Aristotle, *Metaphysics*, VIII, 1045a1–7.

166. Coope and Shields, "Aristotle on Action," 126–27.

167. Aristotle, *Metaphysics*, VII, 1035a30–35.

168. Aristotle, *Metaphysics*, VII, 1033b16.

169. Aristotle, *Physics*, I, 190b6–24.

Another form of change is when a substance remains the same but changes in relation to its quality, quantity, or location: and in these cases the substance continues as before.[170]

Substances can also experience changes in their "accidents" ("accident" is "the thrown together," *tò sumbebēkós*).[171] If a man is cultured, then being cultured is an accident. The man might not have been cultured.[172] Culture is not a substance because it is not separable from the man.[173] Similarly, the size of a brass sphere might be accidental: so the sphere can change without the matter or the form changing. The substance can be modified while remaining the same substance:[174]

> There must always be an underlying something, namely that which becomes, and that this, though always one numerically, in form at least is not one. (By that I mean that it can be described in different ways.) For "to be man" is not the same as "to be unmusical." One part survives, the other does not: what is not an opposite survives (for "man" survives), but "not-musical" or "unmusical" does not survive, nor does the compound of the two, namely "unmusical man."[175]

Aristotle would therefore be able to say to Heraclitus that we *can* step into the same river twice.[176] The form and matter would be the same, and the modification in the substance of the river that the flowing water might bring about would be irrelevant to the fact that it was still the same river.

Kínēsis, "movement," and more generally "change,"[177] whether understood as a process or as an event,[178] appears to be as intrinsic to Aristotle's explorations as are the continuities represented variously by form, matter, essence, and substance: and Aristotle's treatment of it is just as diverse. *Metabolḗ* also connotes a range of kinds of change, and is generally used for change that is not motion: but there appears to be another difference between the meanings of the two words as well. While a change will always be continuous (a

---

170. Aristotle, *Categories*, V, 4a10–34; *Physics*, I, 190a35–b6; Gill, *Aristotle on Substance*, 6.
171. Aristotle, *Metaphysics*, V, 1017a8–9, 17, 19.
172. Aristotle, *Metaphysics*, V, 1017b27–1018a3.
173. Barnes, "Aristotle," 248.
174. Aristotle, *Metaphysics*, IV, 1003b6–10.
175. Aristotle, *Physics*, 1, 190a15–21.
176. Irwin, *Classical Thought*, 126.
177. Barnes, "Aristotle," 254.
178. Kostman, "Aristotle's Definition of Change," 3, 14.

discontinuity, or a period of rest, would represent a distinction between two separate changes[179]), *metabolé* would appear to connote a change from one state to another, with the attention on both the former state and the latter state,[180] whereas *kínēsis* suggests that we should pay more attention to the end or purpose of the change or motion, and to the transition towards the end in view[181]: but both words suggest something active (*metabolé* suggests one situation being thrown into another). In fact, all of the words that Aristotle uses to discuss change—*enérgeia*, *dúnāmis*, *kínēsis*, *metabolé*—would appear to connote action of some kind. Change, whether motion or other kinds of change, functions in a cosmos suffused with action. And another word that connotes action is, perhaps surprisingly, *ousía*, "being." As Kosman puts it:

> Aristotle finds at the heart of all being that which is unmoved, but not inactive. At the heart of the cosmos is that which is full act, total shining forth of being. Substance, that is, *ousía* or being, is an activity, an entity's manifesting what it is; to be a man is to shine forth with humanity, to act one's manhood out in the world.[182]

d. Things that change

What we have here is a conceptual system in which diversity and unity, and change and the unchanging, can all function together, with the fundamental difference from Plato being that the forms (and the species), although theoretically at the "unchanging" end of the spectrum, do not exist independently of particular things, so they do not in fact occupy that extreme end. What might occupy that extreme end is the essence or substance, the *ousía*, of each particular thing; although the fact that any being can be modified by accidents, that substances can change, and that a natural substance can change itself, suggests that in practice each substance or essence is in fact located at some distance from the "unchanging" end of the changing/unchanging spectrum, and that the entire conception of reality might be better described in terms of "action" than in terms of "being": unless, of course, being is understood in terms of action.

179. Bowin, "Aristotle on the Unity of Change."
180. Segvic, "Aristotle's Metaphysics of Action."
181. Charles, *Aristotle's Philosophy of Action*, 36, 58; Waterlow, *Nature, Change, and Agency in Aristotle's* Physics, 93, 96.
182. Kosman, "Aristotle's Definition of Motion," 54.

Matter is diverse (it might be bronze, or it might be something else): but does bronze change? It would appear not: although Aristotle recognises that the matter of a human person changes on the person's death. So yes, perhaps some kinds of matter belong at the unchanging end of the spectrum in the same way that forms belong there: but just as forms do not exist apart from particular things, so matter never exists in isolation from particulars, so again there is nothing that in fact sits at the far static end of the spectrum. We have already seen that motion connects potency and actuality, or activity, and that it is characterized by the *télos*, the "end," towards which something moves. In terms of "being" language: motion "intensifies the being of the potential towards the actual,"[183] suggesting degrees of being: so again, we avoid the ends of a spectrum. On whichever spectrum we are trying to locate Aristotle—the being/action, unity/diversity, or changing/unchanging spectrum—it is difficult to place his work at either of the extreme ends. Aristotle has attempted to understand a world of changing things. There is no sense in which change or action is fundamental, in the Heraclitean sense, because where change does occur it is not necessarily a change in form, matter, essence, or substance: but the change is real nevertheless.

Aristotle's explorations, by refusing to ignore particular things, changes, relationships, and activities that he knows about, cannot result in a clear theoretical structure within which he can comprehend these various notions. Definitions and relationships therefore shift, and there are no final resolutions. What we are left with is a rough working paradigm with revisable components, and one that locates every particular thing away from either end of the various spectrums, with each thing connected in some way to the "unchanging" and "being" ends by its form, matter, and possibly substance, and to the "changing" and "action" ends by various kinds of change and by the thing's activity or actuality. Similarly, diversity belongs to particular things, and "oneness" to substances: so the diversity of accidents and forms connects things to the diversity end of the spectrum, and the substances that constitute the particulars connect them to the unity end of the spectrum even if the particulars are not there themselves:

> In general those things whose concept, which conceives the essence, is indistinguishable and cannot be separated either in time or in place or in definition, are in the truest sense one[184]; and of these such as are substances are most truly one.[185]

---

183. Oliver, *Philosophy, God and Motion*, 45.
184. *málista taūta hén*
185. Aristotle, *Metaphysics*, V, 1016b1–5.

While it is not our immediate task here to study Aristotle's understanding of time, it will serve our general purpose to note that for Aristotle time is not an unchanging framework through which we move and within which events happen, but is rather itself defined by "motion" (which functions as the typical kind of change for Aristotle[186]) and by the order in which events occur:[187]

> But we apprehend time only when we have marked motion[188], marking it by "before" and "after"; and it is only when we have perceived "before" and "after" in motion that we say that time has elapsed.[189]

If we put together these last two passages, we find that the unchanging is defined within a context of change. Aristotle experiences both change and stability, and he is trying to create a coherent metaphysic that takes full account of both. He therefore posits substance, form, and matter as the building-blocks of reality understood as things that change, but never outside a context of constant and ubiquitous change. He has started from the unchanging, and has worked hard to understand change within that conext; and he starts from change and understands the unchanging. Where Aristotle's conceptual structure might be located on our various spectrums is in fact quite easy to say: it is all over them, but never in practice at either end, even if parts of the conceptual structure are in theory at one end of a spectrum.

e. God as Action

> There is something which is eternally moved with an unceasing motion, and that circular motion. This is evident not merely in theory, but in fact. Therefore the "ultimate heaven" must be eternal. Then there is also something which moves it. And since that which is moved while it moves is intermediate, there is something which moves without being moved; something eternal which is both substance and actuality.[190]

---

186. Heinaman, "Alteration and Aristotle's Activity-Change Distinction," 257.
187. Coope, *Time for Aristotle*.
188. *kínēsin*
189. Aristotle, *Physics*, IV, 219a23–25.
190. Aristotle, *Metaphysics*, XII, 7, 1072a21–26. See Aristotle, *Physics*, VIII, 9, on the priority of circular motion.

Aristotle goes on to suggest that because an object of desire has no need to move in order to create movement, the movers of the celestial spheres must be equal in number to the number of the heavenly spheres,[191] and must be objects of desire: desirable in themselves, and not in relation to something else, and therefore good, and "the good itself"[192].[193]

At the end of the *Metaphysics*, the discussion of causes becomes obliquely theological: "there is something—X—which moves while being itself unmoved,[194] existing actually, X cannot be otherwise in any respect":[195] and then *ti*, "something," becomes explicitly theological:

> Hence it is actuality rather than potentiality that is held to be the divine possession of rational thought, and its active contemplation is that which is most pleasant and best. If, then, the happiness which God always enjoys is as great as that which we enjoy sometimes, it is marvellous; and if it is greater, this is still more marvellous. Nevertheless it is so. Moreover, life belongs to God. For the actuality of thought is life, and God is that actuality[196]; and the essential actuality of God is life most good and eternal. We hold, then, that God is a living being, eternal, most good; and therefore life and a continuous eternal existence belong to God; for that is what God is.[197]

Here perhaps we find the root of the tensions between the changing and the unchanging that we have found throughout our study of Aristotle's *Metaphysics*. The particular things—human beings, statues, horses—change, but their substances, their matters, and their forms do not change (although one form might be replaced by another, and a substance might degenerate or be generated). Different sets of causes relate to natural beings (such as horses) and to non-natural beings (such as statues and beds), but both kinds of substance can come into existence and pass out of existence, and both kinds can change.[198] God might be *akínēton*, "unmoved," but at the same

---

191. Aristotle, *Metaphysics*, XII, 8, 1074a15–16.
192. *hautò hairetòn*
193. Aristotle, *Metaphysics*, XII, 7, 1072a26–32. See Barnes, "Metaphysics," 104.
194. *epeì dè ésti ti kinoûn autò akínēton ón, energeíą ón*
195. Aristotle, *Metaphysics*, XII, 1072b8–9.
196. *enérgeia*
197. Aristotle, *Metaphysics*, XII, 1072b23–31. Perl, *Thinking Being*, 93, suggests that "divine" would be a better translation than "God." Aristotle uses the definite article with *theòs*, so it is not clear why "God" should not be the translation.
198. Aristotle, *Metaphysics*, V, 1015a13–19; VIII, 1043b14–23. See Hankinson, "Philosophy of Science," 120.

time God has *zōḕ aristē kaì aḯdios*, "life most good and eternal," and God is *enérgeia*, which means "action, operation, energy,"[199] as well as "actuality."

> The activity[200] of God, which is transcendent in blessedness, is the activity of contemplation; and therefore among human activities that which is most akin to the divine activity of contemplation will be the greatest source of happiness.[201]

Oliver suggests that there can be no community between an unmoved mover and a cosmos characterized by motion:[202] but "unmoved mover" is not Aristotle's only understanding of God. Aristotle finds himself living in a world in which change happens to things that exhibit continuity, and God, even though an unmoved mover, experiences "activity," *enérgeia*. Aristotle was a voracious thinker, in the sense that he could always see the multiple connections between the various things that he was writing about, and also connections with numerous other factors and considerations. Tidy and systematic writing was therefore impossible, and sometimes he would fail to offer a watertight definition of an important concept (such as "action")[203] or to answer what looks to us like an important question (for instance, "What is it to act for a reason?"),[204] because that would not be what had taken his interest, or because he had been waylaid by tangential ideas and connections. What emerges is a creative and somewhat chaotic search for patterns and continuities within the fascinating diversity of the world as Aristotle experienced it. The world, God, and Aristotle, are full of *enérgeia*: an "actuality" which is "action, operation, energy."[205]

f. Diverse positions on the action/being spectrum

By constructing a metaphysics around a diverse set of concepts—substance, form, species, essence, actuality, potential, and cause—Aristotle has taken account of both the continuities and the change. Perhaps we should value the fact that he has achieved this combination, and not complain too much that he has not managed to weld everything into something entirely consistent.

---

199. Liddell and Scott, *An Intermediate Greek-English Lexicon*.
200. *enérgeia*
201. Aristotle, *Nicomachean Ethics*, 1178b22–24.
202. Oliver, *Philosophy, God and Motion*, 45.
203. Ackrill, "Aristotle on Action," 601.
204. Coope, "Aristotle," 445.
205. Liddell and Scott, *An Intermediate Greek-English Lexicon*.

The connections between the changing and the unchanging, in God, and in the universe, are far from clear, and our flexible, changing, and often ambiguous[206] language hinders precise formulation of the problem and of possible solutions, and itself epitomizes the problem. No linguistic formula will ever express the connections that we seek to express. Language is, after all, an integral part of a diverse and changing world, and subject to the same causes as everything else: and perhaps it fulfils its function best when, as rhetoric, it expresses change and action. As Aristotle says in the *Rhetoric*:

> ... few of the propositions of the rhetorical syllogism are necessary, for most of the things which we judge and examine can be other than they are, human actions[207], which are the subject of our deliberation and examination, being all of such a character and, generally speaking, none of them necessary.[208]

In the *Physics* and the *Metaphysics*, just as much as in the *Rhetoric*, Aristotle is employing the language available to him in order to understand the evidence of his senses. He understands the diversity inherent in every field of experience, and that the task is to create order out of the diversity. His attempt is perhaps more intelligent than those that try to reduce everything to a single system: so we constantly find Aristotle's vocabulary and ways of putting things shifting, and a variety of terms used in similar and sometimes different ways. This is particularly true of his fundamental building blocks, *ousía*, "substance"/"essence," *húlē*, "matter," *tí esti*, "essence," and *eîdos*, "form" or "species"; and of the ambiguity inherent in such concepts as *dúnāmis* and *enérgeia*.

It might be thought that Aristotle's major achievements were the inventions of biology and logic. Not so. The *Metaphysics* is his major achievement, for it recognises that his philosophical forerunners could not get it right because they were trying to reduce the diversity to a unity. Aristotle, too, longed for a unity, and he believed that because all beings exist[209] they are in that sense one: but he also knew that diversity—of things, of sciences, and of everything else—is ubiquitous. When Aristotle used the concept of "unity," *toũ henòs*, it was in the context of a discussion of whether "Socrates" and "Socrates seated" should be identified with each other:[210] that is, in relation to particular beings. Each particular being exhibits unity, so unity can

206. Aristotle was well aware of homonymy, or ambiguity: Barnes, "Metaphysics," 74–75.
207. *práttousi*
208. Aristotle, *Rhetoric*, I, 2, 14, 1357a29–35.
209. Aristotle, *Metaphysics*, IV, 1003a1–1003b11, 1003b19–33.
210. Aristotle, *Metaphysics*, IV, 1004b1–7.

be discussed as a general concept, and things can be studied *qua* their unity: but just as there is no Being beyond beings that exhibit being, so there is no unity beyond beings that each exhibit unity.

For Aristotle, change is *real*. It is "a sort of actuality[211], or actuality of the kind described, hard to grasp, but not incapable of existing."[212] But in the end Aristotle could not bring himself to define change *primarily* in terms of action: "There is no motion[213] apart from things[214], for change[215] is always in accordance with the categories of Being"[216].[217] Perhaps if Aristotle had begun his exploration of the nature of particular things with an understanding of their activity and the ways in which they change, and had understood that change changes,[218] and if he had only then thought about the continuities, then we would have had a rather different metaphysic: but it would still not have been entirely consistent, and it would still have given us an understanding of reality all over the different spectrums, giving us yet more diversity. What it might have done, though, is to have tilted Aristotle towards the "action," "diversity" and "change" ends of the spectrums, and to have freed him more thoroughly from Plato's influence. We might then have been in a better position to construct a metaphysic that starts from the "change," "diversity" and "action" ends of the spectrums, rather than being stuck for so many centuries closer to the more "unchanging," "unity" and "being" ends.

D. COMPLEXITY

So far we have studied some remarkable thinkers, all of whom have made substantial contributions to our understanding of the world and of everything else. The inspiration that I for one experience as I read Parmenides and Heraclitus, as they try to create the language that they need in order to understand the very foundations of reality, is tinged with sadness that we no longer possess the books that they wrote. Plato took his inspiration largely from Parmenides, and created a philosophical system—we can only call it that—that has informed, and largely controlled, Western philosophy

---

211. *enérgeian*

212. Aristotle, *Physics*, III, 2, 201a9–15. See Waterlow, *Nature, Change, and Agency in Aristotle's* Physics, 109.

213. *kínēsis*.

214. *prágmata*

215. *metabállei*

216. *toũ óntos katēgorías*

217. Aristotle, *Metaphysics*, XI, 1065b7–8.

218. See Aristotle, *Metaphysics*, XI, 1068a1–7.

for two and a half thousand years: although it is still not clear what is at the heart of Plato's philosophical system: separately existing Forms, or forms as patterns that can only be said to exist when the things that we experience in the world participate in them. We face a similar dilemma when we study a later philosopher substantially influenced by Plato, Plotinus: "Generative of all, The Unity is none of all,"[219] and "we have here one identical Principle, the Intellect, which is the universe of authentic beings, the Truth."[220] It is not clear whether the "One," "the Unity," is here being identified with all that is, or whether it is not. Either interpretation would be possible. The One is an absolute transcendence: "they are Being and the Beings; it therefore transcends Being";[221] and at the same time "all things are from it."[222] This combination suggests that what we have here is a way of seeing the diversity in its totality, rather than a separate reality of some kind.[223]

One clear difference between Plato and Aristotle is that for Plato "The Good" is beyond being and form,[224] and it may be this unifying factor, and Plato's reluctance to get involved in the kind of detailed discussion of different kinds of reality in the things that we experience that Aristotle got drawn into, that secured Plato's place as the originator of the conceptual structure within which so much subsequent philosophy and theology has been carried out. Nobody else has achieved that. Aristotle, being more aware of the complexities of reality, has left us with a complex set of intertwined philosophical concepts and relationships. We can feel rather lost among the complexity, but at the same time we have to recognise the handywork of a philosopher who takes physics as seriously as he takes metaphysics.

The lesson to be learnt is that a neat system that encompasses diversity and unity, change and the unchanging, motion and rest, being and action, is simply not available. We end up either with a neat system that clings to the ends of a variety of spectrums, because, having lost hold of empirical anchorage, it has to set out from a particular place on each spectrum; or with a far from neat system that attempts to take account of empirical reality, of unity and diversity, of change and the unchanging, of movement and rest, and of being and action (and perhaps of Being and Action as well), and

---

219. *oūsa tōn pántōn oudén estin autōn*: Plotinus, *The Six Enneads*, VI, 9, 3, 36–41.

220. *Mía toínun phúsis haútē hēmīn, noūs, tà ónta pánta, hē alḗtheia*: Plotinus, *The Six Enneads*, V, 5, 3, 1–2. It is not clear why the word "authentic" has been inserted into this translation.

221. *Taūta dè tà ónta kaì tò ón; epékeina ára óntos*: Plotinus, *The Six Enneads*, V, 5, 3, 1–6.

222. *ex autoū pánta*: Plotinus, *The Six Enneads*, V, 2, 1, 7–10.

223. Perl, *Thinking Being*, 129.

224. Perl, *Thinking Being*, 105.

leaves us all over the various spectrums. Aristotle straddles these two positions. He leaves us all over the various spectrums, but at the same time he can still leave us with a God attached to the "unmoved" end of the "moving/unmoved" spectrum.

Where Plato has not influenced the road that Western philosophy has taken, Aristotle has done so, which means that we have taken a road that is still influenced by Plato, and is at the same time characterized by incoherence. We won't entirely escape incoherence, but we shall attempt to build something like a coherent actology. An important aspect of this task will be the attempt to connect being and action with each other. We have already found that Aristotle's *energeía*—often translated "in actuality," "actually"—can be understood as expressing an act of becoming, or an act of keeping in being, and we shall find Thomas Aquinas, a millennium and a half later, employing *in actu*, "in act," in a similar way. Over half a millennium later, we shall find Blondel even more clearly understanding *êtres en devenir*, "beings in [their] becoming."[225]

E. THOMAS AQUINAS'S "IN ACT"

The thirteenth century Dominican friar Thomas Aquinas set out to construct the nearest thing that we possess to a medieval theological theory of everything. The metaphysical structure is Aristotelian, not only in its employment of "matter," "form," and so on, but also in its understanding that motion is an important category. Aquinas follows Aristotle in suggesting that "every motion[226] is from something into something,"[227] where, like Aristotle's *kínēsis*, *motus*, "motion," embraces a variety of kinds of change ("local, quantitative or qualitative instances of change"[228]); and Aquinas extends Aristotle's understanding of causes in a somewhat Platonic direction when he suggests that "everything that is being moved is necessarily being moved by some other,"[229] that "every primary cause infuses its effect more powerfully than does a secondary cause,"[230] and that the chain of increasingly

225. Blondel, *L'Être et les Êtres*, 72. Translation by the author.

226. *omnis . . . motus*

227. Thomas Aquinas, *Commentaria in Octo Libros Physicorum*, V, 1, §641. See Oliver, *Philosophy, God and Motion*, 88–93.

228. Oliver, *Philosophy, God and Motion*, 92.

229. *omne quod movetur, ab aliquo alio moveri*: Aquinas, *Commentaria in Octo Libros Physicorum*, VII, 1, §885. See Oliver, *Philosophy, God and Motion*, 91.

230. *Omnis causa primaria plus est influens super suum causatum quam causa secunda universalis*: Aquinas, *Super Librum De Causis Expositio*, lectio 1; English translation from Aquinas, *Commentary on the* Book of Causes, quoted in Oliver, *Philosophy,*

powerful causes extends from local, quantitative, and qualitative change, through the motion of heavenly bodies, to the circular, "diurnal," motion of the heavenly spheres:[231] "The movements of bodies here below, which are various and multiform, must be referred to the movement of the heavenly bodies, as to their cause."[232] The first and most powerful cause, and the cause that infuses everything else, is God, the "first unmoved mover":[233] although given the broad meaning of *motus*, "first unchanged changer" would also be a legitimate translation. The alternative to a first unmoved mover would be an infinite regress, which Aquinas rejects because "then there would be no first mover, and, consequently, no other mover."[234] The argument is flawed in terms of its logic, but like other arguments in an apparently logical form, it expresses a theological conviction: that there is a first cause, and that that cause is God. Aquinas's argument for an unmoved mover does not rely simply on the idea that the circular movement of the heavenly spheres requires an unmoved mover, but rather that *every* movement is moved by God as well as by every other movement in the relevant causal chain.[235] As far as Aquinas is concerned, God, the first and unmoved mover, is the continuous creator of all that is, and the continuous mover of all motion.

The "first mover" moves the heavenly spheres and everything else by "willing and understanding and loving," and not by "motions," because motion is movement from potentiality to actuality, from potency to act, and God is "pure act, without the admixture of any potentiality."[236] The "willing and understanding and loving" by which God causes the heavenly spheres and everything else are "operations" that bring about no change in God:[237] but that is not all that there is to be said, because Aquinas can find within the unmoved mover a kind of movement that is analogous to the movement that we experience:

> Because God understands and loves Himself, in that respect . . . God moves Himself, not, however, as movement and change

---

God and Motion, 95.

231. *motus diurnus*: Aquinas, *Commentary on Aristotle's Metaphysics*, V, 8, §873.

232. *reducuntur in motum corporis caelestis, sicut in causam*: Aquinas, *Summa Theologiae*, 1a, 115, 3, responsio.

233. *primum movens non motum*: Aquinas, *Contra Gentiles*, III, 64, 4.

234. Aquinas, *Summa Theologiae*, I, 2, 3.

235. Aquinas, *Questiones Disputatae de Potentia Dei*, III, 7.

236. Aquinas, *Summa Theologiae*, I, 9, 1.

237. *intelligere et velle et amare*: Aquinas, *Summa Theologiae*, I, 9, 1.

> belong to a thing existing in potentiality, as we now speak of change and movement.[238]

Aquinas is aware that language can have different but related meanings in different contexts, as when he understands that the "divine operation is related to the being of things as the motion of a corporeal mover is to the becoming and passive movement of the things that are made or moved."[239] Aquinas was as interested in the status of the language that he was using as he was in the theology that he was trying to express; and here we have a clear recognition that he is employing analogy: that is, language normally used in one context now used in another, and now with a meaning both like and unlike its normal meaning. There is no direct relationship between the use of "motion" or "cause" used of God and uses of the same words in the context of the world or of human beings: but there *is* a relationship between the *relationship* between "motion" and "cause" language used of God and "motion" and "cause" language used of the physical and the human, and the *relationship* between God and the human and physical. This means that we can speak of "motion" in relation to the "unmoved mover":

> Life also is especially manifested in motion, for we say that self-moving things live and in general we say this of everything which puts itself into operation. If, then, by reason of love, drive and motion[240] are suited to the Holy Spirit, life is also suitably attributed to Him.[241]

> The love by which God is in the divine will as a beloved in a lover proceed[s] both from the Word of God and from the God whose Word He is.[242]

The basis of analogy resides in God, rather than in our attempts to speak of God:

> Whatever is said of God and creatures, is said according to the relation of a creature to God as its principle and cause, wherein all perfections of things pre-exist excellently. Now this mode of

---

238. Aquinas, *Contra Gentiles*, I, 9, 1.

239. *igitur se habet ad esse rerum operatio divina, sicut motio corporis moventis ad fieri et moveri rerum factarum vel motarum*: Aquinas, *Contra Gentiles*, III, 65, 6.

240. *impulsio et motio*

241. Aquinas, *Contra Gentiles*, IV, 20, 6. See Oliver, *Philosophy, God and Motion*, 117, on "a divine dynamism."

242. Aquinas, *Contra Gentiles*, IV, 19, 8.

> community of idea is a mean between pure equivocation and simple univocation[243]

—as is all analogy. So analogical language, like all motion, becomes a participation in the eternal self-movement of God.[244]

Aquinas's language is not only analogical, it is also quite fluid, so we find the causes of "motion" discussed elsewhere in terms of causes of "action":

> The higher the cause the greater its scope and efficacy: and the more efficacious the cause, the more deeply does it penetrate into its effect, and the more remote the potentiality from which it brings that effect into act.[245] . . . Therefore God is the cause of every action,[246] inasmuch as every agent is an instrument of the divine power operating.[247]

More significant for our purposes is the connection that Aquinas constructs between action and being: a connection expressed by the term *in actu* rather than by the word *motus*.

In his *De Ente et Essentia*, "on being and essence," Aquinas distinguishes between the *essentia* of a phoenix and its *esse*:[248] that is, between what it is (whether or not one exists), and its existence: "For I can understand what a man is, or what a phoenix is, and yet not know whether they have existence in the real world. It is clear, therefore, that existence is other than essence . . . ."[249] Essence is therefore a form of potentiality, and one that continues to adhere to a thing once it achieves actuality: that is, once it exists. The essence of a thing is its being something in particular: that is, its being something *in actu*, something actual or "in act":

> That matter alone is not the essence of a real thing is clear, since through its essence a real thing is knowable and assigned to a species or to a genus. But matter alone is neither a principle of knowledge, nor is it that by which something is assigned to a

---

243. Aquinas, *Summa Theologiae*, I, 13, 5; Perl, *Thinking Being*, 175.
244. Oliver, *Philosophy, God and Motion*, 118.
245. *in actum*
246. *Deus est causa omnis actionis.*
247. Aquinas, *Questiones Disputatae de Potentia Dei*, III, 7.
248. On the translation of *esse* see Kenny, *Aquinas on Being*, 34, and Perl, *Thinking Being*, 152–3. Here "existence" is the best translation.
249. *esse est aliud ab essential*: Aquinas, *De Ente et Essentia*, § 77.

> genus or to a species; rather a thing is so assigned by reason of its being something actual.[250]

This is Joseph Kenny's translation. Robert Miller translates the end of this passage somewhat differently:

> ... But matter is not a principle of cognition; nor is anything determined to a genus or species according to its matter but rather according to what something is in act.[251]

Further on in the same passage Aquinas writes:

> For through the form, which is the actuality of matter[252], matter becomes something actual and something individual.[253]

Again, Miller translates *actu* as "in act," and *actus* as "act":

> Through the form, surely, which is the act of the matter[254], the matter is made a being in act and a certain kind of thing.[255]

"A being in actuality" might be the best way to capture the two connected meanings of *actus*: 1. "actuality," that is, really existing, and 2. "act," that is, the act of being.[256] Matter alone does not constitute an individual being; and form alone might constitute a purely intelligible reality, but it could never constitute a being "in actuality." Form and matter together are required for the existence of a particular "individual being," that is, a being "in actuality," or "actually." The *actus*, "action," that occurs might be either a "coming into being," or a constant "act of existing"[257] or "act of being":[258] but most likely *esse*, existing, requires both an act of becoming and an act of being. It is this complex "act" that creates the "actuality."

If this action comes from within the possessor of existence, then it comes from the *essentia*, generating an *actus primus*, a "first actuality": "the essence itself gives *esse* to its possessor, and this actuality is as it were its first

---

250. *sed secundum id quod aliquid actu est*: Aquinas, *De Ente et Essentia*, § 15.
251. Aquinas, *On Being and Essence*, chapter II.
252. *est actus materiae*
253. *materia efficitur ens actu et hoc aliquid*: Aquinas, *De Ente et Essentia*, § 15.
254. *est actus materiae*
255. *materia efficitur ens actu et hoc aliquid*: Aquinas, *On Being and Essence*, chapter II.
256. Kretzmann, "Philosophy of Mind," 149.
257. Wippel, "Being."
258. Wippel, "Metaphysics," 97; Wippel, "Thomas Aquinas and the Axiom That Unreceived Act Is Unlimited," 564.

actuality."²⁵⁹ The *actus secundus*, the "second actuality," is "both the act of its possessor considered as an agent, and also the act of the essence, as the source of action."²⁶⁰ Here we are not far from the idea that essence implies action, and that that action is the essence's existence.

The word *actus* is also central to Aquinas's attempt to show that *Deum non esse corpus*, "God is not a body." God is not a body

> ... because the first being must of necessity be in act, and in no way in potentiality. For although in any single thing that passes from potentiality to actuality, the potentiality is prior in time to the actuality; nevertheless, absolutely speaking, actuality is prior to potentiality; for whatever is in potentiality can be reduced into actuality only by some being in actuality.²⁶¹

The argument is flawed, because something potentially hot can become something actually hot without the involvement of anything that is already actually hot,²⁶² so again Aquinas is expressing a theological conviction: that God is pure actuality, pure "in act."

As Burrell shows, Aquinas employs *actus* in a wide variety of contexts throughout his writings: of human action, of God's action, and of existence itself. *Actus* functions as a "primitive term incapable of being reduced to any other,"²⁶³ and as lying behind all reality. It is a "master metaphor," and "co-extensive with *ens* (being)."²⁶⁴ "Existence is that which actuates all things,²⁶⁵ even their forms."²⁶⁶ *Actus*, "action," is here being used analogically, with the analogy, as always, based on "the relation of a creature to God as its principle and cause."²⁶⁷

---

259. *et iste actus est quasi actus primus*: Aquinas, *Scriptum Super Sententiis*, I, 7, 1; English translation from Kenny, *Aquinas on Being*, 54. See also Kenny, *Aquinas on Being*, 59.

260. *etiam actus habentis essentiam sicut agentis, et essentiae, sicut principium agenda*: Aquinas, *Scriptum Super Sententiis*, I, 7, 1; English translation from Kenny, *Aquinas on Being*, 59.

261. ... *quia necesse est id quod est primum ens, esse in actu, et nullo modo in potentia. Licet enim in uno et eodem quod exit de potentia in actum, prius sit potentia quam actus tempore, simpliciter tamen actus prior est potentia, quia quod est in potentia, non reducitur in actum nisi per ens actu*: Aquinas, *Summa Theologiae*, I, 3, 1.

262. Aquinas, *Summa Theologiae*, I, 2, 3.

263. Burrell, *Aquinas*, 129.

264. Burrell, *Aquinas*, 116–17.

265. *ipsum esse est actualitas omnium rerum*.

266. Aquinas, *Summa Theologiae*, I, 4, 1, 3.

267. Aquinas, *Summa Theologiae*, I, 13, 5; Perl, *Thinking Being*, 175.

However analogical or metaphorical much of Aquinas's writing about *actus* might be—and the same could surely be said of *esse* and *essentia*, because we can gain knowledge of them only through acquaintance with the existence and essences of particular things—we have in Aquinas's philosophy a conceptual structure expressed as much in "action" terminology as in "being" terminology. It is as much an actology as it is an ontology. In this, in general and in particular, Aquinas follows Aristotle's categories and reasoning. Aquinas's use of *actus* mirrors Aristotle's use of *enérgeia*, which generally means "action" or "energy,"[268] as when Aristotle discusses God's activity,[269] but which can also carry the meaning "in action," that is, "in act," or "in actuality," when it appears in the dative, *energeía*: "A thing may exist only actually or potentially, or actually and potentially."[270]

In Aristotle, in Aquinas, and in the English language, we find connections between "action" and "actually," as in "exists actually": that is, something really does exist, rather than existing potentially, or only in thought. The "act" concerned is that something has come into existence: so the "action" is one of "becoming," or rather, of "having become" and of "continually being brought into being."

So while we might still translate both *energeía* and *in actu* as "actually," we might also wish to keep in mind the fact that something exists *actually* because it has come into existence and because there is a constant act of being. Action has occurred, and there is constant action. The consequence is that every being, including God, in order to exist at all, must exist "in actu." Action is prior to being.

F. ACTION EVERYWHERE

Plato could have done things differently. He could have added verb-based universals to his noun-based ones. He could have added "running," "thinking," "making"—and "being"—to "good," "justice," and "man." If he had, then all of the objects of our experience—"a man running," "doing justly," and so on—would have participated in both ends of an Action/Being spectrum. God, too, could have been at both ends of the spectrum, giving birth to the Forms—giving them actuality—as well as contemplating them. As David Bostock has pointed out, if Plato had followed up a line of thought briefly expressed in the *Sophist*, then this might have happened.

268. Liddell and Scott, *An Intermediate Greek-English Lexicon*.
269. *hē toũ theoũ enérgeia*: Aristotle, *Nicomachean Ethics*, 1178b.
270. *ésti dè tò mèn energeía mónon tò dè dunámei tò dè dunámei kaì energeía*: Aristotle, *Metaphysics*, book XI, 1065b.

"When one says 'a man learns,' you agree that this is the least and first of sentences, do you not?"

"Yes."

"For when he says that, he makes a statement about that which is or is becoming or has become or is to be; he does not merely give names, but he reaches a conclusion by combining verbs with nouns."[271]

This means that the verb "to be" is not a name: it does not indicate an object. It says something about something. And similarly for other more general words, such as "good," "justice," and so on. These might not *name* anything. They do not draw our attention to objects with those names. They say something, and therefore function as verbs.[272]

Similarly, Aristotle could have added to the idea that there is no motion without things[273] the notion that there are no things without action, without *enérgeia*, just as there is no God without *enérgeia*. A little more recognition that for Aquinas God and everything else is "in actu" would lead us in the same direction.

In his survey of the philosophies of Plato, Aristotle, and Aquinas, Oliver has found "motion," whether *kínēsis* or *motus*, to imply change of a variety of kinds, and also to imply what we would call motion. He also finds "motion" to be *the* link between God and everything else. As Oliver puts it: for Plato, Aristotle, and Aquinas,

> motion does not constitute the separation of discourses, but is a means of their unity. For Plato, in wholly undualistic fashion, motion is the very means by which we come to know all that is contained in the eternal stability of the Forms; it is, for Aristotle, the means of our passage from potency to actuality; . . . it is, for Aquinas, the means of our participation in the eternal dynamism of the Trinitarian life of God. . . . Motion, when understood analogically, can relate the different sciences one to another. On such an understanding, motion is not a simple category restricted to a single science; there exists a more delicate boundary between, for example, the motion of bodies through space, the motion of thought, and the motionless motion of the divine life. The basis of this understanding of motion is an

---

271. Plato, *Sophist*, 262c–d: . . . dēloī gàr édē pou tóte perì tōn óntōn è gignoménōn è gegonótōn è mellóntōn, kaì ouk onomázei mónon allá ti peraínei, sumplékōn tà rhḗmatatoīs onómasi. . . .

272. Bostock, "Plato on understanding language," 26–27.

273. Aristotle, *Metaphysics*, book XI, 1065b7–8.

analogical and participatory metaphysics which sees all motion in relation to its origin and *telos* in the divine life.[274]

We have found the same as we have surveyed the thought of Parmenides, Heraclitus, Hesiod, Plato, Aristotle, and Aquinas. We have discovered multiple positions on a variety of spectrums: change/the unchanging, motion/rest, and diversity/unity, and we have found readings of these thinkers that interpret being in terms of action, and unity in terms of diversity.

This finding is similar to Lesley Brown's conclusion relating to the verb "to be" in ancient Greek thought. She finds what she calls a "complete" meaning, when the verb means "exists," or "is real," and an "incomplete" meaning when it is used to introduce a predicate or an identity, which means that the incomplete meaning is itself divisible into those instances where the verb expresses an identity, a = b, and those where it introduces a predicate, a is c. Brown concludes that when Parmenides employs the verb "it is"[275] to mean "changelessness," then he is in fact employing it to express an incomplete meaning, because it implies a predicate, "changeless," and so use of the verb is similar to Plato's use when he is discussing opinion of what is and what is not: what is beautiful might not be, so the verb "to be" is used to introduce a predicate and is incomplete. However, when Plato uses the verb of the Forms, it is used with a complete meaning, because it expresses the reality: for instance, that the Form of Beauty exists, it is real. As Brown points out, there is a connection between the complete and the incomplete uses, because, for instance, something is good because the Form of the Good is real, and also the Form of the Good is good.

When we come to Aristotle's rather varied use of the verb "to be,"[276] we can identify different meanings, but they are often somewhat difficult to determine, and equally difficult to categorise. As Brown points out, Aristotle was interested in rather different distinctions: for instance, between essence, substance, and accident. So what we have here is not a simple spectrum strung in a straight line between two easily identifiable endpoints. We have diversity:[277] and we could perhaps add to the diversity our finding that both Heraclitus and Parmenides were working with a verb when they used "to be" in any of its forms, which means that whatever is is changing and active.

Similarly, there is no simple "being/action" distinction or spectrum, and no simple "Action/Being" distinction or spectrum, and no simple "diversity/unity" spectrum. What our discoveries do suggest is that "action"

---

274. Oliver, *Philosophy, God and Motion*, 189.
275. *éstin*
276. *tò eînai, tà ónta, tò òn*
277. Brown, "The verb 'to be' in Greek philosophy."

might be a useful "master metaphor" through which to understand the nature of reality. Change, motion, and being, can all be understood in terms of action; and because Plato and Aristotle employ the concept of *paradeígmata*, "patterns," "actions in patterns" is looking like an increasingly interesting terminology through which to understand reality.

Because analogical understanding is all that we have available to us in any science, the different sciences, including "divine science," can be connected with each other, and we no longer need to assume an impermeable boundary between them. And as we have seen throughout this chapter, a broad conception of motion that includes both change and motion, and that might also be expressed in terms of action, can achieve the same connection, and perhaps a deeper one as well. God can be understood to be constituted by action—by change and movement—and also to be Action, or action itself; and we and the whole cosmos can be understood as constituted by change and motion, by action. This suggests that in relation both to God and to everything else, "action" must be understood first of all as abstracted from all things that act, and only then as the patterned action that we experience. It must be understood as verb rather than noun, and as both Form and particular.

In order to create a metaphysic on the basis of "action," we have no need to abandon Plato, Aristotle, or Aquinas. On the contrary, they offer to us the possibility of an understanding of the cosmos and of God entirely in terms of motion, change, and action: so to measure any metaphysic that we create against their groundbreaking conceptual structures can only be good for it.

In Hesiod, Parmenides, Heraclitus, Plato, Aristotle, and Aquinas, we have found the building-blocks for the kind of metaphysic, or actology, that we shall need. We can now turn to more recent philosophers for an understanding of some of the detail of the actology that we might create.

4

Hegel's dialectic

A. INTRODUCTION

Georg Wilhelm Friedrich Hegel (1770–1831) presents us with massive collections of text. We plunge in, gaining a brief insight, or suffering intense confusion. What is it that we are trying to do? We are attempting to *understand*: to create a structure in our minds within which we can fit the ideas that Hegel was attempting to express. Or perhaps we are hoping that Hegel has grasped the true nature of reality in its many aspects, and that by understanding the text we too will grasp the nature of reality.

To understand our task in this way is in fact to understand Hegel: the man, as well as the text. He is reading his experience—of consciousness, self-consciousness, history, religion, and much else—in order to understand the nature of reality: and he finds, of course, as we necessarily do, that the nature of reality and the process of understanding it cannot be separated from each other. Hegel hopes to arrive at "the Absolute," or "absolute knowledge," and to grasp the *Geist* ("Mind" or "Spirit") that underlies and realises itself in the processes of consciousness and history, in much the same way that I hope to arrive at a clear understanding of Hegel's philosophy. To understand is a goal that I have set myself; and, in much the same way, to gain knowledge of the

Absolute, and a complete grasp of *Geist*'s process of self-realisation, are the goals that Hegel has constructed for his literary activity. Just as Hegel knew that any understanding of a reality beyond himself would be via an understanding of his consciousness, so I shall need to remind myself that any understanding that I gain will be via an understanding of *my* consciousness, for only if I do that shall I have any hope of understanding Hegel, in the sense of understanding his writings. Thus for me, as well as for Hegel, the process of understanding, and what is understood, are intimately connected, and what is known, and the process of gaining knowledge, are intimately connected.

An important question arises: How much of Hegel's text do I need to grapple with? My ultimate aim is to understand the nature of reality: so the questions that need to be addressed are these: Did Hegel understand reality?—and, if he did, how much of his text do I need to understand in order to understand what he understood? Perhaps no such understanding is possible. Hegel's understanding of reality was intimately connected with his understanding of his own consciousness, and, as he developed his understanding, he sought understanding of his self-consciousness. These are forever hidden from me. There is therefore a sense in which I can never grasp Hegel's understanding of reality. But let us suppose that consciousness and self-consciousness are in some sense universals as well as particulars, as Hegel in fact suggests: then to read Hegel might put me in touch with the connection between my understanding of my consciousness and my understanding of my self-consciousness, and might also put me in touch with my understanding of reality. I shall therefore need to read enough of Hegel to introduce me to the *process* through which he sought understanding and knowledge. As we do that, we might discover that consciousness is actions in patterns, that my self-consciousness is actions in patterns, and that reality as a whole is actions in patterns.

To study Marx is also to embark on a vast sea of primary and secondary literature. Again, I shall have to be selective, and I shall be referring to sufficient of Marx's literary output to enable me to outline his understanding of social and economic reality as dialectically-shaped action.

B. HEGEL

a. Geist and the Absolute

As the understanding of reality that I am exploring is one of actions in patterns, I shall interpret Hegel's *Geist* as the pattern that underlies the action that we discover in consciousness, self-consciousness, and objective reality, and in the action that we experience in the process of discovering these: with action here encompassing both motion and change, but not exhausted by them. Sometimes Hegel employs "the Absolute," or "absolute knowledge," to express an end-point to the process:

> Of the Absolute it must be said that it is essentially a result, that only at the end is it what it is in very truth; and just in that consists its nature, which is to be actual, subject, or self-becoming, self-development:[1]

and sometimes as an activity that we experience:

> The Absolute . . . is not to be grasped in conceptual form, but felt, intuited; it is not its conception, but the feeling of it and intuition of it that are to have the say and find expression.[2]

A conception of the Absolute that might combine these descriptions would be to see the Absolute as a direction or pattern that we experience in the action, alongside and intertwined with the pattern of action constituted by *Geist*'s self-realisation: although the way that Hegel uses both of the terms "*Geist*" and "*Das Absolute*" suggests that they express the same actions in patterns, with "the Absolute" expressing the pattern in terms of a direction, and *Geist* expressing the pattern's constantly changing characteristics. So "*Das Absolute*" and "*Geist*" are dynamic realities, just as Reason—a universal at work in every consciousness and self-consciousness—is "*zweckmäßige Tun*,"[3] "purposive activity."[4] It is within this foundational reality that all finite action and things are located, generating a particular kind of "idealism." It is the idea of the whole that provides the reality of the particular: a highly metaphysical claim.[5]

Within the overall patterning of action denoted by "*Geist*" or "the Absolute," we find a particular pattern to the action that Hegel has discovered in consciousness, in self-consciousness, and in the objective reality that he is getting to know. This pattern is "dialectic": a process that I shall explore in relation to a particular passage in Hegel's *Science of Logic*, because here connections with writers whom we have already discussed are explicit, and

---

1. Hegel, *Phänomenologie des Geistes*, Vorrede; Hegel, *Hegel's Phenomenology of Spirit*, § 20.
2. Hegel, *Phänomenologie des Geistes*, Vorrede; Hegel, *Hegel's Phenomenology of Spirit*, § 6.
3. Hegel, *Phänomenologie des Geistes*, Vorrede.
4. Hegel, *Hegel's Phenomenology of Spirit*, § 22.
5. Wartenberg, "Hegel's idealism," 107.

because in this particular dialectical movement "being" finds its fulfilment in action.

First of all, Being is posited:

> *Being, pure being*, without any further determination . . . it has no diversity within itself. . . . It is pure indeterminateness and emptiness. . . . Being, the indeterminate immediate, is in fact *nothing*, and neither more nor less than *nothing*.[6]

"Being" is indeterminate, so we are thinking "nothing," and any "nothing" is determined by whatever has been removed from consideration:

> *Nothing, pure nothing*: it is simply equality with itself, complete emptiness, absence of all determination and content. . . . In so far as intuiting or thinking can be mentioned here, it counts as a distinction whether something or nothing is intuited or thought. To intuit or think nothing has, therefore, a meaning; both are distinguished and thus nothing *is* (exists) in our intuiting or thinking; or rather it is empty intuition and thought itself, and the same empty intuition or thought as pure being. Nothing is, therefore, the same determination, or rather absence of determination, and thus altogether the same as, pure *being*.[7]

The logic here relies both on the way in which our minds are actually working when we think "being" and "nothing,"[8] and on the relationship that Hegel is building between subjectivity and objectivity "*in der ganze Begriff*" ("in the Notion," or concept).[9] Both "being" and "nothing" are either determined by contingencies, or they are empty: so thinking being and thinking nothing are the same, and a contradiction emerges between their opposition and their connection, and "becoming" (the definition of which contains elements of "being" and "nothing"[10]) emerges from them and is seen as what unites them:

> *Pure Being* and *pure nothing* are, therefore, the same. What is the truth is neither being nor nothing, but that being—does not pass over but has passed over—into nothing, and nothing into being. But it is equally true that they are . . . absolutely distinct, and yet that they are unseparated and inseparable and that each immediately *vanishes in its opposite*. Their truth is therefore, this

---

6. Hegel, *Wissenschaft der Logik*, Kapitel 5; Hegel, *Hegel's Science of Logic*, §132.
7. Hegel, *Wissenschaft der Logik*, Kapitel 5; Hegel, *Hegel's Science of Logic*, §133.
8. Burbidge, "Hegel's Conception of Logic," 95.
9. Hegel, *Wissenschaft der Logik*, Kapitel 2; Hegel, *Hegel's Science of Logic*, §78.
10. Forster, "Hegel's dialectical method," 131.

> movement of the immediate vanishing of the one into the other: *becoming,* a movement in which both are distinguished, but by a difference which has equally immediately resolved itself. . . .
>
> It was the *Eleatics,* above all Parmenides, who first enunciated the simple thought of *pure being* as the absolute and sole truth: *only being is, and nothing absolutely is not,* and in the surviving fragments of Parmenides this is enunciated with the pure enthusiasm of thought which has for the first time apprehended itself in its absolute abstraction. . . . Against that simple and one-sided abstraction the deep-thinking Heraclitus brought forward the higher, total concept of *becoming* and said: *being* as little *is,* as nothing is, or, *all flows,* which means, all is a *becoming.* . . .[11]

I have not been able to find a Heraclitus fragment that says that, but Heraclitus's unity of opposites looks as if it lies behind Hegel's dialectic; the consistent principle that Hegel finds in *Geist* structures his system in much the same way as both *lógos,* "reason" or "account," and *pūr,* "fire," structure Heraclitus's; and, for both of them, reality is a constant process of change.[12]

> *Becoming* is the unseparatedness of being and nothing, not the unity which abstracts from being and nothing; but as the unity *of being and nothing* it is this *determinate* unity in which there *is* both being and nothing. But in so far as being and nothing, each unseparated from its other, *is,* each *is not.* They *are* therefore in this unity but only as vanishing, sublated moments [*Aufgehobene*]. They sink from their initially imagined *self-subsistence* to the status of *moments,* which are still *distinct* but at the same time are sublated.[13]

Aufgehoben, translated by Miller as "sublated," is a past participle that expresses the relationship that "being" and "nothing" experience within the unity provided by "becoming." Each is a "moment" of "becoming," and each of these two "moments," "being" and "nothing," is constantly—instantaneously—both abolished and affirmed in the other: they are *aufgehoben,* sublated.[14]

---

11. Hegel, *Wissenschaft der Logik,* Kapitel 5; Hegel, *Hegel's Science of Logic,* §§ 134–36.

12. Heraclitus, *Fragments,* fragments 60, 126, 2, 30, 12. See Williams, *Hegel, Heraclitus, and Marx's Dialectic,* x, 11–13.

13. Hegel, *Wissenschaft der Logik,* Kapitel 5; Hegel, *Hegel's Science of Logic,* § 176.

14. See Hegel, *Phänomenologie des Geistes,* §§ 167, 170; Hegel, *Phenomenology of Mind,* §§ 167, 170. Hegel here also uses the noun *Aufheben,* which Baillie translates as "sublation." Baillie translates *aufgehoben* as "sublated," "superseded," or "removed." See Adams, *Eclipse of Grace,* 32.

The relationship that Hegel establishes between "being," "nothing," and "becoming," in the *Science of Logic*, is just one example of "dialectic": a "logic"[15] that Hegel finds to be ubiquitous, both in the ways in which our minds work, and in the way in which the history of the world unfolds, and therefore in the way in which knowledge has to be pursued.

For Immanuel Kant, phenomena (what we experience) and noumena (things in themselves) are forever divided:

> The conception of a noumenon, that is, of a thing which must be cogitated not as an object of sense, but as a thing in itself (solely through the pure understanding), is not self-contradictory, for we are not entitled to maintain that sensibility is the only possible mode of intuition. Nay, further, this conception is necessary to restrain sensuous intuition within the bounds of phenomena, and thus to limit the objective validity of sensuous cognition; for things in themselves, which lie beyond its province, are called noumena for the very purpose of indicating that this cognition does not extend its application to all that the understanding thinks. But, after all, the possibility of such noumena is quite incomprehensible, and beyond the sphere of phenomena, all is for us a mere void; that is to say, we possess an understanding whose province does problematically extend beyond this sphere, but we do not possess an intuition, indeed, not even the conception of a possible intuition, by means of which objects beyond the region of sensibility could be given us, and in reference to which the understanding might be employed assertorically.[16]

Hegel never achieved a robust refutation of Kant's arguments,[17] but he found Kant's division between phenomena and noumena, and the related division between knowledge and being, inadequate as a basis for knowledge. Hegel's entire philosophical project can be seen as an attempt to combine phenomena and noumena in a single understanding of reality:[18] so what he needed was a conceptual structure that would enable him to connect phenomena with things in themselves. This he attempted through multiple dialectics: through a dynamic process, as opposed to the rather

15. Burbidge, "Hegel's conception of logic," 87.
16. Kant, *Kritik der Reinen Vernunft*, "Der transzendentalen Doktrin der Urteilskraft (Analytik der Grundsätze)," Drittes Hauptstück, "Von dem Grunde der Unterscheidung aller Gegenstände überhaupt in Phaenomena und Noumena"; Kant, *The Critique of Pure Reason.*, "Transcendental Logic," chapter 3, "Of the Ground of the Division of all Objects into Phenomena and Noumena."
17. Guyer, "Thought and Being," 204–5.
18. Guyer, "Thought and being," 183–84.

static "*notwendigen Vorstellungen a priori*," "necessary a priori representations" (of time and space) and the equally static and abstract "*Kategorien*," "categories" (of unity, plurality, causality, etc.), that Kant suggested regulated our knowledge.[19] In Hegel's scheme, at each stage, an apparent certainty generates a negative, and the two become moments in a new certainty: but this is not a complete reconciliation between phenomena and things in themselves, and so it generates its own negative, and the process continues. Nothing escapes the dialectical process, not even truth: "Appearance is the process of arising into being and passing away again, a process that itself does not arise and does not pass away, but is *per se*, and constitutes reality and the life-movement of truth."[20] So, for instance, following a discussion of sense-certainty—a certainty generated by perception of objects in an external world—Hegel argues that

> in the kinds of certainty hitherto considered, the truth for consciousness is something other than consciousness itself. The conception, however, of this truth vanishes in the course of our experience of it. What the object immediately was *in itself*—whether mere being in sense-certainty, a concrete thing in perception, or force in the case of understanding—it turns out, in truth, not to be this really; but instead, this inherent nature proves to be a way in which it is for an other.[21]

This means that what was thought to be certainty about an objective world in fact generates knowledge, not of that world itself, but of objects as they are for us. When consciousness seeks to know itself—self-consciousness—it grasps itself as an object among other objects, and so experiences the same negation that it experiences with any object (it is an object as it is for us, rather than in itself): but it also knows it as itself. Thus again there are two "moments," and in self-consciousness the opposition is *aufgehoben*, that is, "removed" or "sublated":

> Consciousness has, *qua* self-consciousness, henceforth a twofold object—the one immediate, the object of sense-certainty and of perception, which, however, is here found to be marked

---

19. Kant, *Kritik der Reinen Vernunft*, "Der transzendentalen Ästhetik," Erster Abschnitt, "Von dem Raume"; Zweiter Abschnitt, "Von der Zeit"; "Der Analytik der Begriffe," Dritter Abschnitt, "Von den reinen Verstandesbegriffen oder Kategorien"; Kant, *The Critique of Pure Reason*, "The Transcendental Aesthetic": section I, "Of space"; section II, "Of time"; "The Transcendental Analytic," chapter 1, section III, "Of the Pure Conceptions of the Understanding, or Categories."

20. Hegel, *Phänomenologie des Geistes*, Vorrede; Hegel, *Phenomenology of Mind*, § 47.

21. Hegel, *Phenomenology of Mind*, § 166.

by the character of negation; the second, viz. itself, which is the true essence, and is found in the first instance only in the opposition of the first object to it. Self-consciousness presents itself here as the process in which this opposition is removed [or sublated]²², and oneness or identity with itself established.²³

So self-consciousness has two objects, itself and other objects (including itself as an object), and so can unite these objects with itself. It has "removed" the "opposition" between itself and its objects. However, *aufgehoben* implies affirmation as well as abolition of an opposition, so although in self-consciousness a unity is established between self-consciousness and objects of sense-certainty and perception, the opposition between self-consciousness and the object—whether the object that self-consciousness constitutes for itself, or other objects—remains. Yet more *aufgehobenen*, sublations, will be required.

The *Phänomenologie des Geistes*, translated as either *Phenomenology of Spirit*²⁴ or *Phenomenology of Mind*,²⁵ takes us on a journey through the sense-certainty of perception, the self-certainty attempted through relationships between different self-consciousnesses, the certainty of reason, and then ethics, culture, religion, and finally "absolute knowing."²⁶ Thought, which has to employ concepts that apply universally, finds itself enmeshed in particularities and becomes empirical: but by understanding the entire process as the self-realisation of *Geist*, Hegel can maintain a sense of consistency. The particularities become elements in a complete network of dialectical relationships, and thought becomes a process integrated with that network.²⁷

The *Science of Logic* might begin with the "being," "nothing," "becoming" dialectic, which locates "being" within the patterned action of "becoming," but throughout the *Phenomenology* the focus is on *human* patterned action: action which is particular action, which is an individual's action, and which is universal in the sense that every human action is *human* action. If driven by a purpose, the purpose becomes an object to the actor, and because the purpose is the actor's purpose, the human person becomes an object to the actor, and a dialectical process then unites person, purpose, and action. When human action results in an object of some kind,

22. *aufgehoben*.
23. Hegel, *Phänomenologie des Geistes*, IV, "Die Wahrheit der Gewißheit seiner selbst"; Hegel, *Phenomenology of Mind*, § 167.
24. Hegel, *Hegel's Phenomenology of Spirit*.
25. Hegel, *Phenomenology of Mind*.
26. For a description of the different stages, see Singer, *Hegel*, 70–93.
27. Burbidge, *Real Process*, 206–8.

the person is objectified in the object, and knows themselves in the object.[28] And, of course, consciousness and self-consciousness, history, culture, and religion, are human action: so there is a sense in which the whole of Hegel's philosophical system is about human action, and is one in which human action is the typical "actions in patterns" within that system. All of this human action might well be that of an individual, but it will always be located in some social situation[29] that will influence, and pattern, the action, just as the individual's action will influence the pattern that the action that constitutes the social context will take. That social situation will be historical, cultural, religious, and more: so human action, individually and socially, belongs within the vast network of dialectical relationships.

Nothing is ever left out of that network: and particularly intriguing in this respect is Hegel's treatment of philosophy:

> The study of the history of Philosophy is the study of Philosophy itself, for, indeed, it can be nothing else . . . we must not regard the history of Philosophy as dealing with the past, even though it is history. The scientific products of reason form the content of this history, and these are not past. What is obtained in this field of labour is the True, and, as such, the Eternal; it is not what exists now, and not then; it is true not only today or tomorrow, but beyond all time, and in as far as it is in time, it is true always and for every time. . . . The new forms at first are only special modes of knowledge, and it is thus that a new Philosophy is produced: yet since it already is a wider kind of spirit,[30] it is the inward birth-place of the spirit[31] which will later arrive at actual form.[32]

Every aspect of philosophy's history has contributed to philosophy understood as "the scientific products of reason": and these products are then true for all time and beyond time. History gives birth to *Geist*, Spirit; and Spirit realises itself in history: and, as we found in relation to particular readings of Parmenides and Plato, unity is the unity constituted by diversity. And so the development of Hegel's own philosophy (which, for instance, after its earlier period, let go of the theory that there is a one to one correspondence

---

28. Schmidt am Busch, "What Does it Mean to 'Make Oneself Into an Object'?" The different chapters of Laitinen and Sandis, *Hegel and Action*, explore a variety of interpretations of Hegel's treatment of human action (not of action in general).

29. Yeomans, *The Expansion of Autonomy*, 195.

30. *des Geistes*

31. *des Geistes*

32. Hegel, *Vorlesungen über die Geschichte der Philosophie*, 47–50, 75 (A, 3 and B, 1, c); Hegel, *Lectures on the History of Philosophy*, A, 3 and B, 1, c.

between the categories of speculative logic and the phenomenological categories through which the dialectical process evolves[33]) is itself an element of *Geist*'s self-realisation, and becomes an essential constituent of the Absolute.

Here is not the place for a detailed discussion of Hegel's intellectual development,[34] nor of the many dialectical stages of the journey from sense-certainty to absolute knowledge, except to say that what Hegel has given to us is a theory of everything, that it is within the *Geist*-shaped system as a whole that Hegel's many dialectical oppositions can claim not to be flat contradictions,[35] and that if we were to interpret the details of the journey as one possible route towards absolute knowledge—that is, if we were to posit a diversity of possible ways whereby *Geist* might realise itself, and then suggest that we are experiencing one of those possibilities—then we might be able to ameliorate some of the quite proper objections to Hegel's logic,[36] and in particular its totalizing character. The totalizing nature of the theory becomes clear when we read the final section of the *Phenomenology*, on "absolute knowing," and find there an understanding of the many diverse oppositions as moments in the self-realisation of *Geist*. *Geist*,

> the goal, which is Absolute Knowledge or Spirit[37] knowing itself as Spirit, finds its pathway in the recollection of spiritual forms as they are in themselves and as they accomplish the organization of their spiritual kingdom. Their conservation, looked at from the side of their free existence appearing in the form of contingency, is *History*; looked at from the side of their intellectually comprehended organization, it is the Science of the ways in which knowledge appears. Both together, or History (intellectually) comprehended, form at once the recollection and the Golgotha of Absolute Spirit,[38] the reality, the truth, the certainty of its throne, without which it were lifeless, solitary, and alone.[39]

33. Harris, "Hegel's Intellectual Development to 1807," 41.
34. Harris, "Hegel's Intellectual Development to 1807."
35. Forster, "Hegel's Dialectical Method," 141–57.
36. This alternative understanding of the status of Hegel's argument might help to ameliorate some of the quite proper objections to the *Phenomenology of Spirit*'s logic in Pippin, "You Can't Get There from Here."
37. *Geist*
38. *absoluten Geistes*
39. Hegel, *Phänomenologie des Geistes*, VIII, "Das absolute Wissen"; Hegel, *Phenomenology of Mind*, § 808.

Nothing is lost: and significantly, the "unhappy consciousness,"[40] that is, the "pain . . . of spirit . . . not succeeding,"[41] belongs to the same process as the *Geist*-guided progress of history, and is essential to it.

What began as an exploration of the route to knowledge through the mind's consciousness and self-consciousness—and thus through every mind's consciousness and self-consciousness—can now be recognised as elements of a vast network of dialectical relationships across history: a connection made easier for Hegel by the fact that *Geist* means "Spirit," "mind," or "Mind": so in the earlier sections of the *Phänomenologie des Geistes* he can interpret *Geist* as "mind"—the individual human mind, and human minds in general—and in the later sections as a "Spirit" that "knows itself as Spirit." There has been no shortage of critics of the way in which Hegel has combined psychology and history in the *Phänomenologie*:[42] but the combination is not a problem once we recognise that for Hegel the dialectical relationships discoverable in consciousness, self-consciousness, history, culture, and everything else, belong together as means of *Geist*'s self-realisation. The ambiguity of "*Geist*" thus serves a purpose: it combines in a single term the psychological and the historical aspects of the journey to absolute knowledge; and it enables Hegel to construct the same relationship between division and unity in both philosophical and historical contexts.[43]

So *Geist*, or absolute knowledge, which is here identified with *Geist*, is constituted by the whole of the network of dialectical processes that constitute ourselves and the history of our communities. It is a "living community," not a "lifeless loneliness," and so is a continuing process. There is nothing finished here, and there is nothing finished at the end of the *Phenomenology*.[44] "Being" is the first idea to be swallowed by the dialectical journey. "Becoming" is ubiquitous. The dialectical process goes on and is the pattern visible in the ubiquitous action: for, throughout, everything is action. We might be able to speak of "consciousness" as a stable reality through time, but what constitutes it is its action:

---

40. *unglücklichen Bewußtseins*

41. *nicht erreichende Schmerz des Geistes*: Hegel, *Phänomenologie des Geistes*, VII, "Die Religion"; Hegel, *Phenomenology of Mind*, § 673. See Hyppolite, *Studies on Marx and Hegel*, 24.

42. Pippin, "You Can't Get There from Here."

43. Speight, *The Philosophy of Hegel*, 25.

44. Singer suggests that "absolute knowledge" is achieved "when he, Hegel, understands the nature of reality" (Singer, *Hegel*, 93). This, too, is a legitimate interpretation. Perhaps we might regard the ambiguity as the two moments of another dialectical movement.

> Consciousness ... *qua* essential reality, is the whole of this process of passing out of itself *qua* simple category into individuality and the object, and of viewing this process in the object, cancelling it as distinct, appropriating it as its own, and declaring itself as this certainty of being all reality, of being both itself and its object.[45]

Consciousness is action, history and culture are action, *Geist* is action, and the Absolute, which from the word "absolute" we might expect to be a fixed and static end-point, is "community": that is, the opposite of "lifeless." The "being," "nothing," "becoming" dialectic quickly dissolves "being" language into "action" language. Béatrice Longuenesse suggests that there is no "ontology" here in the sense of a science of being *qua* being, but there certainly is a science of "being as being thought," and perhaps multiple ontologies as thought evolves in relation to many different objectivities as the dialectical chain moves through consciousness, self-consciousness, culture, and the rest.[46] Whether or not there is ontology, there is certainly metaphysics, in the sense of a conceptual structure underlying the understanding of reality that Hegel has constructed. As Adams puts it, an "epic" metaphysics, constructed around the idea of "being," has in Hegel's philosophy become a "dramatic" metaphysics, constructed around the central concept of "action."[47] Just as, in Stephen Houlgate's words, "human beings are nothing but the activity of producing and determining themselves and their identity,"[48] so the Absolute is the vast network of such patterned action that is generated by, and provides a context for, particular actions in patterns.

Hegel hardly ever uses the word "metaphysics," and when he does he disowns it:

> Think? Abstractly? ... Even now I can hear a traitor, bought by the enemy, exclaim these words, denouncing this essay because it will plainly deal with metaphysics. For *metaphysics* is a word, no less than *abstract*, and almost *thinking* as well, from which everybody more or less runs away as from a man who has caught the plague.[49]

---

45. Hegel, *Phänomenologie des Geistes*, V, "Gewißheit und Wahrheit der Vernunft"; Hegel, *Phenomenology of Mind*, § 237.
46. Longuenesse, *Hegel's Critique of Metaphysics*, 161.
47. Adams, *Eclipse of Grace*, 14–16.
48. Houlgate, *Freedom, Truth and History*, 21.
49. Hegel, *Wer denkt Abstrakt?*; Hegel, *Who Thinks Abstractly?*

But metaphysics is what Hegel is doing.[50] He is not simply seeking the conditions for knowledge of an objective world: he is describing the way that the world works: he is looking for an understanding that will encompass the whole of reality in a single conceptual system.[51] Whether or not we agree with what he has constructed, it is certainly metaphysics; and it is a metaphysics of actions in patterns: or perhaps, in Hegel's case, actions in a direction.

If we had not come to recognise that Parmenides and Heraclitus are perhaps not as far apart as we might have thought, then we might have wished to say here that Hegel is Heraclitus to Kant's Parmenides.

b. Hegel's God

The purpose of this chapter is to contribute to an understanding of the history of an "actions in patterns" metaphysic: and just as we have sought to understand the theological aspects of the other philosophies that we have studied, so we shall attempt to grasp Hegel's understanding of God. Here, perhaps unsurprisingly, we find dual emphases:

> Being itself and the special sub-categories of it which follow, as well as those of logic in general, may be looked upon as definitions of the Absolute, or metaphysical definitions of God.[52]

So God is here "an alternative theological idiom for absolute metaphysical reality."[53] However, "religion" belongs within the vast network of dialectical relationships that constitute history, and therefore the Absolute: and within religion we find that "God is presented as self-consciousness,"[54] alongside the self, and so as one moment in a dialectical relationship. Because God here belongs *within* the Absolute, within the network of dialectical relationships, rather than being identified *with* the Absolute, Christian doctrine is described in terms of dialectical relationships: ". . . the Divine Being empties Itself of Itself and is made flesh. . . . God, who has assumed shape and form, surrenders again His immediate existence, and returns to His essential Being. The essential Being is then Spirit only when it is reflected into itself."[55]

---

50. Beiser, "Introduction"; Burbidge, "Hegel's conception of logic," 93.

51. Soll, *An Introduction to Hegel's Metaphysics*, 136–37.

52. Hegel, *Enzyklopädie der philosophischen Wissenschaften im Grundrisse*, § 85; Hegel, *Encyclopedia of Philosophical Sciences*, § 85.

53. Soll, *An Introduction to Hegel's Metaphysics*, 137.

54. *der Gott als Selbstbewußtsein vorgestellt wird*: Hegel, *Phänomenologie des Geistes*, VII, "Die Religion," A, "Natürliche Religion"; Hegel, *Phenomenology of Mind*, § 684.

55. Hegel, *Phänomenologie des Geistes*, VII, "Die Religion," C, "Die Offenbare

Hegel was a committed Lutheran Christian, so the same Christian doctrine was both expressible in terms of the network of dialectical relationships, and intimately connected with Christian doctrine as it had evolved through the history of the church: "The Philosophy of Religion cannot, therefore, in the fashion of that metaphysic of the Understanding and exegesis of inferences, put itself in opposition to positive religion, and to such doctrine of the church as has still preserved its content."[56] Thus "God" can represent the whole of the network of dialectical relationships (the Absolute); God is intimately involved in those relationships in their historical contingency;[57] and it continues to be the church's task, as a community of believers, to teach the faith and to enact the sacraments.[58] This is all as we would expect. Reality in general is constituted by a network of dynamic dialectical relationships; each of those relationships exists within that context and contributes to it; and human community—its history, culture, and religion—is where the Absolute emerges and *Geist* realises itself. Perhaps the most important aspect of Hegel's theology—for it is theology—is the combination of "God" as an expression of the Absolute, and God as involved in contingent dialectical relationships in the same way that everything else is. This shows a firm grasp of historic Christian theology, and sets up a new dialectical relationship within which the contingency and the transcendence are moments that are constantly *aufgehoben*, sublated. The dialectical relationship therefore becomes "God as transcendent," "God as incarnate," with their unity in "God."

A further dialectical relationship applies to God, of course, in the same way as it applies to every other instance of our experience. We know the world of particulars as a world of ideas and thus of universals.

> If nothing is said of a thing except that it is an actual thing, an external object, this only makes it the most universal of all possible things, and thereby we express its likeness, its identity, with everything, rather than its difference from everything else.[59]

Religion"; Hegel, *Phenomenology of Mind*, § 780.

56. Hegel, *Vorlesungen über die Philosophie der Religion*, II, "Die Stellung der Religionsphilosophie zur Philosophie und zur Religion," 3, "Verhältnis der Religionsphilosophie zur positiven Religion"; Hegel, *Lectures on the Philosophy of Religion*, A. "The Relation of the Philosophy of Religion to its Presuppositions and to the Principles of the Time," II, "The Position of the Philosophy of Religion Relatively to Philosophy and to Religion," 3, "The Relation of the Philosophy of Religion to Positive Religion," c, γ.

57. Houlgate, *Freedom, Truth and History*, 191.

58. Houlgate, *Freedom, Truth and History*, 202.

59. Hegel, *Phänomenologie des Geistes*, I, "Die sinnliche Gewißheit; oder das Diese und das Meinen"; Hegel, *Phenomenology of Mind*, § 110.

We receive objects as thoughts of universals, thus reconciling being and thought, and enabling us to reconcile God's being with our conception of God. Here is not the place to discuss the detail of Hegel's ontological argument for God's existence, except to say that by theorizing a relationship between thought and being in relation to God, he can claim to have escaped from the flaws of Anselm's argument, which assumed that the idea of "that than which nothing greater can be conceived"[60] could function as a proof of God's existence without a prior proof that the conception of such a being implied its existence. Positively, by uniting being and thought in dialectical relationship, Hegel can reconcile the thought and being of God with each other, and can also reconcile the intrinsic or immanent Trinity (God as he is in himself) and the extrinsic or economic Trinity (God as experienced by us) with each other.[61]

> God, then, is here revealed, as He is; He actually exists as He is in Himself; He is real as Spirit. God is attainable in pure speculative knowledge alone, and only is in that knowledge, and is merely that knowledge itself, for He is spirit; and this speculative knowledge is the knowledge furnished by revealed religion. That knowledge knows God to be thought, or pure Essence; and knows this thought as actual being and as a real existence, and existence as the negativity of itself, hence as Self, an individual "this" and a universal self. It is just this that revealed religion knows.[62]

It is of course true to the religious consciousness that God as thought and God as being belong together: but surely, the religious consciousness is not the only kind of consciousness. A non-religious consciousness can find that the thought of a God who does not exist belongs with a God who does not exist. Hegel seems to me to have offered precisely what Anselm offered: "faith seeking understanding,"[63] rather than an argument for God's existence.

---

60. *id quo maius cogitari nequit*: Anselm, *Proslogion*, Prooemium, and 2, "Quod vere sit Deus"; Anselm, *Proslogium*, Preface, and chapter II.
61. Calton, *Hegel's Metaphysics of God*, 40, 53, 92–93.
62. Hegel, *Phänomenologie des Geistes*, VII, "Die Religion," C, "Die offenbare Religion"; Hegel, *Phenomenology of Mind*, § 761.
63. *fides quaerens intellectum*: Anselm, *Proslogion*, Preface.

Close to the beginning of the *Phänomenologie des Geistes*[64] we find God treated as an example of "the True":[65] and, throughout, it is "the Absolute" that is the fundamental reality. Where we find "the Absolute" we could perhaps substitute "God": but Hegel does not do so. For him, "the Absolute" is the totality of dialectical reality. "God" obeys the same rules as everything else, and, like everything else, God is the unity of thought and being constantly sublated in each other. God is "no doubt undisturbed identity and oneness with itself":[66] but this description plays no part in the argument. God enters the picture to the extent that God contributes to the self-realisation of *Geist* in the Absolute. *Geist* is a religious word: and it is *Geist* that Hegel's philosophy is all about. We are at liberty to interpret *Geist* as "God," but Hegel might not have done so. For Hegel, *Geist* means everything, because it is the internal process of the universe and of every element of it, and so *Geist* is also the process of thought about *Geist* as well as being the process that constitutes material reality, and the direction in which everything moves. Muers and Higton recommend that when we read Hegel we should "forget about the nouns and focus on the verbs and prepositions."[67] Clearly we cannot forget about the noun *Geist*: which suggests that we should count it among Hegel's verbs, and as the verb that constitutes the relationship between God and God's Word, and the relationship between God and the created order, because, as Pattison suggests, "this difference must be reconcilable, and God must be able to enter into the nondivine world . . . and so restore the world to unity with God's own being."[68]

C. MARX'S DIALECTIC

As a student, Karl Marx was deeply influenced by Hegel's philosophy, which he then transformed,[69] as we shall see.

For Hegel, the individual self-consciousness objectifies itself, and it experiences this process as a "negation." It then knows itself as a negation of that objectified self-consciousness; and self-consciousness then "presents itself . . . as the process in which this opposition is [both affirmed and]

---

64. Hegel, *Phänomenologie des Geistes*, Vorrede; Hegel, *Hegel's Phenomenology of Spirit*, §§ 18–19.

65. *das Wahre*

66. *wohl die ungetrübte Gleichheit und Einheit mit sich selbst*: Hegel, *Phänomenologie des Geistes*, Vorrede; Hegel, *Hegel's Phenomenology of Spirit*, §§ 18–19.

67. Muers and Higton, *Modern Theology*, 89.

68. Pattison, *A Short Course in Christian Doctrine*, 32.

69. Singer, *Marx*, 54.

removed."[70] For Marx, human beings cannot help alienating or negating themselves in their work:[71]

> The worker puts his life into the object; but now his life no longer belongs to him but to the object. . . . The *alienation* of the worker in his product means not only that his labour becomes an object, an *external* existence, but that it exists *outside him*, independently, as something alien to him, and that it becomes a power on its own confronting him. It means that the life which he has conferred on the object confronts him as something hostile and alien.[72]

Haarscher finds here a type of worker's "activity" that lies at one end of a spectrum of activity. At the other end is "authentic activity," which is to the ontological essence of human life as the wage laborer's activity in a capitalist economy is to the laborer's alienation.[73] The problem is that no longer is a "negation of the negation" possible, because in a capitalist society it is the owner of the capital—of the machinery and other means of production—who has control of the worker's product. To produce from nature is the authentic activity that is intrinsic to being human,[74] so for someone else to have the use of what we produce prevents the dialectic completing itself, and compromises our very humanity.

Hegel describes the objectification of self-consciousness as a "bondage" in relation to the self-consciousness's "lordship": but then the "master" needs the "slave," and the "slave" becomes its own self-consciousness:

> But just as lordship showed its essential nature to be the reverse of what it wants to be, so, too, bondage will, when completed, pass into the opposite of what it immediately is: being a consciousness repressed within itself, it will enter into itself, and change round into real and true independence.[75]

---

70. *stellt sich hierin als die Bewegung dar, worin dieser Gegensatz aufgehoben*: Hegel, *Phänomenologie des Geistes*, IV, "Die Wahrheit der Gewißheit seiner selbst"; Hegel, *Phenomenology of Mind*, § 167.

71. Bernstein, *Praxis and Action*, 40–42.

72. Marx, *Ökonomisch-philosophische Manuskripte*, XXII, "Die entfremdete Arbeit"; Marx, *Economic and Philosophic Manuscripts*, XXII, "Estranged Labour."

73. Haarscher, *L'Ontologie de Marx*, 134: "*activité authentique*."

74. Holt, *Karl Marx's Philosophy of Nature*, 11.

75. Hegel, *Phänomenologie des Geistes*, "Die Wahrheit der Gewißheit seiner selbst," A, "Selbstständigkeit und Unselbstständigkeit des Selbstbewußtseins; Herrschaft und Knechtschaft"; Hegel, *Hegel's Phenomenology of Spirit*, § 193.

For Marx, the dialectic is similar to Hegel's in structure, but different in content. The capitalist needs the worker, and, for the worker, alienation is externally imposed by a set of political and economic conditions:[76]

> Capital further developed into a coercive relation, which compels the working class to do more work than the narrow round of its own life-wants prescribes. As a producer of the activity of others, as a pumper-out of surplus labour and exploiter of labour-power, it surpasses in energy, disregard of bounds, recklessness and efficiency, all earlier systems of production based on directly compulsory labour.[77]

The consequence is a build-up of alienation or negation that overcomes itself when the working class seizes the means of production from capitalists:[78] a rather more traumatic "negation of a negation" than Hegel expects when self-consciousness overcomes the enmity between "lordship" and "bondage."

For Hegel, the self-realisation of *Geist*—"Spirit" or "Mind"—drives the evolution of history.[79] *Geist* alienates itself in the world's history, and constantly negates negations, as much in the practical life of the world as in the life of the mind:[80]

> The sphere of spirit ... breaks up into two regions. The one is the actual world, that of self-estrangement, the other is that which spirit constructs for itself in the ether of pure consciousness raising itself above the first.[81]

For Marx, it is the first of these two worlds that matters. To turn ourselves into objects in the world might for Hegel be a negation, but for Marx it is the only way to exist in the world.[82] It is history, in the form of individual human beings active in the world, and in the form of technological change

---

76. Bernstein, *Praxis and Action*, 48–9.

77. Marx, *Capital*, volume 1, ch. 11, "Rate and mass of surplus value"; Marx, *Das Kapital*, volume 1, ch.9, "Rate und Masse des Mehrwerts." (Chapter numbering in the English translation is different from that in the German edition.)

78. Marx, *Das Kapital*, volume 1, ch. 24, "Die sogenannte ursprüngliche Akkumulation," 7, "Geschichtliche Tendenz der kapitalistischen Akkumulation"; Karl Marx, *Capital*, volume 1, ch. 32, "Historical Tendency of Capitalist Accumulation"; Singer, *Marx*, 72–74.

79. Hook, *From Hegel to Marx*, 54, 68.

80. Kedourie, *Hegel and Marx*, 75.

81. Hegel, *Phänomenologie des Geistes*, VI, "Der Geist," B, "Der sich entfremdete Geist; die Bildung," I, "Die Welt des sich entfremdeten Geistes"; Hegel, *Hegel's Phenomenology of Spirit*, § 487.

82. Hyppolite, *Studies on Marx and Hegel*, 28.

and its consequences for social relationships, that drives the evolution of consciousness.

> The mode of production of material life conditions the general process of social, political and intellectual life. It is not the consciousness of men that determines their existence, but their social existence that determines their consciousness. At a certain stage of development, the material productive forces of society come into conflict with the existing relations of production or . . . with the property relations within the framework of which they have operated hitherto. From forms of development of the productive forces these relations turn into their fetters. Then begins an era of social revolution. The changes in the economic foundation lead sooner or later to the transformation of the whole immense superstructure.
>
> In studying such transformations it is always necessary to distinguish between the material transformation of the economic conditions of production, which can be determined with the precision of natural science, and the legal, political, religious, artistic or philosophic—in short, ideological forms in which men become conscious of this conflict and fight it out.[83]

History is here a ferment of change and conflict: and, as Hook puts it: "The recognition of the primary character of change, process and development on every plane of existence appears ever more strongly in Marx's philosophy than in Hegel's."[84] A change in the "forces of production" will generate a "negation" in the realm of social relations, which will then seek resolution in a new social order: and so a dialectical process occurs that drives history forwards. Marx was interested in the influence of the material conditions of society on individual and collective consciousness, rather than in the just as important influence in the opposite direction,[85] because for Marx it was the historical material existence of human beings that was real. The ideas that we might have about society appear to be less real. Marx himself recognised that this difference from Hegel's idealism was crucial:

> In direct contrast to German philosophy, which descends from heaven to earth, here we ascend from earth to heaven. That is to say, we do not set out from what men say, imagine, conceive, nor from men as narrated, thought of, imagined, conceived, in

---

83. Marx, *Zur Kritik der Politischen Ökonomie*, Vorwort; Marx, *A Contribution to the Critique of Political Economy*, Preface.

84. Hook, *From Hegel to Marx*, 55.

85. Singer, *Marx*, 50–54.

order to arrive at men in the flesh. We set out from real, active men, and on the basis of their real life-process we demonstrate the development of the ideological reflexes and echoes of this life-process. The phantoms formed in the human brain are also, necessarily, sublimates of their material life-process, which is empirically verifiable and bound to material premises. Morality, religion, metaphysics, all the rest of ideology and their corresponding forms of consciousness, thus no longer retain the semblance of independence. They have no history, no development; but men, developing their material production and their material intercourse, alter, along with this their real existence, their thinking and the products of their thinking. Life is not determined by consciousness, but consciousness by life.[86]

But however much Marx might have differed from Hegel, there remain deep connections between their theoretical constructions. Just as Hegel envisaged a culmination of the dialectical process through which *Geist* will achieve self-realisation or self-knowledge in the Absolute, so Marx envisaged a culmination of the dialectical process in the emancipation of human beings brought about by a revolution instigated by the working class:

> The capitalist mode of appropriation, the result of the capitalist mode of production, produces capitalist private property. This is the first negation of individual private property, as founded on the labour of the proprietor. But capitalist production begets, with the inexorability of a law of Nature, its own negation. It is the negation of negation. This does not re-establish private property for the producer, but gives him individual property based on the acquisition of the capitalist era: i.e., on cooperation and the possession in common of the land and of the means of production.[87]

We shall have to wait to see whether highly fallible human beings will ever be capable of achieving "socialized production" and "socialized property,"[88]

---

86. Marx and Engels, *Die Deutsche Ideologie*, Band I, "Feuerbach," "Gegensatz von materialistischer und idealistischer Anschauung," A, "Die Ideologie überhaupt, namentlich die deutsche"; Marx and Engels, *The German Ideology*, Vol. I, Part I: "Feuerbach: Opposition of the Materialist and Idealist Outlook," A, "Idealism and Materialism," 4, "The Essence of the Materialist Conception of History: Social Being and Social Consciousness."

87. Marx, *Das Kapital*, ch. 24, "Die sogenannte ursprüngliche Akkumulation." 7, "Geschichtliche Tendenz der kapitalistischen Akkumulation"; Marx, *Capital*, volume 1, ch. 32, "Historical Tendency of Capitalist Accumulation."

88. Marx, *Das Kapital*, ch. 24, "Die sogenannte ursprüngliche Akkumulation," 7, "Geschichtliche Tendenz der kapitalistischen Akkumulation"; Marx, *Capital*, volume 1,

but in the meantime we have in Marx's writings a theory that reality is the ubiquitous dialectical process of human society. This is somewhat different from Hegel's theory that the real is *Geist*, "Spirit" or "Mind." As Peter Singer puts the connection between Marx and Hegel:

> Like Hegel, Marx has a view about what is ultimately real. His materialism is the reverse of Hegel's idealism. The materialist conception of history is usually regarded as a theory about the causes of historical change, rather than a theory about the nature of ultimate reality. In fact, it is both—as Hegel's idealist conception of history was both.[89]

For Marx, ultimate reality is constant and ubiquitous historical change. The real is action in dialectical patterns. As Bernstein puts it:

> What might at first seem to be a chaotic array of meanings—*praxis* as human activity, production, labour, alienation, relentless criticism, and revolutionary practice—are aspects of a single, comprehensive and coherent theory of man and his world.[90]

However, Marx's "materialism" is not of the mechanistic variety: it is human diverse goal-directed activity, and the products of this activity are its "concrete embodiments."[91] The human being is what the human being does, and, in particular, is what the human being makes.

We might have a problem with the ways in which Josef Stalin translated Marx's literary works into political action, but Slavoj Žižek's summary of Stalin's essay "Dialectical and Historical Materialism" reveals an understanding of the metaphysical underpinnings of Marx's conception of history. For Stalin, "nature" is a

> connected whole ... in a state of constant movement and change ... change is not a gradual qualitative drifting, but involves qualitative jumps and ruptures ... this qualitative development is not a matter of harmonious development, but is propelled by the struggle of the opposites. ... [92]

---

ch. 32, "Historical Tendency of Capitalist Accumulation,"

89. Singer, *Marx*, 55.
90. Bernstein, *Praxis and Action*, 76.
91. Bernstein, *Praxis and Action*, 44.
92. Žižek, *Less than Nothing*, 71–2: a summary of Josef Stalin, "Dialectical and Historical Materialism," in *History of the Communist Party of the Soviet Union (Bolsheviks): Short Course*, edited by Commission of the Central Committee of the C.P.S.U (B) (New York: International Publishers, 1939), 106–7.

This understands Marx as the critic of Hegel that he was. Far from seeing reality as an essentially quite harmonious patterned activity, Marx saw it as human, historical, relational, conflictual, and social,[93] with everywhere tensions and contradictions in need of resolution via revolution.[94] "Activity," or "action," is *the* reality for Marx. It is the axiom that informs everything else. As Haarscher puts it, "we act in order to act."[95] Marx has constructed an actology[96] that informs everything that he wrote about nature, history, economics, work, and philosophy. It is this actology that connects his work into a coherent whole:[97] and behind this actology lies Hegel's ubiquitous dialectic. And as for Hegel, the end-point that Marx envisages constantly provides the character of the process towards it. As Haarscher puts it, "the end of history for Marx—that which must be realised—is the ontological essence of activity."[98]

D. ACTION IN TRAJECTORIES

Whether in the form of Hegel's dialectic of the mind and of Mind, or in the form of Marx's social and economic dialectic, everything is action, and in both cases the action is in dialectical patterns and is driven by an inner momentum shaped by an end-point that is itself action in patterns. In Hegel's case the Absolute is both aim and trajectory, and in Marx's case social and economic revolution is both aim and trajectory: and, in the case of both authors, dialectic is the character of a ubiquitous pattern of the action. In neither case does anything appear to escape the dialectic or the trajectory: but in fact in both cases there is an important non-dialectical element. Dialectic itself would seem not to be subject to a dialectical process: so in both cases there is a pattern that escapes action and change. Not until we discuss John Boys Smith shall we find an understanding of this dilemma, and a partial resolution of it.

---

93. Kleinbach, *Marx via Process*, 117.
94. Wood, "Hegel and Marxism," 416.
95. Haarscher, *L'Ontologie de Marx*, 59: "*agir pour agir.*"
96. Haarscher, *L'Ontologie de Marx*, 15: "*ontologie de l'action.*"
97. Haarscher, *L'Ontologie de Marx*, 151, 255, 276.
98. Haarscher, *L'Ontologie de Marx*, 133: "*le but de l'histoire pour Marx, ce qu'elle doit réaliser, c'est l'essence ontologique de l'activité.*" (Author's translation)

5

Maurice Blondel

"Action"

A. INTRODUCTION

In 1893 Maurice Blondel defended and published his doctoral thesis, *L'Action*.[1] This provided the foundation for his later metaphysical project, published between 1935 and 1937, the last part of which was a second version of *L'Action* that was little changed from the thesis.[2] Blondel had started and finished with action. This is at least some justification for being highly selective in our survey of Blondel's huge output, and for restricting our focus to what he meant by "action" and to how he used the idea to construct both a metaphysic and the outline of a theology. He had found in "action" a way of reconciling his two vocations—to be a philosopher, sympathetic to the evolutionary direction of contemporary science, and at the same time to be a faithful Roman Catholic Christian:[3] so the integration between philosophy, science and religion had to be a philosophy that could incorporate both

---

1. Blondel, *L'Action*.
2. Blanchette, "Introduction," xiii.
3. Saint-Sernin, *Blondel*, 11.

real science and the real religion of dogma and practice.⁴ We might find "action" to be equally capable of mediating between the Christian Faith and the modern world.

B. ACTION

> *Action*⁵ appears to me to be that "substantial bond" which constitutes the concrete unity of each being while assuring its communion with all. Is it not, indeed, the confluence in us of thought and life, of individual originality and of the social and even the total order, of science and of faith? . . . It comes from the universal, it returns to it, but by introducing something decisive into it: It is the geometric locus where the natural, the human and the divine all meet.⁶

"Action," for Blondel, is always primarily the particular actions of the individual human being. Our actions are a fact, they are a necessity,⁷ and they are unique to each person and to each time and place. But at the same time, "action" is a universal, naming a category in which every particular action belongs. "Action" is in one sense a Platonic Form, as every particular action participates in action. If Plato's Forms are interpreted as unchanging realities in which the world that we experience participates, then "Action" is different from a Platonic Form in that every particular action contributes to the universal, which is, after all, "action," which means that it changes, and is changed by, every particular action in the category of action. However, if Plato's Forms are interpreted in a more Aristotelian direction, then the Forms are as much constituted by the world that we experience as that world is constituted by the Forms, so to call Blondel's "Action" a Platonic Form becomes entirely legitimate. The boundary between phenomenology (in this context the study of our experience of action), and an "ontology" or actology in which being is understood as action, has therefore become porous, if it exists at all.⁸

---

4. Conway, *The Science of Life*, xvii–xxiv.

5. *L'Action*.

6. Blondel, *L'Itinéraire Philosophique de Maurice Blondel*, 66–67. English translation in Blanchette, "Maurice Blondel's Philosophy of Action," xvi.

7. Preparatory documents for Blondel's thesis suggest that human action's status as both a fact and a necessity was an important reason for taking *l'action* as the subject of his thesis: Virgoulay, *L'Action de Maurice Blondel*, 11.

8. Saint-Sernin, *Blondel*, 50.

It is particular actions that Blondel has in mind when in *L'Action* he sets out to construct a dialectic similar in structure to Hegel's.[9] First of all, he discovers action as a fact:

> To take stock of the immediate evidence, action, in my life, is a fact, the most general and the most constant of all, the expression within me of a universal determinism; it is produced even without me.[10]

As Bernard Saint-Serin puts it: "Action is not treated as an idea that we need to analyze, but as a slice of the reality into the depths of which we need to penetrate."[11] Blondel finds action everywhere:[12] but as he sets out to study this inexhaustible field, he begins with human action, and in particular human consciousness, because that is where human action originates. There he finds freedom—a freedom no doubt important to someone who wished to be a philosopher at the same time as remaining a Roman Catholic:[13] "Nothing acts upon us or through us, unless it is truly subjective, unless it has been digested, vivified, organized in us"[14]—and what determines the human action is the activity of our reason:

> and the act that will proceed from this interior labor is the one we ordinarily call . . . the human act, the reasonable act, the voluntary act, the free act, or simply the act or action.[15]

But when the will to act results in action, that action finds itself embroiled in a particular and determined context. Autonomy therefore gives birth to heteronomy,[16] and freedom finds itself constrained:

> The will . . . claims to be emancipating itself from all the obstacles that stand in the way of its expansion and it goes off to commit itself to the determinism of external powers.[17]

---

9. Blondel does not mention Hegel in *L'Action*, although he does mention him in preparatory papers for the thesis: Blondel, *L'Action*; Virgoulay, *L'Action de Maurice Blondel, 1893*, 18.

10. Blondel, *L'Action*, viii; Blondel, *Action*, 3.

11. Saint-Sernin, *Blondel*, 77. English translation by the author. I have not been able to discover a published English translation.

12. Saint-Serin, *Blondel*, 78.

13. Van Parys, *La Vocation de la Liberté*, 1, 17.

14. Blondel, *L'Action*, 105; Blondel, *Action*, 111.

15. Blondel, *L'Action*, 116; Blondel, *Action*, 121.

16. Brouillard, *Blondel and Christianity*, 6.

17. Blondel, *L'Action*, 137; Blondel, *Action*, 139.

And so yet more action is required, and then again more, in order to impose limits on nature's determinism and continually to strive after freedom:[18]

> Action is the intention living in the organism and fashioning the obscure energies from which it had emerged. Freedom, in effect, has to unfold and embody itself in order to preserve itself and develop. Acclimatizing the life of the spirit in brute determinism, it induces spontaneous life to produce motives and movements more and more in conformity with its profound aspiration. All the progress of science and of consciousness proceeds from action, but only to tend once again to action, which alone sustains and animates it.[19]

Blondel ponders on the relationships between will, body, psychology, and action, and finds that

> whatever power takes the initiative in us, from the moment an act is consented to, from the moment it is accomplished, an intimate cooperation pulls even the opposed tendencies into line and establishes an effective solidarity among all the parts of the physical and mental mechanism.[20]

Thus action constitutes human life as a unity. At the same time it constitutes us as living in an environment, and as members of a community of action:

> Our action is never only our action. It is not enough for it to be led to go out of the individual confines, it must also arouse, through a sort of natural affinity and through *coaction*, powers alien to ourselves; and its work or its phenomenon has to result from a convergence and from a synthesis of operations coming from different origins.[21]

Family, country, and the whole of humanity, are constituted by "coaction"[22] and, ultimately, "to act is in a way to entrust oneself to the universe."[23] However, none of this explains moral action, which "finds within itself something that comes neither from nature nor from thought."[24] If we seek some agent that will explain "this surplus of the human act that always exceeds sensible

---

18. Van Parys, *La Vocation de la Liberté*, 43.
19. Blondel, *L'Action*, 144; Blondel, *Action*, 145.
20. Blondel, *L'Action*, 181; Blondel, *Action*, 177.
21. Blondel, *L'Action*, 215; Blondel, *Action*, 207.
22. Blondel, *L'Action*, 253–78; Blondel, *Action*, 241–62.
23. Blondel, *L'Action*, 280; Blondel, *Action*, 263.
24. Blondel, *L'Action*, 301; Blondel, *Action*, 281.

facts and social life," then we find ourselves inventing gods and undertaking an accompanying "superstitious action,"[25] only to have science demolish both the gods and the superstitious activity, leaving an "abyss."[26] "The one thing necessary"[27] to fill this abyss can only come from beyond ourselves: "Absolutely impossible and absolutely necessary for man, that is properly the notion of the supernatural."[28]

By reasoning on the basis of the human experience of action, Blondel has recognised the necessity of an order of action beyond both human action and the action of the whole created order,[29] and he has reached the remarkable conclusion that "to will all that we will, in full sincerity of heart, is to place the action and the being of God within ourselves."[30] The question of religion has not only been raised,[31] but has been settled in a quite striking way. Whether we accept this final step of the argument is up to us—and I do not—the steps that lead up to it succeed in fashioning a way of understanding ourselves and our situation in the world as constituted by action, and as opening the door to a consideration of a source of action beyond the phenomena that we experience.

C. BEING AS ACTION

In his *L'Action*, "action" has taken Blondel on a journey towards the necessity of a "supernatural," and it is "action" that has constituted everything else along the way, including ourselves as human beings. Blondel spent the years after 1893 responding to the gaps and questions left hanging in *L'Action*,[32] and in particular to the substantial unanswered question: Can we understand everything—the universe and everything in it—in terms of action? He supplies an affirmative answer by defining beings in terms of action, and by understanding Being—being itself—in terms of Action, or action itself. No longer is being constituted by some substance or essence: rather, it is constituted by multi-layered action.[33] "The role of action, then,

---

25. Blondel, *L'Action*, 309; Blondel, *Action*, 289.
26. Blondel, *L'Action*, 318–22; Blondel, *Action*, 296–99.
27. Blondel, *L'Action*, 344; Blondel, *Action*, 318
28. Blondel, *L'Action*, 388; Blondel, *Action*, 357.
29. Saint-Sernin, *Blondel*, 110, 139.
30. Blondel, *L'Action*, 491; Blondel, *Action*, 445.
31. Blanchette, "Maurice Blondel's Philosophy of Action," xxi–xxii.
32. Farraux, *Une Philosophie du Médiateur*, 9.
33. Somerville, *Total Commitment*, 351.

is to develop being and to constitute it."³⁴ *L'Action* is already an "ontological phenomenology":³⁵ and in the later *L'Être et les Êtres* Blondel develops a "phenomenological ontology."³⁶ By the time *L'Être et les Êtres* was written, Henri Bergson's explorations of the possibility of everything being constituted by action had largely dissolved beings and Being. Blondel preferred to retain the consistency that "Being" could deliver—the "solidarity of all phenomena"³⁷ implied by *être* ("to be")—while recognising action's ubiquity, by understanding "beings in [their] becoming."³⁸ Underlying this understanding is the knowledge that beings change, and that they are therefore different at different points in time:

> Is it not at least necessary to say that a being is not only that which it appears to be at a particular moment or in a particular place, but that to know it, and legitimately to affirm [its existence and/or nature], we ought to put together the totality of all of its becoming? Yes, it is.³⁹

We can therefore understand beings in terms of their history of becoming up to the present moment, which of course raises the question as to whether we should apply the term "being" to what something is still becoming rather than simply to what it has already become.⁴⁰

> In fact, to know through its becoming the being that is finding itself, it is not just a question of stopping at each of its isolated momentary appearances: and it seems to be equally impossible to sum up or to understand this being by reuniting all of the snapshots of its metamorphoses. Do we not need rather to untangle this mixture of becoming and being, and to suggest that, under all of the appearances of which its character seems to be made up—a character that seems to be knowable only in this way—hides a certain *je ne sais quoi*? But then, would it be for this pure unknown that we would reserve the term "being"? And would it be this *x* that would be the suspected link, the cause, the

---

34. Blondel, *L'Action*, 467; Blondel, *Action*, 425.
35. Virgoulay, *L'Action de Maurice Blondel*, 81–4. This is less clear in *L'Action* itself than in the preparatory papers for the thesis, and in a Latin text submitted alongside it.
36. Virgoulay, *L'Action de Maurice Blondel*, 90.
37. Virgoulay, *L'Action de Maurice Blondel*, 95.
38. *êtres en devenir*: Blondel, *L'Être et les Êtres*, 72. Translations of *L'Être et les Êtres* are by the author, who was unable to find a published English translation.
39. Blondel, *L'Être et les Êtres*, 92.
40. Blondel, *L'Être et les Êtres*, 102.

inaccessible reason, for our failure to construct a unity out of the multiplicity of momentary appearances?[41]

Blondel's ambition spans space as well as time, so he also suggests that "it is out of the entire universe, its total development, its empirical truth or its metaphysic, that we are claiming to make solid and sufficient reality."[42] We again find ourselves understanding unity as constituted by a totalized diversity:

> If it is a matter of offering a complete explanation of what this total becoming is that appears to include or even to constitute all that has been, is, or will be, then do we not have to admit that this is very being itself, in its unity and totality, and that perhaps there is no other being than this being, in its immanence and inexhaustible creativity?[43]

As in *L'Action*, Blondel takes a final and equally unnecessary theological step:

> The very idea of becoming, we have shown, necessarily implies that of a being that transcends change, and that could not be conceived without positing the idea of the absolute: so we now need to add that this conceptual requirement constitutes an ontological affirmation: that becoming implies not only a before and after in the idea of change, but also a reality indivisible from and higher than what is moving or moved.[44]

While the theological step is not required by the argument, because it is perfectly possible for diverse becomings to continue into the indefinite future; and although this step poses a number of complex questions—such as whether the individual's will is free to will as it wishes, or whether what it wills has been given to it from beyond itself:[45] the theological proposal does enable Blondel to formulate a way of understanding the "consistency,"[46] or the "solidification," that we experience in beings: in ourselves, and in the world around us. He locates the required consistency in the being's "destiny":[47]

---

41. Blondel, *L'Être et les Êtres*, 105.
42. Blondel, *L'Être et les Êtres*, 111.
43. Blondel, *L'Être et les Êtres*, 118.
44. Blondel, *L'Être et les Êtres*, 120.
45. Longton, "A Reconsideration of Maurice Blondel and the 'Natural' Desire," 923.
46. *consistence*
47. *destin*: Blondel, *L'Être et les Êtres*, 229, 230, 241.

> The various contingent and interdependent beings ... together attach themselves to the absolute Being which alone can serve as a foundation and destiny for all that is, but without anything that exists ceasing to retain its own separate existence and being incommensurable with the absolute Being.[48]

There will be "an infinite perfection"[49] that does nothing to prevent the becomings that we experience from having multiple causes: "Beings ... develop ... along with others ... through others ... according to their own plan":[50] or perhaps "their own pattern" might be a better way of putting it; or perhaps their own *configuration*.[51]

D. BLONDEL'S GOD

Blondel and Aquinas suggest different routes towards knowledge of God. Blondel sets out from human action, encompasses action in general, and comes to understand God in terms of action.[52] Action thus provides us with our access to God. Aquinas, on the other hand, approaches God via our desire to know.[53] However, Aquinas's and Blondel's underlying metaphysics prove to be rather similar, suggesting that Blondel's is a route that Aquinas might have taken if his philosophical context had been different. As we discovered in chapter 3: for Aquinas, something exists "in act" or "actually" because it comes to be. For Blondel, the crucial term is similarly *devenir*, "to become":

> The field of becoming is without assignable limit; and new perspectives will always open up, with new theories that will not exhaust the object to be known since they constitute it in part.[54]

Blondel's "action" dialectic has led him to open a philosophical door for theism, and now the centrality that he has assigned to will and action, and his recognition that there can be no "assignable limit" to becoming, find him defining our relationship to God in terms of "becoming":

---

48. Blondel, *L'Être et les Êtres*, 254.
49. Blondel, *L'Être et les Êtres*, 272.
50. Blondel, *L'Être et les Êtres*, 251.
51. The French *configuration* is closer than *modèle* or *dessin* to what we are trying to express by the word "pattern."
52. Blondel, *L'Action*, 491; Blondel, *Action*, 445.
53. Le Grys, "The Christianization of Modern Philosophy according to Maurice Blondel," 455–84.
54. Blondel, *L'Action*, 94; Blondel, *Action*, 101.

> God's only reason for being for us is that He is what we cannot be ourselves or do with our own strength; and yet we appear to have being, will and action only in view of willing Him and becoming Him.[55]

There will always be many influences on the development of any particular being, but it is now the overall direction given to a being's development by its relationship with the absolute Being that provides the framework for Blondel's discussion of beings: and again a theological step is taken: "Being . . . the same as God."[56] But "to be is to act,"[57] and because this applies as much to God as to us, to God belongs an "incessant creativity."[58]

Blondel had already recognised that change itself changes:

> On things that become, change, and disappear, we superimpose a "becoming" which itself seems to contain—and also to control—everything in the ubiquity of an idea in which all successive states are wrapped up. But this is to replace the vivid reality of changing by a fixed type of change: that is to say by an impoverished representation and even a fundamentally unnatural one. If there is movement in the universe, does this mean that this movement is its purpose or its being? Is it not simple, normal even, to examine instead whether this trend is not the first entrance, the birth . . . a conquest or a welcome of Being communicating or offering itself to what is not yet in order to make really exist what was nothing without it, and meanwhile to provide it with existence—or perhaps to accept it by co-operating with it . . . ?[59]

So both the constant changing of change, and the many different changings of different beings, are preserved at the same time as all of this diverse activity finds its reality in Being, which is also Action: which raises the question as to whether God's "incessant creativity"[60] implies that God changes. While in his own quite conservative religious context it is no surprise that Blondel does not deal with this issue explicitly—and where he gets close to it he refers to "the divine"[61] rather than to "God"[62] in order to distance

---

55. Blondel, *L'Action*, 354; Blondel, *Action*, 327.
56. *l'Être . . . Dieu même*: Blondel, *L'Être et les Êtres*, 333.
57. *être, c'est agir*: Blondel, *L'Être et les Êtres*, 341.
58. Blondel, *L'Être et les Êtres*, 333.
59. Blondel, *L'Être et les Êtres*, 393–94.
60. Blondel, *L'Être et les Êtres*, 333.
61. *le divin*
62. *Dieu*

himself from possible criticism from conservative Roman Catholics—it is clear where his ideas are leading:

> It is a matter of knowing whether, from becoming to the divine, and from the divine to becoming, an exchange and a reciprocity, a sort of communion, can be properly conceivable and intelligibly achievable.[63]

In his *L'Itinéraire Philosophique* Blondel proposes a "metaphysic of love."[64] As Farraux puts it, this implies that love is integral to Being;[65] or, as we might put it: at the heart of the action that constitutes Being, or being itself—which we now understand as Action, or action itself—is a pattern of action[66] that we might identify as love. In more theological language: God, who is Being and therefore Action, is "three and one, one because three, three in order to be one, not as a theoretical construction, but as a single intimate and luminous life, eternally creative, perfectly loving and happy."[67]

E. EVERYTHING IS ACTION

So now nothing is excluded from action and becoming. Being, beings, and God: everything is constituted by action, which encompasses both becoming and change. Blondel had recognised this possibility in a short work published between *L'Action* and *L'Être et les êtres*, *L'Illusion Idéaliste*, in which he suggests that

> from the point of view of action, all of the traditional problems might seem to be transposed; that this change might not be arbitrary, optional, or detached from human thought's historical evolution; that this idea might not be simply juxtaposed to or substituted for others, but rather might be an employment and an extension of traditional philosophy; and that from this point of view the contradictions that we find in most previous systems of thought might be reconciled with each other.[68]

---

63. Blondel, *L'Être et les Êtres*, 442.

64. *métaphysique de la charité*: Blondel, *L'Itinéraire Philosophique de Maurice Blondel*, 247.

65. Farraux, *Une Philosophie du Médiateur*, 368, 372.

66. *un configuration de l'action*

67. Blondel, *La Philosophie et l'Esprit Chrétien*, 24. The translation is by the author who could not find a published English translation.

68. Blondel, *L'Illusion Idéaliste*, 99. The translation is by the author, who could not find a published English translation.

Blondel's aim was a philosophy that was both Christian and autonomous,[69] and in which philosophy, theology, human action, and his own human action, could relate to each other.[70] This he achieved. He also achieved a philosophy of action: not just human action, but action, and Action. It would not be the only such philosophy, because Bergson, whom we shall study next, was working in the same field: but certainly it was one of the first two consistent "action philosophies," and, in its continual dialogue between the languages of "action" and "being," it was unique.

Equally important is the fact that Blondel had constructed a metaphysic that could encompass both God and the whole of human life. As Virgoulay puts it: "*L'Action* is not just a book to read: it is a way to practice, a 'science of practice' and a practice of science."[71] It might be true, as Conway suggests, that initially Blondel was in fact somewhat sceptical about the natural sciences, and only later came to evaluate them more positively; and it might also be true that the science that he attempted to integrate with theology operated at a rather generalized level, rather than in relation to the particular actions, perceptions, sensations, and so on, that are the subject matter of real science. It was always the ontology—or rather, the actology—that informed the science, rather than vice-versa, whereas real science informs ontology, and ought to inform actology. But this is all understandable. Blondel was creating a narrative—"*l'Action*"—and it was this that controlled the ontology. There was little conceptual space left for science to influence.[72]

Blondel's "Action" is a true universal, a Platonic Form, constituting and naming a category in which every particular action belongs: but, as we have already recognised, this Form is itself constituted by action, so it changes constantly, forever taking on new configurations. Even more so than in Hegel, "to be is to act,"[73] and Being, because it encompasses the total becoming across time and space, and therefore all action across time and space, is Action. There is nothing fixed about Being, because action is ubiquitous, and every action remains independent and with multiple causes, and so continues to influence the totality of action and thus Being: unless of course there is an endpoint at which action ceases to be action. There is no suggestion that there might be such a finality, and every suggestion that there is not, because God is as much constituted by action as is anything

---

69. Brouillard, *Blondel and Christianity*, vii.
70. Blanchette, "Maurice Blondel's Philosophy of Action," xxiv.
71. See Virgoulay, *L'Action de Maurice Blondel, 1893*, 51.
72. Conway, *The Science of Life*, 215, 242, 245.
73. *être, c'est agir*: Blondel, *L'Être et les Êtres*, 341.

else. All of this in combination results in the remarkable conclusion that Being is Action, that Action, understood in its totality, is Being, and that "Being . . . the same as God."[74] "To be is to act":[75] and because this applies as much to God as to us, to God belongs an "incessant creativity"[76] characterized by the particular configuration or pattern of action that we call "love," creating communion between God and all becoming,[77] and bonding a trinity of persons into a unity.

None of this philosophy or theology requires a proof of God's existence. It is better off without it, because such a proof would suggest a fixed entity, the existence of which is being proved, rather than the God that emerges from Blondel's philosophical theology: a God involved in action and change, and the source and end of action and change.

We have found in Blondel a conceptual structure to which the philosophers whom we have studied have offered significant signposts. This is particularly true of Hegel. But in Blondel we have discovered an action-based conceptual structure that is unique in its consistency and breadth. There will still be new things to learn about an actology constructed on the basis of actions in patterns, but there is now a sense that all of it will be commentary and a discovery of implications.

---

74. *l'Être . . . Dieu même*: Blondel, *L'Être et les Êtres*, 333.
75. *Être, c'est agir*: Blondel, *L'Être et les Ê`tres*, 341.
76. *incessante fécondité*: Blondel, *L'Être et les Êtres*, 333.
77. Blondel, *L'Être et les Êtres*, 442.

6

Henri Bergson

Time, Space, and Action

A. THE DEBT TO HERACLITUS

From 1884 to 1885 Henri Bergson lectured on Greek philosophy, and in the lecture on Heraclitus he said this:

> Heraclitus's system is a radical dynamism portraying a universal changing, the transformation of all of the instants of things into all of the others. We must not believe that this transformation applies only to things available to the senses ... for it is certain that in Heraclitus's era the distinction between things available to the senses and intelligible things did not exist. So the dynamism is not simply radical: it is also universal.[1]

Of Heraclitus's "fire" he said this:

> There is a material principle which is transformed and which transforms itself, which is at the root of the universal transformation: fire. This is the element that is the most appropriate to creation and to change ... There is war and harmony ... Indeed,

---

1. Bergson, *Cours sur la Philosophie Grecque*, 167. The translation is by the author, who could not find a published English translation.

it is thanks to the action of discord and harmony on fire that fire eternally transforms itself.[2]

This is not necessarily how Heraclitus would have related strife and fire, but at least it recognises that at the heart of Heraclitus's thought there is a "continual changing":

> Heraclitus was struck by the universal flow of things, by the perpetual change which today has so vividly struck supporters of the doctrine of evolution. Guided by this idea, they have said that this universal changing is perhaps the most important aspect, the foundation, and the very existence of things. But what proves that Heraclitus never thought to completely identify opposites with each other is that he finally agrees that there is a permanent substance underlying the universal flow of things: fire—which constantly transforms itself as a human being does, which passes through a series of states, which changes continuously, and yet always remains itself.[3]

According to Bergson, Heraclitus's originality was in the importance that he attributed to the idea of change: "The originality of the system lies in the importance attributed to what, until then, had been a secondary consideration: the idea of change, of universal transformation."[4]

There is a strong possibility that Bergson's reading of Heraclitus led him into fashioning his own philosophical system (for it *is* a system) on the basis of the notions of movement and change: a system that would serve both science and metaphysics. Bergson had started out as a mathematician, but that did not mean that he believed that science should necessarily take mathematics as its model, and he came to believe that more recent science, and particularly the biological and psychological sciences, had begun to break free from that model and to be searching for a new basis.[5] Noting that by the time he wrote the teleological section of the *Critique of Judgment* Kant had somewhat revised his earlier view that metaphysics was no longer possible because there is (scientific) knowledge only of phenomena and not of *noumena* (things in themselves), Bergson suggested that the biological and psychological sciences might have their own more intuitive methods: and on this basis he set out to study change, movement, and time.

2. Bergson, *Cours sur la Philosophie Grecque*, 167.
3. Bergson, *Cours sur la Philosophie Grecque*, 168.
4. Bergson, *Cours sur la Philosophie Grecque*, 168.
5. Lindsay, *The Philosophy of Bergson*, 10.

B. CHANGE AND MOVEMENT

In 1911 Bergson delivered two lectures in Oxford, in French, under the title *La Perception du Changement*.[6] In these lectures, "*changement*" and "*mouvement*" appear to be used interchangeably, and change or movement functions as the primary reality. Bergson could even say that "movement is reality itself."[7] What we perceive as "immobility" is like the experience of sitting in a moving train alongside another train travelling in the same direction at the same speed: an abnormal situation that we wrongly assume to be the norm. Movement is the fundamental reality: it is not a mechanism to link a series of somehow more real states of affairs. Movement is indivisible,[8] and any fixity or stability is merely "an ephemeral arrangement between mobilities."[9] What is primary is the movement and not any of the states of affairs along the way, for they never exist as static states. Bergson even goes so far as to say that "*there are changes, but there are underneath the change no things which change.*"[10] Bergson seems to have experience on his side in his discussions of music, of the elementary particles of matter, and of the human person, for whom *durée*, duration, is constituted by continuous change: for time, like movement, is continuous: "Our present falls back into the past when we cease to attribute to it an immediate interest. . . ."[11]

As Keith Ansell-Pearson puts it, Bergson is asking us to

> overcome certain ingrained habits of mind . . . the view that change is reducible to an arrangement or rearrangement of parts, or that change merely involves a change of position regarding unchangeable things . . . that time has only as much reality for a living system as an hour-glass.[12]

The human person is, like all other reality, constant change: not a thing that changes (for how would we identify or define such a thing?), but change after change, the change being continuous. As Bergson puts it:

---

6. Bergson, "La Perception du Changement"; Bergson, *The Creative Mind*.

7. *le mouvement est la réalité même*: Bergson, *La Pensée et le Mouvant*, 102; Bergson, *The Creative Mind*, 169.

8. Bergson, *La Pensée et le Mouvant*, 103; Bergson, *The Creative Mind*, 169.

9. *un arrangement éphémère entre des mobilités*: Bergson, *La Pensée et le Mouvant*, 106–7; Bergson, *The Creative Mind*, 177.

10. *Il y a des changements, mais il n'y a pas, sous le changement, de choses qui changent*: Bergson, *La Pensée et le Mouvant*, 104; Bergson, *The Creative Mind*, 173. Italics in the original.

11. Bergson, *La Pensée et le Mouvant*, 108; Bergson, *The Creative Mind*, 179.

12. Ansell-Pearson and Urpeth, "Bergson and Nietzsche on Religion," 37–38.

there is neither a rigid immovable substratum nor distinct states passing over it like actors on a stage. There is simply the continuous melody of our inner life—a melody which is going on and will go on, indivisible, from the beginning to the end of our conscious existence.[13]

In order to make his point that there are no fixities underlying change, Bergson redefines the word "substance" in terms of change: "change is . . . the very substance of things . . . substance is movement and change . . . movement and change are substantial. . . ."[14]

C. DURÉE

If "there is neither a rigid immovable substratum nor distinct states passing over it like actors on a stage,"[15] then time cannot be a "rigid immovable substratum": and Bergson's discussion of time as *durée*, as experienced duration, is both presupposition and consequence of his view that "change is . . . the very substance of things."[16]

According to Bergson, we must not confuse "duration[17] with extensity, succession with simultaneity, quality with quantity."[18] In *durée*, everything is connected. Bergson is able to suggest that the past is carried into the present, and that the past is continuous with the present, because points that touch each other are the same point, so to talk of a point in time is nonsense. This is very different from space, which Bergson believes to be external to us, and in which the thing occupying a position can be distinguished from the position itself. Time-processes are unities, so cannot be broken down into numbered parts: so whenever we try to measure physical states we end up evacuating them of any temporal element. But measure we must, so we map time onto space: we represent it by a line, and we divide up the line. As Lindsay puts it, "we mark time by the concurrence of an event, whether it be our own action or some event of the outside world, with a certain

---

13. Bergson, *La Pensée et le Mouvant*, 106; Bergson, *The Creative Mind*, 176.

14. *le changement tel qu'il est, . . . est la substance même des choses . . . la substance est mouvement et changement . . . le mouvement et le changement sont substantiels*: Bergson, *La Pensée et le Mouvant*, 110; Bergson, *The Creative Mind*, 184.

15. Bergson, *La Pensée et le Mouvant*, 106; Bergson, *The Creative Mind*, 176.

16. Bergson, *La Pensée et le Mouvant*, 110; Bergson, *The Creative Mind*, 184.

17. *la durée*.

18. Bergson, *Essai sur les Données Immédiates de la Conscience*, 8; Bergson, *Time and Free Will*, preface.

simultaneity in space."[19] Bergson describes what he takes to be a normal scientific procedure:

> Two intervals of time are equal where two identical bodies in identical condition at the beginning of each of the [two] intervals, and subject to the same actions and influences of every kind, have traversed the same space at the end of these intervals.[20]

This is possible because every moment in a time-process can be mapped onto space and thus become an element in a space simultaneity; and also because, as Bergson makes clear, movement reconciles space and time. While recognising that measurement is both useful and necessary, Bergson emphasises that time is not a sum or aggregate of simultaneities. In space there is no time, because at any simultaneity nothing is left of the past[21] and so there is no *durée*.

In the context of more recent debates on whether time flows from the future to the past or whether we travel through time,[22] Bergson is clearly on the "time flows" side of the argument. For him, the future does not exist, and he requires this because he, like Kant, had an ethical purpose: the maintenance of the individual's freedom. For Bergson, the universe and every part of it is a creative process, so the future cannot be something already determined and towards which we travel. And there are consequences for the free creativity of the individual and of the cosmos, for if time is psychological, then the universe's *durée* and evolution display mind-like properties,[23] memory is real and is what carries the past into each new moment, and the mind is independent of the body.

Just as *durée* makes genuinely creative evolution possible, so the concept itself evolved in Bergson's thought. In his *Essai sur les Données Immédiates de la Conscience* (translated into English as *Time and Free Will*),[24] time and space are *radically* separated: *durée* is qualitative, heterogeneous, and dynamic, and space is quantitative, homogeneous, and static. In this situation, the individual's time and action are divorced from those in the world.

19. Lindsay, *The Philosophy of Bergson*, 126.

20. Bergson, *Essai sur les Données Immédiates de la Conscience*, 63; Bergson, *Time and Free Will*, 115.

21. Bergson, *Essai sur les Données Immédiates de la Conscience*, 60; Bergson, *Time and Free Will*, 108.

22. Prior, "Changes in Events and Changes in Things."

23. Kolakowski, *Bergson*, 3.

24. Bergson, *Essai sur les Données Immédiates de la Conscience*; Bergson, *Time and Free Will*.

But by the time *Matière et Mémoire* (*Matter and Memory*)²⁵ was written, space and time had been reconciled somewhat through the notion of movement. At the same time, *durée* had been extended into matter, thus giving matter a subjectivity of its own. Bergson believed this transition to conform to contemporary scientific developments:

> They show us pervading concrete extensity, *modifications, perturbations,* changes of *tensions* or of *energy,* and nothing else. It is by this, above all, that they tend to unite with the purely psychological analysis of motion.²⁶

Thus the dualism is reconciled by turning matter into mind, and in *L'Évolution Créatrice, Creative Evolution,*²⁷

> intellect and materiality are derived from a wider and higher form of existence . . . [a single process that] cut out matter and intellect, at the same time, from a stuff that contained both.²⁸

Not only is *durée* dynamic and located in the mind, but it is also asymmetrical, as the past and the present are *different*: the present is novel whereas the past is "mnemic survival."²⁹ So the past is neither built up from elements of the present, nor are both past and present elements of a deterministic unified laid-out time:³⁰ rather, the past forms the still-existing context for novelty. Bjelland sums up the creatively evolutionary process to which Bergson's notion of *durée* had led him: "The becoming of continuity and the emergence of novelty are twin facets of a present synthesis which, in its very presentness, is both mnemic and creative."³¹

D. EINSTEIN'S SPECIAL THEORY OF RELATIVITY

Believing that Newton's treatment of time was inimical to his own prioritizing of time as *durée*, Bergson valued Einstein's Special Theory of Relativity because it privileged no particular time-system, but rather regarded relative motions as interchangeable, enabling the observer to stand at any point within a moving system. However, Bergson was never able to resolve

25. Bergson, *Matière et Mémoire*; Bergson, *Matter and Memory*.
26. Bergson, *Matière et Mémoire*, 139; Bergson, *Matter and Memory*, 196.
27. Bergson, *L'Évolution Créatrice*.
28. Bergson, *L'Évolution Créatrice*, 131, 151; Bergson, *Creative Evolution*, 653, 664
29. Bjelland, "Durational Succession and Proto-mental Agency," 21.
30. Bjelland, "Durational Succession and Proto-mental Agency," 24.
31. Bjelland, "Durational Succession and Proto-mental Agency," 27.

the paradoxes to which Einstein's theory led, as he had hoped to be able to do, nor to reconcile Einstein's theory with his own ideas without making a colossal new assumption: that every *durée* belongs within a single universal *durée*, thus unpsychologizing the concept and so destroying it.

As we have seen, in *Duration and Simultaneity,* Bergson describes the relationship between time and space as an "analogy" through which "we use space to measure and symbolise time":[32] but it is not purely an analogy, because

> to each moment of our inner life there ... corresponds a moment of our body and of all environing matter that is "simultaneous" with it; this matter then seems to participate in our conscious duration.[33]

The universe seems to be a single whole, so we develop the idea of "the singleness of an impersonal time":[34] but still time itself must be a personal *durée*, because without a memory to connect two moments, they will each remain isolated, with "no before or after, no succession, no time."[35] Comparison, though, is possible because of *our durée*:

> We call the external flows that occupy the same duration "simultaneous" because they both depend on the duration of a like third, our own; this duration is ours only when our consciousness is concerned with us alone, but it becomes equally theirs when our attention embraces the three flows in a single indivisible act.[36]

Einstein's Special Theory of Relativity understands Lorentz's equations, drawn from the Michelson-Morley experiment (which showed that the relative speed of a light source does not affect the speed of light), as a statement that space, time and motion are related in such a way that the time experienced by an object depends on its velocity. In order to join in the debate, Bergson had to offer an understanding of how, with his psychologized time, two clocks at a distance could be compared. It is here that his concept of a single universal *durée* comes in useful. He suggested that simultaneity between two clocks at a distance depends on "a consciousness coextensive with the universe, capable of embracing the two events in a unique and

---

32. Bergson, *Durée et Simultanéité*, 10; Bergson, *Duration and Simultaneity*, xxviii.
33. Bergson, *Durée et Simultanéité*, 42; Bergson, *Duration and Simultaneity*, 30–31.
34. Bergson, *Durée et Simultanéité*, 44; Bergson, *Duration and Simultaneity*, 32.
35. Bergson, *Durée et Simultanéité*, 44; Bergson, *Duration and Simultaneity*, 33.
36. Bergson, *Durée et Simultanéité*, 47; Bergson, *Duration and Simultaneity*, 36.

instantaneous perception,"[37] thus relating *durée* to the universe as a whole, and making the experienced *durée* secondary and thus no longer the basis of his understanding of time. But for Bergson, time as a fourth dimension (for that is what the Special Theory of Relativity treats it as) was still a "purely mental view,"[38] for it required time to be spatialized, which Bergson still could not allow, as that would have meant that the future was already created, whereas he believed that the universe was "a continuity of creation."[39]

Thus while Bergson did his best to relate his view of time to Einstein's theory by effectively destroying *durée* as experienced time, he found that he could not in the end let go of time as experienced time, as that would have been the end of our freedom: so in fact he forbade himself the possibility of genuine debate with Einstein.

At first sight it might seem strange that Bergson did not keep hold of the different *durées* that Einstein's theory suggested, as well as positing the universal *durée* that would enable clocks to be compared: but maybe the problem was that for Bergson *motion* was the primary reality, and motion was what reconciled space and time at the same time as leaving them as very different entities: the one a visual perception, and the other an element of the inner life.[40] For time and space to be already parts of the same continuum would have made both *durée* and motion secondary to the space-time continuum: but it is still difficult to see why Bergson did not try to run *with* Einstein's theory rather than against it.

E. THE ÉLAN VITAL

However much motion or change was at the heart of his philosophical system, Bergson could not fail to be aware of continuities between events. He therefore posited an "*élan vital*,"[41] variously translated as "vital impulse," "vital impetus," "vital force," "creative impulse," or "living energy."[42]

The *élan vital* is not easy to interpret. Either it is directional, with some goal in mind, or it is not, and is simply the drive to innovate. Kolakowski describes it as "a kind of intentionality . . . in the evolutionary process"[43] and

37. Bergson, *Durée et Simultanéité*, 49; Bergson, *Duration and Simultaneity*, 38.
38. Bergson, *Durée et Simultanéité*, 53; Bergson, *Duration and Simultaneity*, 42.
39. Bergson, *Durée et Simultanéité*, 54; Bergson, *Duration and Simultaneity*, 43.
40. Scharfstein, *Roots of Bergson's Philosophy*, 42.
41. Bergson, *L'Évolution Créatrice*, 419.
42. Kreps, *Bergson, Complexity and Creative Emergence*, 65.
43. Kolakowski, *Bergson*, 57.

as an "original drive" which "divides itself into a growing variety of forms, but retains a basic direction."[44] Ansell-Pearson recognises that Bergson regards metaphysics and natural science as different disciplines with different methods, but still interprets the *élan vital* as a hypothesis expressed as a psychological analogy; and he also understands it as a regulative principle in a rather Kantian sense.[45] Osman Chahine *begins* his interpretation of Bergson's thought with the *élan vital*, and regards it as itself a unity that enables evolution to occur and that gives to society a direction. As he summarises a passage from Bergson's *Creative Evolution*: "Evolution marks out a direction, a continuous progress, and it has a goal to attain."[46] And David Kreps interprets the *élan vital* as the forerunner of modern complexity science, and as "explosively emergent self-organisation."[47]

The *ordered* nature of movement becomes clear when Bergson tackles such issues as perception and consciousness:

> To recognise a common object is mainly to know how to use it . . . But to know how to use a thing is to sketch out the movements which adapt themselves to it; it is to take a certain attitude, or at least to have a tendency to do so. . . . There is no perception which is not prolonged into movement[48]

—and similarly, "the orientation of our consciousness towards action appears to be the fundamental law of our psychical life. . . ."[49] Indeed, there is no perception which is not *itself* action, for if perception is real, and if change is reality, then perception and everything else is movement.

As we have seen, and as Kolakowski suggests, Bergson eventually mitigated some of the more radical aspects of his thought. In the earlier works, *durée* was entirely individual, but by the time of *Duration and Simultaneity* the *world* was experiencing *durée* and each individual's *durée* fitted into that experience. Similarly, Bergson came to value a little more fully the mapping of time onto space: for, after all, we need to measure time in order to function.[50] But the radical edge never quite disappeared, and in the later *The Two Sources of Morality and Religion* Bergson was still able to say "Action on the move creates its own route, creates to a very great extent

---

44. Kolakowski, *Bergson*, 58.
45. Ansell-Pearson, *Philosophy and the Adventure of the Virtual*, 136–39.
46. Chahine, *La Durée chez Bergson*, 19.
47. Kreps, *Bergson, Complexity and Creative Emergence*, 77.
48. Bergson, *Matière et Mémoire*, 65; Bergson, *Matter and Memory*, 111.
49. Bergson, *Matière et Mémoire*, 124; Bergson, *Matter and Memory*, 192.
50. Kolakowski, *Bergson*, 23.

the *conditions* under which it is fulfilled, and thus baffles all calculation."[51] For Bergson, there was no level of abstraction at which change ceases, or at which change ceases to change:[52] and it is when abstraction occurs that reality is revealed, as when individual movements have their particularities removed and "movement itself"[53] is discovered.[54]

F. BERGSON'S FOLLOWERS

Bergson had his enthusiastic followers, some of whom tried to put the evolving ideas spread across the various books into some kind of order. Among these was H. Wilden Carr, one of whose favourite texts was Bergson's "*La Perception du Changement*" ("The Perception of Change").[55] In Carr's *The Philosophy of Change*,[56] chapter VI is entitled "A World of Actions," and it declares reality to be "an original movement, not the purely relative movement, which we call movement or translation, but the absolute movement which we call change, and which characterizes life."[57] "Living action" is where time and space are related to each other.[58] Carr notes that our experience assures us that there are "real movements,"[59] and agrees with Bergson that the act of apprehending movement intellectually reduces movement to immobility. In reality, there are movements and not things, and "reality is movement."[60] We do experience *things*, of course, so a metaphysic is needed that takes this into account: but still, "life is an order of reality that is real, matter an order that is derived";[61] and Carr draws from contemporary science the view that atoms are electricity, and from Bergson the priority of change, and decides that "what we call matter is a form of movement."[62]

---

51. Bergson, *Les Deux Sources de la Morale et de la Religion*, 181; Bergson, *The Two Sources of Morality and Religion*, 255–56.
52. Mullarkey, *Bergson and Philosophy*, 6.
53. *le mouvement*
54. Bergson, *La Pensée et le Mouvant*, 105; Bergson, *The Creative Mind*, 167.
55. Bergson, "La Perception du Changement"; Bergson, *The Creative Mind*.
56. Carr, *The Philosophy of Change*.
57. Carr, *The Philosophy of Change*, 122.
58. Carr, *The Philosophy of Change*, 123.
59. Carr, *The Philosophy of Change*, 134.
60. Carr, *The Philosophy of Change*, 144.
61. Carr, *The Philosophy of Change*, 145.
62. Carr, *The Philosophy of Change*, 35.

Where Carr was interested in what we have called actology, Emmanuel Levinas was more interested in the ethical implications of Bergson's writings. Bergson was concerned to prevent the withering of subjectivity and of freedom by preventing the replacement of *durée* by determinism, of movement by psychophysics, and of the *élan vital* (understood as creativity) by biological determinism.[63] As Bergson put it, "the whole history of life until man has been . . . to create with matter . . . an instrument of freedom, to make a machine which should triumph over mechanism, and to use the determinism of nature to pass through the meshes of the net which this very determinism had spread."[64] Similarly, Levinas—for whom ethics is "first philosophy"[65]—regarded Being as a homogenizing of reality, and looked for

> a diversity all of whose terms would maintain reciprocal relations among themselves, exhibiting thus the totality from which they proceed, and in which there would on occasion be produced a being existing for itself, an I, facing another I.[66]

There is a "multiplicity in being, which refuses totalization but takes form as fraternity and discourse."[67] Levinas had read Bergson, but he then left behind the continuities that he found in his philosophy:

> The Bergsonian conception of freedom through duration . . . preserves for the present a power over the future: duration is creation . . . [but the *élan vital*] tends towards an impersonal pantheism, in the sense that it does not sufficiently note the crispation and isolation of subjectivity.[68]

Just as Bergson believed that we cannot know anything or anyone other than ourselves, as we would need to know every element of their *durée*,[69] so the whole of Levinas's work was in the cause of the otherness of the other. The other person is Other, and the future is Other in relation to the present.

---

63. Bergson, *Mélanges*, 495.
64. Bergson, *L'Évolution Créatrice*, 178–79; Bergson, *Creative Evolution*, 264.
65. *philosophie première*: Levinas, *Éthique comme Philosophie Première*.
66. Levinas, *Totalité et Infini*, 190–91; Levinas, *Totality and Infinity*, 215.
67. Levinas, *Totalité et Infini*, 191; Levinas, *Totality and Infinity*, 216.
68. Levinas, *Le Temps et L'Autre*, 72, 86–87; Levinas, *Time and the Other*, 80, 91–92.
69. Bergson, *Essai sur les Données Immédiates de la Conscience*, 118; Bergson, *Time and Free Will*, 185.

G. MOVING ON FROM BERGSON

Julien Benda[70] offers a rather different critique of Bergson's work on movement and *durée*. She lists the descriptions of the *act* of evolution (*l'acte vital*) in *L'Évolution Créatrice, Creative Evolution*[71]—liberty, novelty, incommensurability, and so on[72]—and then points out that in Bergson's book there is more on the *states* of evolution than on the *act* of evolution. Bergson had not delivered on what he had promised: "M. Bergson explains nothing";[73] and Benda decides that he is a mystic, and that mystics are not scientists.[74]

Yes, Bergson *is* a mystic, but not one who thinks that he can reach a permanent reality, for he knows full well that everything changes, including his own ideas. As Mullarkey points out, "in a creative universe with no static foundations, there will never be a first philosophy for anything or anyone to claim. In other words, if *everything* is changing, then this must be true for philosophy as well,"[75] and it must be true for knowledge.[76] In particular, Bergson's depictions of time are highly temporal,[77] which rather suggests that time is both diverse and changing, and is explicable in terms of a variety of theories. Bergson knew that philosophy, ideas, and everything else, changes constantly: so it is a pity that he did not similarly regard *space* as diverse and changing, for by doing so he would have unrigidified time as measured, and would have retained time's character as radically and unmeasurably *durée*. More importantly, he would have made it easier for movement to reconcile time and space without movement ceasing to be movement.[78] Similarly, it is a pity that, while he sometimes regarded change and movement as the primary categories, Bergson sometimes regarded time as the place to start. Maybe if he had kept his attention more firmly on movement and change—which is, after all, how we experience reality—he would have found it easier to understand time as a diverse phenomenon, and would not have expended so much energy fighting Einstein's Special Theory of Relativity.

---

70. Benda, *Le Bergsonisme ou Une Philosophie de la Mobilité*.
71. Bergson, *L'Évolution Créatrice*.
72. Benda, *Le Bergsonisme ou Une Philosophie de la Mobilité*, 90–91.
73. Benda, *Le Bergsonisme ou Une Philosophie de la Mobilité*, 97.
74. Benda, *Le Bergsonisme ou Une Philosophie de la Mobilité*, 101.
75. Mullarkey, *Bergson and Philosophy*, 4.
76. Mitchell, *Studies in Bergson's Philosophy*, 37.
77. Mullarkey, *Bergson and Philosophy*, 2.
78. Lindsay, *The Philosophy of Bergson*, 152–53.

Another way to see the whole picture is to understand both time and space as diverse patterned movement and change, with layers of patterns marking out the different elements of the diversity. Thus the time and space mapped out by the change which is the expanding universe is the fairly stable pattern of the time and space of physics; the time and space mapped out by the action that *I* am is my *durée* and my spatial relationships. As Arthur Mitchell points out, we can compare one time interval with another, we *can* remember previous time intervals (as when we watch a pendulum swinging and know that the swing that we saw was not the only one), and we can add one time interval to another: so there must be something homogeneous about time.[79] The fundamental difference between time and space is not that one is personal and the other a rigid external reality, but rather that in space patterns of movement and change are reversible, but in time they are not.

If movement and change take place in a variety of differently patterned layers, measurement is possible (against the fairly stable larger patterns), the patterns are connected (as they are all related to action), and Einstein's Special and General Theories of Relativity express patterns of action that relate to other levels, and are neither false nor necessarily ultimate.

Bergson was right about *durée* being the time that we experience, but wrong to privilege this particular member of the diversity; and he was similarly wrong to regard space as a rigid matrix. Bergson tended to choose one side of an abstract polarity, when in fact they often belong together.[80] Time is both discrete and continuous, just as space is. To have concentrated more on movement and change might have enabled Bergson to be more flexible on space and time, for movement and change require different levels of patterning in both time and space: we need the flexible and internal time and space of change or motion, and also the other layers of patterns within which they occur.

H. BERGSON'S GOD

Verging on the theological is Bergson's discussion of "living eternity,"[81] within which our own *durée* is like "perturbations in light."[82] There is nothing unchanging here. Eternity is as active as our own *durée*. Eternity is also open. There is nothing determined about it. Neither *durée* nor an eternity

---

79. Mitchell, *Studies in Bergson's Philosophy*, 43, 49.

80. Mitchell, *Studies in Bergson's Philosophy*, 50.

81. *éternité vivante*

82. *vibrations dans la lumière*: Bergson, *La Pensée et le Mouvant*, 115; author's translation. See Gouhier, *Bergson dans L'histoire de la Pensée Occidentale*, 68.

modelled on *durée* allows access to the past: only to an unknown future. This is the understanding of time that we find in the Judaeo-Christian tradition,[83] which might suggest religious roots for the idea, and a way into theology.

When Bergson turns to God, he is clear that he does not believe in Aristotle's God, "necessarily immutable, and apart from what is happening in the world."[84] For Bergson, "God has nothing of the ready-made, he is uninterrupted life, action, freedom. And the creation, so conceived, is not a mystery; we experience it in ourselves when we act freely."[85] Such a God is himself active, suggesting that action is indeed *the* fundamental idea for Bergson. This is a God Bergson could not find in Plato or Aristotle. It is a God discovered in a dynamic religion,[86] and in a mysticism defined by the *élan vital*:[87] a God that he could find in a Christian tradition defined by action; a God who propelled Christians into action: "We think of the accomplishments, in the field of action, of a St. Paul, a St. Theresa, a St. Catherine of Siena, a St. Francis . . ."[88] Jesus is the origin of Christianity, and reveals "everyone's divinity,"[89] but there is no attempt at a Christology, or even at a theology.[90] All that matters is that God should conform to the philosophical position, which is all about change and movement. As Gouhier puts it, "Christian mysticism is therefore complete because it extends into action; Greek mysticism is incomplete because it ends up in contemplation."[91]

For us, too, action, and the changing patterns of action that we might discover, will be a fruitful way of seeing all of reality: God, the universe, humanity, the macrocosm and the microcosm; for actions in patterns gives us a means of comprehending time, space, movement, the universe—and God.

I. ACTIONS IN PATTERNS

We can conclude that Bergson was reaching for an overall vision of reality, a metaphysic, but that he did not reach or achieve that. There are three difficulties: the complex relationship between movement and change; Bergson's

---

83. Jankélévitch, "Bergson and Judaism," 239.
84. Bergson, *L'Évolution Créatrice*, 188; Bergson, *Creative Evolution*, 322.
85. Bergson, *L'Évolution Créatrice*, 169; Bergson, *Creative Evolution*, 249.
86. Ansell-Pearson and Urpeth, "Bergson and Nietzsche on Religion," 251.
87. Ansell-Pearson and Urpeth, "Bergson and Nietzsche on Religion," 263.
88. Bergson, *Les Deux Sources de la Morale et de la Religion*, 122. Author's translation.
89. Bergson, *Les Deux Sources de la Morale et de la Religion*, 128. Author's translation.
90. Gouhier, *Bergson dans L'histoire de la Pensée Occidentale*, 119.
91. Gouhier, *Bergson dans L'histoire de la Pensée Occidentale*, 117. Author's translation.

understanding of space; and the priority given to *durée*. All three problems can be resolved if the focus of attention is shifted.

We have already noted that in the lectures published as *La Perception du Changement*,[92] change and movement, "*changement*" and "*mouvement*," seem to be used interchangeably. But should they be? "Movement" is a change of position in space, whereas "change" is a broader concept that encompasses both movement and a variety of other kinds of change: for instance, a change of color. And while it might be true that "*There are changes, but there are underneath the change no things which change*,"[93] the concept of change does in fact assume that there is something that changes, and the concept of movement does assume that there is something that moves. It is a pity that although Bergson and Blondel knew each other's work, they remained at a distance from each other both geographically and intellectually.[94] If they had not done so, then Bergson might have found in "action" a more basic concept than either movement or change. Admittedly, we can find it as difficult to abstract action from things that act or are acted upon as we do to abstract movement and changes from things that move and change, but both change and movement are actions at some level, so for Bergson to have developed Blondel's concept of action so that it could encompass both change and movement might have enabled him to work out a more appropriate relationship between movement and change.

Bergson reached the position that *durée* is both a psychological and a universal reality, and that space is a rigid matrix within which movement and change occur. This is a somewhat inconsistent position to have reached, particularly in the light of the space-time continuum with which Einstein and others were then working. Bergson's *élan vital* gives a sense of direction to the whole evolving configuration (somewhat mitigating the personal freedom that was an important aim), but without a clear relationship to either space or time. With a new starting-point in action, Bergson might have been able to co-ordinate his ideas rather better. Both movement and change could then have been experienced as diverse patterned action; *durée* could have been experienced as diverse personal experiences of sequential and simultaneous actions, and could also have been understood as the universe's experience of sequential and simultaneous action, with the patterns of action defining *durée*, rather than vice versa; space could have been our experience of relationships between simultaneous patterned actions; and

92. Bergson, *La Pensée et le Mouvant*; Bergson, *The Creative Mind*.

93. *Il y a des changements, mais il n'y a pas, sous le changement, de choses qui changent*: Bergson, *La Pensée et le Mouvant*, 104; Bergson, *The Creative Mind*, 173. Italics in the original.

94. Dupont, *Phenomenology in French Philosophy*, 94–95.

the *élan vital* could have been understood as one of an indefinite number of possible patterns of action, and as itself subject to change. Putting Blondel's and Bergson's conceptual structures together could have resulted in a powerful metaphysic that would have enabled us to experience ourselves, the evolving universe, and everything else, as actions in patterns. It is a pity that Bergson and Blondel appear to have decided not to work together. If they had, then they might have arrived at something like Pierre Teilhard de Chardin's understanding of humanity, the universe, and God: the subject of the next chapter. As Bergson did in fact put it:

> Reality no longer appears then in the static state, in its manner of being; it affirms itself dynamically, in the continuity and variability of its tendency. What was immobile and frozen in our perception is warmed and set in motion. Everything comes to life around us, everything is revivified in us.[95]

J. MUHAMMAD IQBAL: BERGSON'S EASTERN DISCIPLE

Muhammad Iqbal was a poet and philosopher who lived in British-ruled India and died just a few years before independence. Many regard him as the spiritual father of Pakistan.

> Rest and immobility are mere illusions,
> Every particle of the universe pulsates with life.
> The caravan of life never stops;
> At every stage it manifests itself in a new form.
> You think life is a mystery (No!)
> It is nothing but a continuous flow.[96]

Iqbal recognised his debt to Bergson, whom he read in the light of the Quran, but he found Bergson's *élan vital* rather goalless. For Iqbal, life's driving force, the emergent evolution that characterized all of life, was driving towards creativity and freedom.[97]

> Life is preserved by purpose:
> Because of the goal its caravan-bell tinkles.
> Life is latent in seeking and striving,
> Its origin is hidden in desire.[98]

---

95. Bergson, *La Pensée et le Mouvant*, 111; Bergson, *The Creative Mind*, 186.
96. Iqbal, "Bāl-i Jibrīl," 171.
97. Dar, *A Study in Iqbal's Philosophy*, 35.
98. Iqbal, "The Quest."

The goal is never imposed, and it is never the same: it is always new, because to live is to shape and change ends and purposes as well as to be governed by them.

Unsurprisingly, a further inspiration was A.N. Whitehead's process philosophy, which we shall study in chapter 8:

> Nature is . . . a structure of events possessing the character of a continuous flow which thought cuts up into isolated immobilities out of whose mutul relatedness arise the concepts of space and time.[99]

Bergson is more likely to have written about process in that way than Whitehead was, because, as we shall see, Whitehead does not appear to have thought the flow of life to be as continuous as Iqbal's summary makes out. For Iqbal, everything changes, from the universe to someone's inner life,[100] so he was reading Whitehead through a Bergsonian lens.

Although Iqbal was a barrister, he regarded intuition rather than mechanistic reason to be our access to the very heart of life, as Bergson did. Iqbal took as an example of constant change the way in which Islamic law has constantly changed in response to new problems, and the way in which it has always been characterized by diversity.[101] There is nothing that does not change.

---

99. Iqbal, *Six Lectures on the Reconstruction of Religious Thought in Islam*, 47.
100. Ashraf, *A Critical Exposition of Iqbal's Philosophy*, 109
101. Iqbal, *Six Lectures on the Reconstruction of Religious Thought in Islam*, 230.

7

A Single Fire

Pierre Teilhard de Chardin's Search for Synthesis

A. INTRODUCTION

Pierre Teilhard de Chardin's mind must have been one of the most versatile of the twentieth century. As a palaeontologist, he contributed to major advances in anthropology and geology; as a priest he was steeped in the philosophy and doctrine of the Roman Catholic Church; and as a theologian (even though he always said that he wasn't one) he was both conservative and innovative, seeking always new understandings of the church's traditions: understandings that would achieve *synthesis*, between human action and God's action, between science and religion, and between cosmology and theology. In the early *Le Milieu Divin*[1] (where *milieu* means both "source" and "environment"), God is active in the world, and Christ is the world's source of energy, thus reconciling the world to God. In *Le*

---

1. Teilhard de Chardin, *Le Milieu Divin*; Teilhard de Chardin, *Le Milieu Divin* (Eng.). The English translation retained the original French title. Subsequent translations were titled *The Divine Milieu*. (The short form reference for the original French *Le Milieu Divin* will be Teilhard de Chardin, *Le Milieu Divin*, and the short form for the English translation will be Teilhard de Chardin, *Le Milieu Divin* (Eng.).)

Phénomène Humain (The Human Phenonemon)[2] the "Omega point" is the aim of the evolutionary process, and the "Christian phenomenon" is the focal process of history: so it rather looks as if synthesis has been achieved from the cosmic and human end as well: although Teilhard does not unambiguously say this, possibly because of his church's insistence that revelation is God's breaking into history: a breaking in at a particular point in time, so one that might invite new interpretation, but not one that continues to evolve.[3]

Teilhard's synthesis was always a synthesis between two elements of a duality: so we shall discuss Teilhard's cosmology, then the theology, and then the attempts at synthesis.

B. COSMOLOGY

In 1908 Teilhard read Bergson's *L'Évolution Créatrice (Creative Evolution)*,[4] and in 1919 he met Blondel and subsequently corresponded with him:

> With Blondel I [have] been in touch . . . Certain features of his thought certainly had their effect on me: the vale of action (which became for me a quasi-experimental energenetics of the biological forces of evolution), and the notion of pan-Christ-hood[5] (at which I had arrived independently, without daring at the time to name it so appropriately).[6]

For both Blondel and Teilhard de Chardin, this "pan-Christism" related God both to the world and to the Eucharist,[7] and Teilhard subsequently incorporated the idea into his *Le Phénomène Humain (The Human Phenomenon)*: a description of the evolutionary process from matter to life

---

2. Teilhard de Chardin, *Le Phénomène Humain*; Teilhard de Chardin, *The Phenomenon of Man*. Subsequent editions of the English translation were published under the title *The Human Phenomenon*.

3. Wildiers, *An Introduction to Teilhard de Chardin*, 14.

4. Bergson, *L'Évolution Créatrice*.

5. *la notion de "panchristisme."* It might have been better to have retained Teilhard's own expression "panchristism," and to have translated *"une énergétique quasi-expérimentale"* as "a sort of experiential energizing."

6. Letter, 15th February 1955, quoted in Cuénot, *Teilhard de Chardin*, 55–6; Cuénot, *Teilhard de Chardin* (Eng.), 39. (The short form reference for the original French will be Cuénot, *Teilhard de Chardin*, and the short form for the English translation will be Cuénot, *Teilhard de Chardin* (Eng.).)

7. Saint-Sernin, *Blondel*, 87; Rideau, *Teilhard de Chardin*, 2.

(the biosphere), to persons (the noosphere: *nóos*, Greek for "mind"), and onwards to an "Omega point": a final consummation of the evolutionary process.

Bergson and Teilhard start in different places: Bergson with the *durée* experienced by the individual consciousness, and Teilhard with the evolution of the cosmos; and they come to different conclusions: for instance, Teilhard de Chardin finds consciousness throughout reality, whereas for Bergson it remains a characteristic of living beings: but, for both of them, evolutionary change is at the heart of their projects.[8]

For Teilhard, matter is both plural and a unity—"this unity reveals itself in an astonishing similarity of the elements"—a homogeneity, with each unit only defined "by virtue of its influence on all around it"; and "a mysterious identity," connecting the units together. And matter is energy, "a unifying power"[9] and "a kind of homogeneous, primordial flux in which all that has shape in the world is but a series of fleeting vortices."[10] The "plural" and "unity" understandings of matter define it more in terms of being or beings than diversify and change, but the "energy" understanding comprehends it as action in changing patterns: so here we have a complex understanding of matter that is inspired by both the "being" and "action" streams within Western philosophy.

Throughout this cosmos of matter Teilhard finds a whole, a system, and interconnections.[11] As matter complexifies, so critical moments occur, first giving birth to life (the biosphere), and then to the noosphere (human beings): a whole new stage of being. But that is not where the process stops, for in *L'Avenir de L'Homme*, *The Future of Man*, Teilhard writes of a new kind of evolution driven by the development of the human social group rather than by biological transformations. Evolution thus looks as if it "rebounds"[12] on itself,[13] acting with "reflective purpose": "It is only through reflective [purpose],[14] slowly acquired, that Life can henceforth

8. Barthélémy-Madaule, *Bergson et Teilhard de Chardin*, 265, 237.

9. *pouvoir de liaison*

10. *une sorte de flux homogène, primordial, dont tout ce qui existe de figure au Monde ne serait que de fugitifs "tourbillons"*: Teilhard de Chardin, *Le Phénomène Humain*, 29–30; Teilhard de Chardin, *The Phenomenon of Man*, 45–47.

11. Teilhard de Chardin, *Le Phénomène Humain*, 30; Teilhard de Chardin, *The Phenomenon of Man*, 49.

12. *rebondit*

13. Teilhard de Chardin, *L'Avenir de L'Homme*, 262, 271; Teilhard de Chardin, *The Future of Man*, 212, 221.

14. *la finalité réfléchie*: Teilhard de Chardin, *L'Avenir de L'Homme*, 258. The translation in Teilhard de Chardin, *The Future of Man*, 209, reads "purposiveness." However,

hope to raise itself yet higher, by auto-evolution, in the twofold direction of greater complexity and fuller consciousness."[15]

In *L'Avenir de L'Homme,* Teilhard offers a series of "theorems": Life is the central phenomenon of evolution[16] (a possibility because matter has a "within" which is already pressing towards the formation of the biosphere, the noosphere, and beyond);[17] "Human reflection is not an Epi-phenomenon of the organic world but the central phenomenon of vitalisation";[18] "Socialisation is not an Epi-phenomenon in the sphere of reflective life but the Essential Phenomenon of Hominisation";[19] and the church is "the . . . axis (or nucleus) about which [the growth of the human social organism] forms."[20] These theorems are most easily understood within a conceptual framework within which matter is comprehended as action in changing patterns, as that framework makes most sense of the centrality of evolution, human reflection, socialisation, and the church. It would therefore appear that by this stage in the evolution of his thought Teilhard has largely abandoned the "beings that change" framework in favour of "actions in patterns."

For Teilhard de Chardin, Christ is related to the "Omega point" at the end of the evolutionary process,[21] and the "Christian phenomenon" is present already as "the palpable influence on our world of *another* and supreme someone . . . Is not the Christian phenomenon, which rises at the heart

---

"finalité" might be better translated as "purpose." The Collins French-English dictionary (www.collinsdictionary.com/dictionary/french-english) gives this as a possible translation; and to read the sentence as suggesting that it is the purpose towards which evolution is driving that draws evolution towards that purpose—the purpose "rebounding," and functioning "reflectively"—coheres with the general tenor of Teilhard de Chardin's thought. Teilhard is offering a final cause argument. A further reason for choosing "purpose" as the translation is that it can be ambiguous, as Teilhard's "finalité" might be: that is, it might refer both to a purpose that draws evolution towards itself, and to the answering purposiveness that we experience.

15. Teilhard de Chardin, *The Future of Man,* 209.

16. Teilhard de Chardin, *L'Avenir de L'Homme,* 223.

17. Teilhard de Chardin, *Le Phénomène Humain,* 42; Teilhard de Chardin, *The Phenomenon of Man,* 59.

18. Teilhard de Chardin, *L'Avenir de L'Homme,* 279; Teilhard de Chardin, *The Future of Man,* 226.

19. Teilhard de Chardin, *L'Avenir de L'Homme,* 282; Teilhard de Chardin, *The Future of Man,* 229.

20. *L'église n'est pas un épi- ou para-phénomène, mais elle forme l'axe même (ou noyau) du rassemblement*: Teilhard de Chardin, *L'Avenir de L'Homme,* 285; Teilhard de Chardin, *The Future of Man,* 231.

21. Teilhard de Chardin, *Le Phénomène Humain,* 262; Teilhard de Chardin, *The Phenomenon of Man,* 286.

of the social phenomenon, precisely that?"[22] Yes, it is precisely that: but if it is that, then already we are in the theological world, whatever Teilhard might say to the contrary; and so here already we experience him stepping back from possibilities of synthesis, presumably because of his own and his church's unwillingness to recognise that cosmology and theology cannot be kept separate, and that if the relationship goes in one direction (from theology to cosmology) then there exists a relationship that cannot prevent movement in the opposite direction, from cosmology to theology.

The process of evolution, from matter to life, from instinct to thought, has now moved from hominisation[23] to divinisation, with the universe and the personal growing in the same direction, culminating in each other,[24] and putting us in touch with *all* centres of consciousness and with *all* matter: for throughout this process consciousness has been struggling to appear,[25] and throughout it all the Omega Point has been drawing the process towards its future.

C. THEOLOGY

We have discovered that Teilhard's cosmology leads inexorably to theology. We shall now find that the theology leads just as inexorably towards cosmology, except where Teilhard decides not to let it do so.

In *Le Milieu Divin* we experience clearly metaphysical and theological work, although Teilhard will not allow it to be called metaphysics, and will not even permit the description "apologetics": "I shall not attempt to embark on metaphysics or apologetics."[26] In *Le Milieu Divin* we find an explicit desire for synthesis, because for Teilhard the "divine milieu" "harmonises with itself qualities which appear to us contradictory,"[27] and this "harmonisation" is God-achieved, for the "divine milieu" *is* God: "God reveals himself everywhere, beneath our groping efforts, as a *universal milieu*, only because

---

22. Teilhard de Chardin, *Le Phénomène Humain*, 300–301; Teilhard de Chardin, *The Phenomenon of Man*, 327.

23. Teilhard de Chardin, *Le Phénomène Humain*, 160, 170–71; Teilhard de Chardin, *The Phenomenon of Man*, 182, 193.

24. Teilhard de Chardin, *Le Phénomène Humain*, 256–65; Teilhard de Chardin, *The Phenomenon of Man*, 284–90.

25. Gatliffe, "Jung and Teilhard de Chardin," 2002.

26. Teilhard de Chardin, *Le Milieu Divin*, 16; Teilhard de Chardin, *Le Milieu Divin* (Eng.), 46.

27. *harmonise en soi les qualités qui nous paraissent les plus contraires*: Teilhard de Chardin, *Le Milieu Divin*, 122; Teilhard de Chardin, *Le Milieu Divin* (Eng.), 113.

he is the *ultimate point* upon which all realities converge."[28] Because God is everywhere, we can "seize him everywhere,"[29] and because there is *one* God, and one incarnation, there is one Eucharist and one communion.[30]

As we shall see, while Teilhard de Chardin will not allow God to be *completely* embroiled in the struggles of the physical world, there is genuine involvement, for the divine milieu discloses itself to us as "a modification of the deep being of things":[31] but then a more Platonic "being" worldview informs the language of "principles" and "the purity, faith and fidelity" which are the means to a relationship with the divine milieu.[32] The theology remains theology, just as the cosmology remains cosmology: but the cosmology merges into the theology, and we have seen that in *The Divine Milieu* (—and this is also true of "the Mass on the World"[33]) the theology becomes cosmology to the extent that it is allowed to do so, thus introducing a reconciliation between the two spheres of thought which leads us to question whether they really are two separate spheres at all.

D. UBIQUITOUS INCARNATION

As Wildiers suggests, Teilhard's work is about "God and the universe"[34] and the connection between them. He seeks a totality: an understanding of God and the universe which comprehends them within a single conception. Teilhard had found in Bergson's *L'Évolution Creatrice*, *Creative Evolution*, the idea that matter evolves towards complexity and consciousness, driven by an *élan vital*. As he writes:

> Is it by chance (as Bergson said in his *Creative Evolution*) that the Welfstoff [matter] presents itself to us, scientifically, as endowed with a special sort of "gravity" that makes it take advantage of

---

28. Teilhard de Chardin, *Le Milieu Divin*, 123; Teilhard de Chardin, *Le Milieu Divin* (Eng.), 114.

29. *le saisir universellement*: Teilhard de Chardin, *Le Milieu Divin*, 134; Teilhard de Chardin, *Le Milieu Divin* (Eng.), 121.

30. Teilhard de Chardin, *Le Milieu Divin*, 138; Teilhard de Chardin, *Le Milieu Divin* (Eng.), 124.

31. Teilhard de Chardin, *Le Milieu Divin*, 148; Teilhard de Chardin, *Le Milieu Divin* (Eng.), 130.

32. Teilhard de Chardin, *Le Milieu Divin*, 151; Teilhard de Chardin, *Le Milieu Divin* (Eng.), 132.

33. Teilhard de Chardin, "La Masse sur le Monde"; *Hymn of the Universe*, 17–37.

34. Wildiers, *An Introduction to Teilhard de Chardin*, 21.

every chance always to fall (or rather rise) through greater complexity to greater consciousness?[35]

But this still does not reconcile the cosmic consciousness and the Christic consciousness to each other. As far as Teilhard was concerned, these had arisen separately but were moving towards an eventual reconciliation: for, as Wildiers has put it, "Christ had a comsic function and . . . the evolution of the cosmos had to be seen as a movement orientated upon a cosmic central point."[36] It is in Christ, and not through the evolution of the cosmos left to its own devices, that Teilhard seeks reconciliation, the Omega Point: because, as Mooney suggests, there is one divine plan, from creation out of nothing and towards a "plenitude in Christ," so that the "Christogenesis" can be understood both as God's creativity and as our action, with throughout it a movement from God to humanity and from humanity to God.[37] This could be interpreted as an "incarnational" reconciliation understood from within a thoroughly Catholic theology:

> Christ, principle of universal vitality because sprung up as man among men, put himself in the position (maintained ever since) to subdue under himself, to purify, to direct and superanimate the general ascent of consciousness into which he inserted himself. By a perennial act of communion and sublimation, he aggregates to himself the total psychism of earth,[38]

so that eventually "God shall be in all"—or rather, "there will only be God, all in all"[39]—and there will be a "perfect unity, steeped in which each element will reach its consummation at the same time as the universe."[40] In this context, "incarnation" would encompass not only God living a particular human life, but God incarnate in every aspect and every moment of the

35. Cuénot, *Teilhard de Chardin*, 368; Cuénot, *Teilhard de Chardin* (Eng.), 304: quoting a letter from Teilhard de Chardin dated the 27th February 1953.

36. Wildiers, *An Introduction to Teilhard de Chardin*, 23.

37. Mooney, *Teilhard de Chardin and the Mystery of Christ*, 187.

38. Teilhard de Chardin, *Le Phénomène Humain*, 296; Teilhard de Chardin, *The Phenomenon of Man*, 322.

39. *il n'y aura plus que Dieu, tout en tous*: cf. 1 Cor 15: 28: *hína ȩ̃ ho theòs [tà] pánta en pāsin*, ". . . that God may be all in all"; Eph 1: 23: *hḗtis estìn tò sō̃ma autoū̃, tò plḗrōma toū̃ tà pánta en pāsin plērouménou*, "which is his body, the fullness of him who fills all in all." Teilhard de Chardin's translator has been led by the text of the New Testament to translate Teilhard's French as "God shall be in all," rather than by Teilhard de Chardin's significant adaptation of it: "There will be no more than God, all in all," or "there will only be God, all in all."

40. Teilhard de Chardin, *Le Phénomène Humain*, 296; Teilhard de Chardin, *The Phenomenon of Man*, 322.

evolution of the cosmos, with every aspect and every moment of that evolution being found in God.

But Christ remains at the heart of this incarnation, for it is he that is at work, "directing" and "superanimating" consciousness: and because matter has a "within," and thus already a consciousness, matter as well as consciousness is the object of Christ's reconciling activity. This is why in the "Mass on the World," written in 1923, Teilhard is able to offer the world in its entirety to Christ, and to dedicate himself to Christ incarnate in matter:

> It is to your body in this its fullest extension . . . that is, to the world become through your power and my faith the glorious living crucible in which everything melts away in order to be born anew; it is to this that I dedicate myself;[41]

and why, in the "Hymn to Matter,"[42] written in 1919, Teilhard even addresses himself to matter itself, acclaiming it as the "universal power which brings together and unites, through which the multitudinous monads are bound together and in which they all converge on the way of the Spirit."[43]

But still the consummation remains future: an "Omega" that is "autonomy, actuality, irreversibility, and thus finally transcendence,"[44] the "Prime Mover ahead."[45] Thus Omega might be "already in existence,"[46] but still the consummation is future, prepared for by a "love" that "is nothing more, and nothing less, than the more or less direct trace marked on the heart of the element by the psychical convergence of the universe upon itself,"[47] which leads us

> to conceive a noogenesis rising upstream against the flow of entropy; to provide evolution with a direction, a line of advance

---

41. Teilhard de Chardin, "La Masse sur le Monde," 156; Teilhard de Chardin, *Hymn of the Universe*, 35.

42. *Hymne à la Matière*.

43. Teilhard de Chardin, *Le Coeur de la Matière*, 90; Teilhard de Chardin, *Hymn of the Universe*, 64.

44. Teilhard de Chardin, *Le Phénomène Humain*, 272; Teilhard de Chardin, *The Phenomenon of Man*, 297.

45. Teilhard de Chardin, *Le Phénomène Humain*, 273; Teilhard de Chardin, *The Phenomenon of Man*, 298.

46. Teilhard de Chardin, *Le Phénomène Humain*, 293; Teilhard de Chardin, *The Phenomenon of Man*, 319.

47. Teilhard de Chardin, *Le Phénomène Humain*, 266; Teilhard de Chardin, *The Phenomenon of Man*, 291.

and critical points, and finally to make all things double back upon *someone*.⁴⁸

In this process, "God arises": that is, the idea of God emerges, and perhaps *God* emerges:

> The last phase of this vast revelation, whose history is one with that of the world, cannot be other than the history of union, which will take place when the attraction of God, victorious over the material resistance caused by unorganized plurality, will once and for all have rescued from inferior determinizing the Spirit slowly nourished by all the sap of the earth.⁴⁹

At the heart of the process is action—our action⁵⁰—for "each one of our works, by its more or less remote or direct effect upon the spiritual world, helps to make perfect Christ in his mystical totality";⁵¹ and it is through *action* that communion is achieved, and the Christian

> not only [encounters] God in the entire field of his actions in the perceptible world, but in the course of this first phase of his spiritual development, the divine *milieu* which has been uncovered absorbs his powers in the proportion in which these laboriously rise above their individuality.⁵²

As we have discovered, Bergson's philosophy was one capable of informing religion. Teilhard de Chardin's is inherently and totally religious.⁵³ For him, cosmology and theology meet not only in Christ present and future, but also in action that is both God's and ours,⁵⁴ thus achieving reconciliation: and then Teilhard steps back, claims not to be constructing a metaphysic or a theology, and locates in the Christian and the priest the action that

---

48. Teilhard de Chardin, *Le Phénomène Humain*, 292; Teilhard de Chardin, *The Phenomenon of Man*, 318.

49. Teilhard de Chardin, *L'Énergie Humaine*, 57; Teilhard de Chardin, *The Human Energy*, 47.

50. Teilhard de Chardin, *Le Milieu Divin*, 21, 28–29; Teilhard de Chardin, *Le Milieu Divin* (Eng.), 49, 53.

51. Teilhard de Chardin, *Le Milieu Divin*, 42; Teilhard de Chardin, *Le Milieu Divin* (Eng.), 62.

52. Teilhard de Chardin, *Le Milieu Divin*, 58; Teilhard de Chardin, *Le Milieu Divin* (Eng.), 73.

53. Barthélémy-Madaule, *Bergson et Teilhard de Chardin*, 640–41.

54. Teilhard de Chardin, *The Making of a Mind*, 58, 210.

matters: although reference to God as "Act"⁵⁵ suggests where a little more metaphysical exploration might have taken Teilhard de Chardin.

Jacques Fabre shows that "the question of being leads Teilhard to posit a hierarchy of evolutionary levels . . . levels of reality":⁵⁶ "prelife, biosphere, noosphere,"⁵⁷ between which "disruptive mutations" occur.⁵⁸ The system cries out for an "action" metaphysic: an understanding of reality as actions in patterns, with periods of relative stability in the patterns, and periods of "disruptive mutations": but, always and everywhere, actions in patterns understood as evolutionary change. And the system cries out for completion: for God to be as defined by and as embroiled in the actions in patterns as everything else; and for the Omega Point to be equally defined by actions in patterns, rather than as the still point that is often implied.

E. REACTIONS AND PROBLEMS

The Society of Jesus, of which Teilhard de Chardin was a member, refused him permission to publish his more speculative work during his lifetime. The work was not condemned as heretical: it was simply that caution led his superiors to forbid publication, which meant that following his death in 1955 publication of books and of collections of papers was rapid, and made available a substantial body of important work: but unfortunately did not give to Teilhard himself the benefit of criticism.

Following publication, the Roman Catholic Church, and especially the Jesuits, set about domesticating Teilhard's ideas. Thus Mooney suggested that Teilhard had achieved no synthesis between science and theology, because science is a specialized and separate discipline, and Teilhard's "specialized spiritual experience" had limited his theological achievement. Mooney's verdict is that we are still seeking a synthesis.⁵⁹ Similarly, Speaight declared Teilhard to have been "a practical geologist and very much a practising priest," and so decided that "his thought [both] sprang from action [and] was equally directed to it."⁶⁰ He tried to evacuate Teilhard's thought

---

55. Teilhard de Chardin, *Writings in Time of War*, 135.

56. Fabre, "Les Niveaux du Reel et les Mechanismes de l'Évolution," 47, 49. Author's translation.

57. Fabre, "Les Niveaux du Reel et les Mechanismes de l'Évolution," 48. Author's translation.

58. Fabre, "Les Niveaux du Reel et les Mechanismes de l'Évolution," 48. Author's translation.

59. Mooney, *Teilhard de Chardin and the Mystery of Christ*, 212.

60. Speaight, *Teilhard de Chardin*, 118.

of theological meaning, as did Grenet, by placing rather too much weight on Teilhard's statements about not intending to be a theologian.[61] Rideau employed another tactic: he suggested that Teilhard's theology had its own (orthodox) sources, and was independent of his cosmology, and criticized him for those occasions on which he did try to relate his theology to his cosmology: for this kind of theology simply could not be reconciled with the Christian tradition.[62]

Teilhard de Chardin was a cosmologist: and that cosmology was one of the roots of his theological statements, and of his search for reconciliation between science and religion and between cosmology and theology. His superiors understood this perfectly well, which is why they forbade publication at the same time as not condemning Teilhard's writings. It is a pity that they did not positively value what he wrote as the important apologetics that it could have been, which is not to say that there are not problems with what Teilhard wrote.

Teilhard's spiritual journey began in 1908, but it was also informed by the trenches of the First World War in which he was a stretcher-bearer, so it is rather strange that a discussion of evil appears only as an appendix to *Le Phénomène Humain, The Human Phenomenon*,[63] and that that discussion is of different types of evil, with the last line taking the cross as an analogy to people's sufferings.[64] In *L'Énergie Humaine, The Human Energy*, the world "is under construction,"[65] so that it is inevitable that there should be pain:

> The world, seen by experience at our level, is an immense groping, an immense search, an immense attack: its progress can take place only at the expense of many failures, of many wounds."[66]

Here the stretcher-bearer's experience gives priority to the battle rather than to the victims: and we have to ask whether the experience of war was just too painful to be incorporated into either the cosmology or the theology

---

61. Grenet, *Teilhard de Chardin*.

62. Rideau, *La Pensée du Père Teilhard de Chardin*, 370–72; Rideau, *Teilhard de Chardin*, 188–89.

63. Teilhard de Chardin, *Le Phénomène Humain*, 315–18; Teilhard de Chardin, *The Phenomenon of Man*, 339–42.

64. Teilhard de Chardin, *Le Phénomène Humain*, 318; Teilhard de Chardin, *The Phenomenon of Man*, 342.

65. Teilhard de Chardin, *L'Énergie Humaine*, 61; Teilhard de Chardin, *The Human Energy*, 48.

66. Teilhard de Chardin, *L'Énergie Humaine*, 63; Teilhard de Chardin, *The Human Energy*, 50.

in anything like a personal fashion. It is true that Teilhard recognises that *sometimes* sufferers are "driven out of themselves,"[67] and that they are therefore "compelled to depart from the prevailing forms of life";[68] and it might be true that Jesus' death is creative and is a part of the process—

> The cross is the symbol and the place of an action whose intensity is beyond experience . . . [Jesus] bears the weight and draws ever higher towards God the universal march of progress . . . Let us act like him, in order to be in our whole existence united with him[69]

—but Teilhard knew the horrors of war, and this hardly seems adequate. Here is no Studdert Kennedy, with his "comrade God" who suffers with the suffering.[70] Here is someone who *could* have involved God in the suffering, but did not, to our theological loss.

The second problem is related. Teilhard's evolution is convergent, on an Omega point: but our experience could easily lead us to believe that human society's evolution is now divergent, and that we are causing the same to be true for matter and the biosphere. Teilhard suggests that

> we have gone deeply into these new perspectives: the progress of the universe, and in particular of the human universe, does not take place in competition with God, nor does it squander energies that we rightly owe to him. The greater man becomes, the more humanity becomes united, with consciousness of, and master of, its potentialities, the more beautiful creation will be, the more perfect adoration will become, and the more Christ will find, for mystical extensions, a body worthy of resurrection.[71]

The earth thus becomes the body of Christ, the body "of him who is and of him who is coming . . . the divine milieu."[72]

---

67. *se trouvent chassés hors d'eux mêmes*: Teilhard de Chardin, *L'Énergie Humaine*, 64; Teilhard de Chardin, *The Human Energy*, 50.

68. *poussés à émigrer hors des forms présentes de la Vie*: Teilhard de Chardin, *L'Énergie Humaine*, 64; Teilhard de Chardin, *The Human Energy*, 50.

69. Teilhard de Chardin, *L'Énergie Humaine*, 65–66; Pierre Teilhard de Chardin, *The Human Energy*, 52.

70. Studdert Kennedy, Geoffrey, *The Unutterable Beauty*, 30.

71. Teilhard de Chardin, *Le Milieu Divin*, 184; Teilhard de Chardin, *Le Milieu Divin* (Eng.), 153–54.

72. Teilhard de Chardin, *Le Milieu Divin*, 186; Teilhard de Chardin, *Le Milieu Divin* (Eng.), 155.

As I write, the coronavirus crisis is revealing the depth of societies' inequalities, wars continue, Europe is trying to keep out increasing flows of migrants, the UK is leaving the European Union, and the United States has elected a protectionist, isolationist and erratic president. It is difficult to call this *convergent* evolution, and difficult to see how it contributes to Christogenesis.

The third problem is metaphysical. Teilhard was a scientist, interested in phenomena.[73] Rideau calls his cosmology of progressive spheres an "ontology": it is not: it is a cosmology, because it does not discuss *how* the within of matter drives the process forwards. Teilhard constantly wrote that he was not doing metaphysics, but because he used metaphysical terms such as being, non-being, absolute, and unity,[74] he left his readers somewhat perplexed.

> In hominised evolution, the physical and the psychic, the without and the within, matter and consciousness, are all found to be functionally linked in one tangible process. Setting aside the metaphysics, the two terms in each of these pairs are articulated in a quasi-measurable fashion with one another, with the two-fold result not only of at last affording us a unified concept of the universe, but also of breaking down the two barriers behind which Man was coming to believe himself to be for ever imprisoned—the magic circle of phenomenalism and the infernal circle of egocentrism.[75]

Setting aside the metaphysics seems to have led Teilhard in a most metaphysical direction. Where it did not finally lead him was towards asking whether the action that he would have found to be central to Blondel's and Bergson's philosophies might have served his own philosophical and theological purposes. "Action," for Teilhard de Chardin, remained human action.[76]

Why was this? Melvyn Thompson suggests that "the problem of action"—meaning "the problem of human action"—lies at the heart of Teilhard de Chardin's intellectual project. The "problem" was this:

---

73. Rideau, *La Pensée du Père Teilhard de Chardin*, 546; Rideau, *Teilhard de Chardin*, 237.

74. Rideau, *La Pensée du Père Teilhard de Chardin*, 55; Rideau, *Teilhard de Chardin*, 43.

75. Teilhard de Chardin, *L'Avenir de L'Homme*, 268; Teilhard de Chardin, *The Future of Man*, 218.

76. De Lubac, *La Pensée du Père Teilhard de Chardin*, 255–56, 365–70; De Lubac, *The Religion of Teilhard de Chardin*, 177–78, 262–66.

that man, because of his ability to think and reflect, would cease to act unless he could see that his action would produce some appropriate end result. He therefore feared that man would lose his natural incentive to live and develop unless he could see a specific goal to which evolution was moving.[77]

Le Phénomène Humain, The Human Phenomenon, contains an entire section on "the problem of action"[78] which exhibits "a sense of helplessness unless there is evolution towards some final goal:"[79]

If progress is a myth, that is to say, if faced by the work involved we can say: "What's the good of it all?" our efforts will fall flat. With that the whole of evolution will come to a halt, because we are evolution.... Either nature is closed to our demands for futurity, in which case thought, the fruit of millions of years of effort, is stifled, still-born in a self-abortive and absurd universe. Or else an opening exists: that of the super-soul above our souls; but in that case the way out, if we are to agree to embark on it, must open out freely onto limitless psychic spaces in a universe to which we can unhesitatingly entrust ourselves.[80]

Thompson suggests that "the problem of action" is "existentially motivated and shaped":[81] it expresses Teilhard's own anxieties about the purpose of human life, and of his own life in particular, in the context of an evolution that could easily look as if it had no purpose beyond itself. It was not Blondel, and it was not the intellectual challenge of building a coherent relationship between theology and science, that drove the structure of Teilhard's oeuvre and his focus on human action: it was his anxieties, and the vision and commitment that he constructed to deal with them.[82] However, it is not inconsistent with this insight to suggest that other motives contributed to Teilhard de Chardin's thought-processes. One of those is surely the need to reconcile two vital parts of his life: science and religion, evolution and

---

77. Thompson, *A Critical Analysis,* 6.

78. Teilhard de Chardin, *Le Phénomène Humain,* 226–34; Teilhard de Chardin, *The Phenomenon of Man,* 249–57.

79. Thompson, *A Critical Analysis,* 41.

80. Teilhard de Chardin, *Le Phénomène Humain,* 232–3; Teilhard de Chardin, *The Phenomenon of Man,* 256.

81. Thompson, *A Critical Analysis,* 231.

82. Thompson, *A Critical Analysis,* 233, 238.

Christian faith:[83] and not only his science and religion, or science and religion in general, but the very subject matters of science and religion:[84]

> Religion and science are two conjugated faces or phases of one and the same complete act of knowledge . . . The end of the world; . . . detaching the mind, fulfilled at last, from its material matrix, so that it will henceforth rest with all its weight on God-Omega.[85]

A further driver of Teilhard's intellectual journey might have been a desire to reconcile the one and the many.[86] In *Le Milieu Divin*, "the true God . . . will invade the universe . . . without mixture, without confusion."[87] The cosmos would be reconciled in the Omega, the many in the one, and the problem that had driven Western philosophy for two and a half thousand years would be solved.

F. THE SINGLE FIRE

While there is no explicit metaphysics underlying the theology, the fact that the cosmology flows into the theology, and vice versa, implies a metaphysic that counts the divine and the human as belonging to the same universe, and as describable in terms of each other. Within a particular understanding of a more Platonic theological system this cannot be done, for the divine is the unchanging, and the human lies in the changing world of appearances. But there are hints that Teilhard had pondered on a possible solution to this problem. His "*La Messe sur le Monde*," "the Mass on the World," begins with "offertory," and closes with "communion." Between the two we might have expected to find the usual Sanctus, but instead we find "*Le Feu au-dessus du Monde*" and "*Le Feu dans le Monde*," "Fire over the Earth" and "Fire in the Earth."[88]

---

83. Raven, *Teilhard de Chardin*, 185–86; Towers, *Concerning Teilhard*, 53.

84. Lyons, *The Cosmic Christ*, 39.

85. Teilhard de Chardin, *Le Phénomène Humain*, 287, 290; Teilhard de Chardin, *The Phenomenon of Man*, 312–13, 316.

86. Gray, *The One and the Many*, 162, 182.

87. Teilhard de Chardin, *Le Milieu Divin*, 18; Teilhard de Chardin, *Le Milieu Divin* (Eng.), 47.

88. Teilhard de Chardin, *Le Coeur de la Matière*, 139–56; Teilhard de Chardin, *Hymn of the Universe*, 17–37. "Fire over the world" and "Fire in the world" might have been better translations.

> Fire,[89] the source of being . . . once again the Fire[90] has penetrated the earth . . . the flame has lit up the whole world from within. All things individually and collectively are penetrated and flooded by it, from the inmost core of the tiniest atom to the mighty sweep of the most universal laws of being: so naturally has it flooded every element, every energy, every connecting link in the unity of our cosmos, that one might suppose the cosmos to have burst spontaneously into flame.[91]

There is plenty of biblical "fire" imagery with which Teilhard would have been familiar. The tribal God of the children of Israel, conquering the promised land for them, "is the one who crosses over before you as a devouring fire";[92] and in the book of the prophet Isaiah,

> The sinners in Zion are afraid;
> trembling has seized the godless:
> "Who among us can live with the devouring fire?
> Who among us can live with everlasting flames?"[93]

The New Testament applies a fair share of "fire" language to the devil: in terms of fire prepared for the devil and his angels,[94] and as a description of the place to which the "rich man," who has taken no notice of poor Lazarus at his gate, has been sent.[95] And then in the New Testament, the fire of God is both a judgement and a cleansing:

> The work of each builder will become visible, for the Day will disclose it, because it will be revealed with fire, and the fire will test what sort of work each has done. . . . If the work is burned, the builder will suffer loss; the builder will be saved, but only as through fire;[96]

---

89. *Le feu*

90. *le Feu*

91. Teilhard de Chardin, *Le Coeur de la Matière*, 143, 145; Teilhard de Chardin, *Hymn of the Universe*, 23–4.

92. Deut 9:3.

93. Isa 33:14.

94. Matt 25:41.

95. Luke 16:24.

96. 1 Cor 3:13, 15.

and in the Letter to the Hebrews, it is God who is "a consuming fire":[97] a complex echo of the way in which God, or the angel of the Lord, appeared to Moses in a burning bush that was *not* consumed.[98]

In a letter to Auguste Valensin, a longstanding friend and a fellow Jesuit, steeped in Blondel's philosophy,[99] Teilhard suggests that

> through his incarnation, [God] *made himself* in some way an element of our universe—a superior element, to be sure, a super-element, but one which may be understood by analogy with our elements (or with what would constitute a "soul of the world") ... the Fire of Heaven, which consumes us, reaches us in (and after) embracing the world: consequently the fire is, in part, Fire of the Earth; and the universe, [become] Fire,[100] now counts fire among its analogical but real constituent parts.[101]

Has Teilhard been reading Heraclitus as well as the New Testament? If he has, then he has found there a fire underlying both God and the cosmos, suggesting a metaphysic of action within which God, the evolution of the cosmos, Christogenesis, and the evolution towards the Omega point, can all be understood: provided, of course, that the Omega is not a still point, but is rather the action that is Christ, drawing matter (which is action) into an Omega symphony of action. Thus the Mass on the World becomes the Eucharistic action offering the world's actions to the world's destiny, and the question as to whether evolution is convergent or divergent becomes irrelevant.

For Teilhard de Chardin, none of this is a theoretical or even an objectively empirical issue. It is intensely personal.

> If the Fire has come down into the heart of the world it is, in the last resort, to lay hold on me and to absorb me. Henceforth I cannot be content simply to contemplate it or, by my steadfast faith, to intensify its ardency more and more in the world around me. What I must do, when I have taken part with all my energies in the consecration which causes its flames to leap

---

97. Heb 12:29.

98. Exod 3:2.

99. Cuénot, *Teilhard de Chardin*, 7; Cuénot, *Teilhard de Chardin* (Eng.), 19.

100. *devenu le Feu*: The translation in Teilhard de Chardin and Blondel, *Correspondence*, 49, has "born of fire." "become fire" is probably a better translation, so here I have substituted that.

101. De Lubac, *Blondel et Teilhard de Chardin*, 45; Teilhard de Chardin and Blondel, *Correspondence*, 49.

forth, is to consent to the communion which will enable it to find in me the food it has come in the last resort to seek.

So, my God, I prostrate myself before your presence in the universe which has now become living flame: beneath the lineaments of all that I shall encounter this day, all that happens to me, all that I achieve, it is you I desire, you I await.[102] [103]

As Anthony Hanson suggests, Teilhard de Chardin is a theologian and a philosopher who sought to hold together both the Christian Faith and openness to the world around him,[104] and he invites us to do the same: in particular, "to examine the metaphysical and theological implications of new deliverances in science, whether in physics, biology, or any other branch, a work which Teilhard so brilliantly attempted."[105] This suggests that we should agree with d'Armagnac in calling Teilhard de Chardin an apologist.[106] Teilhard might have written that *Le Milieu Divin* was not apologetics,[107] but it clearly was, as was the whole of his attempt to reconcile the Christian Faith both with the findings of modern science and with contemporary philosophy. The book that you are reading now belongs in that tradition, and Teilhard de Chardin is clearly one of the giants on the shoulders of whom we all need to try to stand.

G. AN ALL-ENCOMPASSING THEOCOSMOLOGY

This chapter contains no section on "Teilhard's God." This is because, as we have discovered, the theology becomes cosmology, and the cosmology becomes theology. Separating them is impossible. "Theocosmology" might therefore be the best way to describe Teilhard's aim and achievement.

---

102. Teilhard de Chardin, *Le Coeur de la Matière*, 149–50; Teilhard de Chardin, *Hymn of the Universe*, 29.

103. Author's note: Ever since I had to conduct the funeral of three children who died in a fire, I have had a problem with the idea of fire consuming us (Torry, "Being and Doing."). Teilhard de Chardin was in the trenches of the First World War just five years before he wrote the Mass on the World. I am a little surprised that he finds the imagery of fire consuming us so easy to use. But maybe fire was such an appropriate expression for his understanding of God's relationship with the cosmos and with us, and such an appropriate way to describe the nature of the cosmos, that he had to use it.

104. Hanson, "Ecclesia Quaerens," 176–78.

105. Hanson, "Ecclesia Quaerens," 177.

106. d'Armagnac, "La Pensée de Pierre Teilhard de Chardin."

107. Teilhard de Chardin, *Le Milieu Divin*, 16; Teilhard de Chardin, *Le Milieu Divin* (Eng.), 46.

If Teilhard de Chardin had not been held back by what he understood to be the requirements of his church's doctrinal position, if he had not allowed his understanding of evolution to be controlled by his need for a sense of purpose, and if he had not been trammelled by the remaining Platonic elements in his system—and particularly the evolutionary convergence on a still point—then he might have delivered an even more fruitful metaphysic, theology, and cosmology—a theocosmology—that could have encompassed everything (or rather, every action) within a single conception. To have understood God and everything else as actions in patterns would have offered to Teilhard the possibility of an evolution constituted by ubiquitous chaotic action (understood initially as abstracted from all being, beings, things, and stabilities) in constantly changing patterns; an Omega defined as constantly changing patterns of action, drawing all reality towards itself and propelling it onwards as action in yet more changing patterns; and a God as Action, and as the source of all action, and of all of the patterns that we and the cosmos experience. As Heraclitus suggested, and as Teilhard de Chardin recognised, "fire" might be the best way to envisage such a theocosmology.

Teilhard's cosmological and theological journey was no doubt sufficient for his own purposes, and many of us have found Teilhard's theology and cosmology to be invigorating: but if he had allowed himself to admit that he was writing metaphyics, theology, and, yes, apologetics, then he might have exercised a little more purposiveness in those directions, and might have understood that a God understood as Action and as the source of all action might not have provided the stability that he craved, but might instead have carried him along on God's journey with the evolving universe, a journey infused with pain as well as hope, and thus a journey on which Teilhard de Chardin might have found his sublimated wartime experiences revisited and reconciled with God, the evolving universe, and the Christ-shaped Omega that would usher in the Kingdom of God: a far from static reality.

8

Process Philosophy and Theology

Towards a suffering God

A. PROCESS METAPHYSICS: AN ADEQUATE FRAMEWORK?[1]

While Alfred North Whitehead is rightly honoured as having given birth to process philosophy, in this chapter I shall take as my guide to process philosophy Nicholas Rescher: because, as we shall see, there are reasons for regarding him as more of a process philosopher than Whitehead was.

Rescher defines process metaphysics as a set of "concepts and principles that makes it possible to devise a synoptic and unified yet detailed and substantially adequate descriptive and explanatory account that at once integrates and illuminates our cognitive attainments in science."[2] There is a "stronger" form of process metaphysic in which "process has primacy over things. Substance is subordinate to process. Things are simply constellations of processes";[3] and a "weaker" form: "process has *priority* over substance. Things are always subordinate to processes because processes inwardly engender, determine, and characterize the things there are.

---

1. For a brief comparison between process philosophy and an "actions in patterns" metaphysic, see Torry, "Testing Torry's Model."
2. Rescher, *Process Metaphysics*, 1–2.
3. Rescher, *Process Metaphysics*, 2.

But processes as such transcend the realm of things since there are also substance-detached processes."[4]

Rescher and other process thinkers look on Heraclitus as the founder of process philosophy. Interestingly, they also regard Plato as living in a Heraclitean conceptual world:[5] and, as we have seen, there are readings of Plato that would support this view. For Aristotle, the basic question was the same as for Heraclitus and Plato, that is: How can things change and remain the same? And how can different things belong in a single category? But Aristotle's answers are "scientific" in the sense of "exploratory," and no coherent metaphysic emerges: so while his world might be a process world, his philosophy is not a process metaphysic: or, if it is, then it is of the "weaker" variety.

B. MONADS

Both Rescher and Whitehead regarded Leibniz's "Monadology" as the original inspiration for process philosophy. This is not an obvious connection, for while the monads *might* be regarded as "bundles of activity,"[6] they are also "windowless," their properties are mental states or "perceptions," and the objects of these perceptions are "ideas." Connections between monads are "ideal," and are constituted by God's intervention: and so we return to Plato's distinction between a world of change and another more real unchanging world or way of seeing. For Leibniz, beings are collections of monads, with one monad being the "entelechy," or soul, which has clear perceptions of the other monads and brings them into an organism: but, again, the physical world's order is located in God and communicated by God, and there are no intrinsic spatial relationships between the worlds, except for that given by God to our souls. Similarly, causal laws relate to the world of appearances, not to the monads.[7] (Here we are not far from Malebranche's occasionalism: that is, all perceptions are immediately given by God, thus dislocating perception and reason from any real world that might exist.)

Leibniz's monads are certainly active, but their actions do not affect other monads, for it is God who makes the adjustments in surrounding monads and, in particular, keeps the soul in harmony with the body. Thus God chooses a whole universe, and Leibniz thinks that it is "the best" of worlds, full of monads, each internally changing, and each with their own point of view.[8]

4. Rescher, *Process Metaphysics*, 2.
5. Rescher, *Process Metaphysics*, 10.
6. Rescher, *Process Metaphysics*, 12.
7. Leibniz, "Monadology."
8. Leibniz, "Monadology."

Yes, there are processes within the monads, and each monad somehow contains the whole world within itself: but relationships between monads are all God-mediated, making them essentially isolated, as Rescher realises: "Physically, monads are centers of force or activity: loci characterized by a dynamic impetus to change. Metaphysically, monads are existing items (units of reality), whose identities lie in their descriptive uniqueness."[9] He thinks that it is "better" to think of monads as "processes,"[10] meaning that the world's substances "become phenomenal, immersed in a sea of process,"[11] giving them a "physical aspect in which monads are units of process" and "a metaphysical aspect in which monads are units of concrete existence that admit of descriptive individuation."[12]

C. WHITEHEAD'S CONCEPTS

Hegel's attachment to historical development, Peirce's "pragmatism" and concentration on evolutionary processes,[13] William James's understanding of the psychic as organized process, and John Dewey's lectures on Bergson and James, all influenced Alfred North Whitehead's basic concepts: but, as we shall see, the "Monadology" was particularly influential.

"Process" is *the* basic concept, for process is ubiquitous in the world that we experience. We experience "becoming," not "being," which is only ever an abstraction from experience.[14] In a lecture delivered in 1919, Whitehead described "nature" as a "process":

> Each duration happens and passes. The process of nature can also be termed the passage of nature ... The passage of nature is exhibited equally in spatial transition as in temporal transition. It is in virtue of its passage that nature is always moving on.[15]

Bergson's influence is even clearer when Whitehead adds that "the passage of nature" "is only another name for the creative force of existence."[16] Leibniz's influence is equally clear when Whitehead writes that events are made up of "event particles," and that "the aggregation of event particles

---

9. Rescher, *Process Philosophy*, 121.
10. Rescher, *Process Philosophy*, 130.
11. Rescher, *Process Philosophy*, 131.
12. Rescher, *Process Philosophy*, 132.
13. Peirce, *Collected Papers*, volume 6, section 6:169.
14. Pittenger, *Alfred North Whitehead*, 21.
15. Whitehead, *The Concept of Nature*, 54.
16. Whitehead, *The Concept of Nature*, 73.

forms a four-dimensional manifold."[17] Just as "particles" suggests a static aspect to reality, so Whitehead's description of "objects" as ingredients of events, as "without passage,"[18] and as being situatable in different events and so in different durations,[19] suggests that events are as much constructed by basically fixed objects as they are by whatever is changing. We are here in an Aristotelian world. Whitehead is asking himself how to conceptualize the fact that things change, with equal emphasis on "thing" and "change." In this early lecture, "event" and "process" are already important concepts. They will remain important, and the ways in which they are constructed will prevent Whitehead from reaching the "change" end of the unchanging/changing spectrum.

> "Actual entities"—also termed "actual occasions"—are the final real things of which the world is made up. There is no going behind actual entities to find anything more real. They differ among themselves: God is an actual entity, and so is the most trivial puff of existence in far-off empty pace.[20]

Norman Pittenger suggests that "actual entity" is a

> somewhat unhappy term, because it suggests a "thing," whereas something like an "energy event" is what was intended. We experience events as change, and a world marked by a social quality in which everything affects and influences everything else. The past perishes in one sense, but its consequnces are not lost since each given moment in that past has its place in what follows after . . . This influence is . . . "prehension," in that every occasion grasps or feels that which makes its impact upon it.[21]

Unlike the monads, Whitehead's "actual entities" are "interdependent," and they are the root of all meaning.[22] They relate to each other through "prehensions": "any characteristic of an actual entity is reproduced in a

---

17. Whitehead, *The Concept of Nature*, 97, 100.
18. Whitehead, *The Concept of Nature*, 143.
19. Whitehead, *The Concept of Nature*, 157.
20. Whitehead, *Process and Reality*, 27–8; Whitehead, *Process and Reality: corrected edition*, 18.
21. Pittenger, *The Divine Trinity*, 103.
22. Whitehead, *Process and Reality*, 28; Whitehead, *Process and Reality: corrected edition*, 18–19.

prehension";[23] and they involve each other "by reason of their prehensions of each other."[24] There are thus

> real facts of the togetherness of actual entities which are real, individual, and particular, in the same sense in which actual entities and the prehensions are real, individual and particular.[25]

The "togetherness" creates new actual entities out of the manifold of prehensions. As Kraus puts it:

> The actual entity arising from the final synthesis of its many prehensions represents the transformation of the original incoherence of its manifold data into the coherence of its drop of unitary experience, of its one synthetic feeling.[26]

So the prehensions can get together to create new actual entities, but the fact that Whitehead feels the need of the concept of *nexus* suggests that the entities themselves remain isolated:

> Any . . . particular fact of togetherness among the actual entities is called a *nexus* . . . The ultimate facts of immediate actual experience are actual entities, prehensions, and *nexūs* [plural]. All else is, for our experience, derivative abstraction[27]

—which rather suggests that "process" itself is, for Whitehead himself, an "abstraction." No wonder Rescher thinks that Whitehead should have managed without the isolating notion of the *nexus*.[28]

Once Whitehead concentrates on the idea of process, it becomes clear that he could indeed have abandoned the *nexus* and the actual entity's isolation. The first of his twenty-seven "categories of explanation" is "that the actual world is a process, and that the process is the becoming of actual entities. Thus actual entities are creatures."[29] The word "process" might be thought to connote a set of actions already prescribed, for that is what

---

23. Whitehead, *Process and Reality*, 29; Whitehead, *Process and Reality: corrected edition*, 19.

24. Whitehead, *Process and Reality*, 29; Whitehead, *Process and Reality: corrected edition*, 20.

25. Whitehead, *Process and Reality*, 29–30; Whitehead, *Process and Reality: corrected edition*, 20.

26. Kraus, *The Metaphysics of Experience*, 48.

27. Whitehead, *Process and Reality*, 30; Whitehead, *Process and Reality: corrected edition*, 20.

28. Rescher, *Process Metaphysics*, 55.

29. Whitehead, *Process and Reality*, 33; Whitehead, *Process and Reality: corrected edition*, 22.

"process" often means: but for Whitehead, "creativity" and "novelty" are ubiquitous:" "'Creativity' is the universal of universals characterizing ultimate matter of fact . . . 'creativity' is the principle of *novelty*,"[30] with novel entities constantly being created as actual entities come "together."

> The ultimate metaphysical principle is the advance from disjunction to conjunction, creating a novel entity . . . the novel entity is at once the "together" of the "many" which it finds, and also it is one among the disjunctive "many" which it leaves; it is a novel entity, disjunctively among the many entities which it synthesizes. The many become one, and are increased by one.[31]

And so each person is a series of entities, unified by a personal identity constructed out of the prehensions between them.[32]

Alongside the concepts of "actual entity," "event," "*nexus*," and "prehension," Whitehead develops concepts to distinguish between two different kinds of process: "concrescence" and "transition." "Concrescence" is "the production of novel togetherness,"[33] and "transition" is a process operating when existents give way to new successors:[34] or, as Whitehead puts it, "from particular content to particular existent."[35] In both of these cases of process, the new actual entity formed (and, in fact, *every* actual entity) "is at once the subject experiencing and the superject of its experience":[36] that is, it is its own object.

D. EVALUATION

Reading some parts of *Process and Reality* might lead the reader to the view that Whitehead's philosophy *is* all about process: about macroscopic process in which there is constant transition from actuality to actuality, about microsopic process in which sets of conditions result in "determinative

---

30. Whitehead, *Process and Reality*, 31; Whitehead, *Process and Reality: corrected edition*, 21.

31. Whitehead, *Process and Reality*, 32; Whitehead, *Process and Reality: corrected edition*, 21.

32. Hamilton, *The Living God and the Modern World*, 88.

33. Whitehead, *Process and Reality*, 32; Whitehead, *Process and Reality: corrected edition*, 21.

34. Rescher, *Process Metaphysics*, 20.

35. Whitehead, *Process and Reality*, 320; Whitehead, *Process and Reality: corrected edition*, 210.

36. Whitehead, *Process and Reality*, 43; Whitehead, *Process and Reality: corrected edition*, 29.

actuality,"[37] about "the expansion of the universe in respect to actual things," and about "each actual entity itself [being] only describable as an organic process."[38] Indeed, Rescher insists that the "existents" are not substances, but are "items of existence" to which change and temporality are basic, and that for Whitehead everything is "novelty and innovation" within a world that is an organic and processual whole.[39] Rescher goes on to show how Wilmon Sheldon, Charles Hartshorne, and other process thinkers, agree with Whitehead in "seeing time, process, change, and historicity as among the fundamental categories for understanding the real."[40]

However, Whitehead's attachment to "concrescence," which connotes substance, and the boundaries that he gives to actual entities by using the term *nexus*, suggest things in process rather than process itself: that is, Aristotle's changing substances rather than Heraclitus's cosmic fire or Bergson's *changement*. Here there is no chaos out of which transient order emerges on the way to no fixed entity: instead there are "existents" and "entities." As Rescher suggests, process philosophy has itself been in process, but rather than "instantiating and vividly illustrating process philosophy's message that we live in a world where nothing stands still and that change is of the very essence of reality,"[41] it illustrates a progressive complexification towards a *variety* of fundamental concepts of which "process" is only one. The direction in which Whitehead might have taken his ideas, but did not, might be best represented by Lancelot Law Whyte's "unitary principle," about which he was writing between Whitehead and Rescher:

> On the unitary view there is one universal formative process; matter, energy, life and mind, are names which man has given to different aspects of that universal process. There is process; but there is no essence, no substance, and no static existence.[42]

Whyte believed that in the "process," "structure" emerged: that is, an "effective pattern of relationship," that "beneath the apparently haphazard motions of particles may lie a formative tendency, or tendency toward simplicity of form, order and regularity," and that "in the future it may be necessary . . . to

---

37. Whitehead, *Process and Reality*, 326; Whitehead, *Process and Reality: corrected edition*, 214.

38. Whitehead, *Process and Reality*, 327; Whitehead, *Process and Reality: corrected edition*, 215.

39. Rescher, *Process Metaphysics*, 20–21.

40. Rescher, *Process Metaphysics*, 24–25.

41. Rescher, *Process Metaphysics*, 25.

42. Whyte, *The Unitary Principle*, 56.

regard change as changes of form."[43] Apart from the slippage into "particles" language, this would be a useful expression of the "actions in changing patterns" actology that we are developing in this book.

For Rescher, "becoming and change—the origination, flourishing and passing of the old and the innovative emergence of ever-new existence . . . constitute the central themes of process metaphysics,"[44] whether we are studying the weaker (conceptual) or the stronger (ontological) form of process thought; and this begins to be true of Rescher's summary as he starts to distance himself from Whitehead, abandoning the *nexus*[45] and discrete events, and insisting that "verb-entities have as good a claim to reality as noun-entities."[46] For Rescher,

> "activity" is prioritized over "substance," process over product, change over persistence, novelty over continuity . . . process philosophy does not—or need not—deny the reality or validity of the second member of these pairs, but rather maintains that in the order of significance they must be subordinated to the first:[47]

or at least *Rescher's* process philosophy does. So here we have a metaphysic that employs "process" terminology to enable it to operate close to the "change" end of the change/unchanging spectrum, but not at the extreme end of it.

The next step, surely, is to recognise that product *is* process, that persistence *is* that of change, that continuity *is* that of novelty, so that "process" becomes not *a* "principal category of ontological description,"[48] but *the* principle. Certainly, God, nature, persons, and material substance, *can* be understood in terms of Whitehead's "process," but the system then ends up in complexity as different kinds of process are delineated,[49] the persistences have to be reconciled to change, and Aristotle's considerable abiding influence leads the philosophy in the direction of "things that change."

Yes, there *are* persistences, but only changing ones "on the way," and thus not really persistences at all; and there are "dispositions,"[50] but they are best understood as patterns of action, and not merely as "potential action."

43. Whyte, *Accent on Form*, 27, 67.
44. Rescher, *Process Metaphysics*, 28.
45. Rescher, *Process Metaphysics*, 55.
46. Rescher, *Process Metaphysics*, 29.
47. Rescher, *Process Metaphysics*, 31.
48. Rescher, *Process Metaphysics*, 31.
49. Rescher, *Process Metaphysics*, 41.
50. Rescher, *Process Metaphysics*, 47.

And there are patterns that change: a situation that Rescher hints at with his "systemic wholes."[51] We are indeed "what we do," and not only dispositionally so: that is, we are what we do, and not merely what we "dispositionally can do and normally would do."[52]

What Rescher clearly wants to see is a "one-tier" ontology (which he might have called an actology) rather than an ontology of "things and change"; but, wherever we look, there is more than one tier, and particularly the two tiers of action and things, of process and entity, of change and things that change. Rescher thinks that processes flow into each other rather than requiring *nexūs* [plural] through which to relate:[53] but still he can write about "concrete (physical) particulars ... which arise in a "processual setting ... but don't seem themselves to be in process."[54] We are suffering from Peirce's "synchrism": "that tendency of philosophical thought which insists upon the idea of continuity as of prime importance in philosophy."[55] Time, however, *is* constituted by "the interlocking structure of individual process," and space is "itself an actual complex or state of process,"[56] showing that Rescher and other process thinkers are perfectly capable of contemplating the ubiquity of change, even though they might step back from making it *the* fundamental philosophical principle. Similarly, for Rescher, quantum physics is about small processes[57] and not small things, and knowledge is "fluid and ever-changing."[58]

Rescher's definition of "process" is "a co-ordinated group of changes in the complexion of reality, an organized family of occurrences that are systematically linked to one another either causally or functionally."[59] So there is *already* a pattern to the action, and we might therefore do best to regard process philosophy as a *second*-order activity: as a study of patterns of action as those patterns change, rather than of the more fundamental reality, action itself. Patterns of action are both in process and isolable (conceptually if not in fact), and so might well be described as events, enabling events and processes to be discussed together, different kinds of processes to be compared, "dispositions" in relation to processes to be discussed,

---

51. Rescher, *Process Metaphysics*, 37.
52. Rescher, *Process Metaphysics*, 47.
53. Rescher, *Process Metaphysics*, 55.
54. Rescher, *Process Metaphysics*, 51.
55. Peirce, *Collected Papers*, volume 6, section 6:169.
56. Rescher, *Process Metaphysics*, 95.
57. Rescher, *Process Metaphysics*, 91.
58. Rescher, *Process Metaphysics*, 123.
59. Rescher, *Process Metaphysics*, 38.

the relationship between one process and another to be studied, continuities and elements of chaos to be compared and related, "lawful order" to be debated, and process understood to "encompass change without itself changing,"[60] thus showing that this way of seeing reality is at some distance from the "change" end of the changing/unchanging spectrum. Rescher asks for a "taxonomy of processes,"[61] and recognises that this will be complex. Indeed, it will be, for "process" is a second-order matter, and the *basic* reality is action. To see process in this way as secondary is to attempt a break with an "unchanging Forms" reading of Plato, but the greater the element of changelessness and inate and unchanging order that we can find within the process or processes, the nearer to that reading of Plato it becomes.

At the beginning of his survey of process thought Rescher suggests that

> process metaphysics as a general line of approach holds that physical existence is at bottom processual; that processes rather than things best represent the phenomena that we encounter in the natural world about us[62]

—or, as Bracken puts it, Whitehead's metaphysics is about "the overall fluidity of reality and . . . the interrelation of everything with everything else in the forward movement of the cosmic process."[63] We might wish to go further and put it like this:

> Action metaphysics as a general line of approach holds that physical existence is at bottom actions in patterns; that action and patterns rather than things that change best represent the phenomena that we encounter in the natural world about us; and that Action, actions, and actions' changing patterns, are what constitute the evolution of the universe.

E. A GOD IN PROCESS

Process theology has given birth to a "process theology," which, by envisioning God as involved in the processes of the universe, and as affected by them, has laid one of the foundations for the modern understanding of a God who suffers.

60. Rescher, *Process Metaphysics*, 38–41.
61. Rescher, *Process Metaphysics*, 42.
62. Rescher, *Process Metaphysics*, 2.
63. Bracken, *The One and the Many*, 104.

In his *Process and Reality*, Whitehead posits a "dipolar" God.[64]

> God's "primordial nature" is abstracted from his commerce with particulars . . . It is God in abstraction, alone with himself. As such it is a mere factor in God, deficient in actuality. . . But God, as well as being primordial, is also consequent . . . By reason of the relativity of all things, there is a reaction of the world on God . . . [God's] derivative nature is consequent upon the creative advance of the world.[65]

The primordial nature is "free, complete, primordial, eternal, actually deficient and unconscious," the consequent nature is "determined, incomplete, consequent, 'everlasting,' fully actual, and conscious."[66] There is a real difference between God and the world, for in God permanence is primordial and flux is derived from the world, whereas in the world flux is primordial and permanence is derived from God: but the outcome is that both God and the world share a process in which they both affect each other. As Rescher puts it: "God does not constitute part of the world's matrix of physical processes, but nevertheless in some fashion or other, *participates* in it," "persuading" and "influencing" it.[67] For Whitehead, God is an "actual entity," that is, an element of the world as well as being outside it.[68] For Norman Pittenger, "God is the dynamic, living, event-full, related, free reality who is not the only but who is the chief causative principle."[69] This is the God of the Bible: one "prehended" by the early Christians, and one by whom they were prehended, and of whom "they came to speak in threefold idiom."[70] God is a Trinity, with the persons in process, relating to each other as interpenetrating processes.[71] A consequence of God's relating to persons, and of God's internal relation to Jesus, is that God is subject to the world's temporality,

---

64. Whitehead, *Process and Reality*, 524; Whitehead, *Process and Reality: corrected edition*, 345.

65. Whitehead, *Process and Reality*, 50, 523; Whitehead, *Process and Reality: corrected edition*, 34, 345.

66. Whitehead, *Process and Reality*, 524; Whitehead, *Process and Reality: corrected edition*, 345.

67. Rescher, *Process Metaphysics*, 155.

68. Whitehead, *Process and Reality*, 28; Whitehead, *Process and Reality: corrected edition*, 18; Rescher, *Process Metaphysics*, 156.

69. Pittenger, *The Divine Trinity*, 106.

70. Pittenger, *The Divine Trinity*, 106.

71. Rescher, *Process Metaphysics*, 158.

that God is changed, and that God cannot experience foreknowledge, as his consequent nature is "consequent upon the course of events."[72]

For Whitehead, the consequent and primordial poles do not exhaust God, for God has a "superjective" nature that unites the various aspects, resulting in a God who is "the outcome of creativity, as the foundation of order, and as the goad towards novelty."[73] So God is utterly involved *and* alone with himself. This is no different from what Whitehead says about actual entities that have their own identity as well as being affected by neighbouring actual entities through their prehensions of them. But then Whitehead writes: "In the subsequent discussion, 'actual entity' will be taken to mean a conditioned actual entity of the temporal world, unless God is expressly included in the discussion."[74] The term "actual occasion" will always exclude God from its scope.[75] The problem is that the "primordial nature" must remain *outside* the world's influences, and thus separate from prehensions of other actual entities. Whitehead posited a "primordial" nature for God because he wanted to protect his theism from pantheism: that is, he wanted to ensure that God did not become entirely immanent. I agree that we should continue to be able to distinguish God from the universe, but wonder whether there might be other ways of doing that. Might it not be possible to conceive of God as activity, and maintain the difference between God and the universe by defining God in terms of God's own patterns of action and in terms of God as Action, the source of all action?

Whitehead's theological work spawned a movement that we now call "process theology," exemplified in the UK by Norman Pittenger, and in the United States by John Cobb. Pittenger confesses debts to John Boys Smith, to Whitehead, and to Charles Hartshorne, and also recognises Teilhard de Chardin's genius in relating evolutionary ideas to Christian theology. There are many theological threads that flow into process theology, and many that flow out of it.

Pittenger, like Whitehead, assumes that science reveals a dynamic rather than a static reality, and that we cannot isolate one event from another. On this basis, he expounds a theology that he believes lies closer to biblical roots than theologies based on more traditional Platonist presuppositions.

72. Rescher, *Process Metaphysics*, 160.

73. Whitehead, *Process and Reality*, 135; Whitehead, *Process and Reality: corrected edition*, 88.

74. Whitehead, *Process and Reality*, 135; Whitehead, *Process and Reality: corrected edition*, 88.

75. Whitehead, *Process and Reality*, 135; Whitehead, *Process and Reality: corrected edition*, 88.

Pittenger draws out the theological consequences of Whitehead's process philosophy in terms of a God who is "love because he is infinitely related,"[76] a God who is "omnipotent" in the sense of "Cosmic Love's supreme capacity to work in and through, as well as with, the world, indefatigably and indefeasibly," a God who is "infinite" in the sense that "God's Love knows no limit,"[77] and a God who

> will be the lure that is active in all enticement towards fulfilment . . . the recipient of the good that is achieved in the world . . . participant in the frustrations and disappointments that follow when wrong goals are chosen, limited results are obtained, and the total good is not promoted. Finally, he will use that which has been contributed by creaturely occasions: having taken those contributions into his consequent nature . . . he can and does plough them back into the world in order to bring about more good in the process of creative advance.[78]

This is a God who is revealed "in act" in Jesus Christ; and perhaps it is in the notion of the suffering God that a God who is action has impinged most profoundly on the Christian tradition.[79]

For Pittenger, "the central ethical principle and the only ethical absolute is . . . God as Love and as Lover."[80] Here we are in the territory of God's consequent pole, of a God who feels the suffering of others, of a self-emptying God. This theology requires a *kenosis*, an emptying, for it requires first of all that there will be an other to love,[81] and that there will be a *network* of relationships:[82] a network already in action within God.[83] Whether we regard God's love as a metaphysical attribute or as an ethical attribute (as Isaak Dorner did, thinking God's ethical being to be the location of any immutability, and to be prior to God's metaphysical attributes, which exist for the sake of love[84]), love is a changing pattern of action, and an obvious basis for a Christian process theology.

This theology is certainly based on the notion of process, but Pittenger's theology, like Whitehead's, still operates within a subject-object

76. Pittenger, *Process Thought and Christian Faith*, 11.
77. Pittenger, *The Lure of Divine Love*, 94.
78. Pittenger, *Cosmic Love and Human Wrong*, 38.
79. Pittenger, *Process Thought and Christian Faith*, 11.
80. Pittenger, *Loving Says It All*, 77.
81. Ellis, "Kenosis as a Unifying Theme for Life and Cosmology," 114.
82. Walker, "Romantic Love, Covenantal Love, Kenotic Love."
83. Moltmann, "God's Kenosis in the Creation and Consummation of the World."
84. Drewer, "Dorner's Critique of Divine Immutability."

context that retains a focus on the subject or object who/which is in process, rather than on the process itself. Whitehead's theology is complex because he wished to retain notions of the unchanging. If he had left those notions to one side, then he might have offered precisely the philosophy and theology that we shall need if we are to speak of God who is grace, a God from whom Whitehead was not so very far when he called God "the great companion, the fellow-sufferer who understands."[85]

There have been other attempts at a process theology. Charles Hartshorne has developed out of Whitehead's cosmology a natural theology for our times[86] in which he tries to answer the question: "Can technically precise terms be found which express the supremacy of God, among social beings, without contradicting his social character?"[87] The consequence is that God cannot be a single actual entity, as Whitehead originally suggested, but must, like us, be a series of actual entities connected by their prehensions.[88] In Whitehead's "completely social philosophy" Hartshorne has found a God relative to every historical event,[89] and he concludes that talk of God is rational, and that philosophy of religion and natural theology are thus possible. Language is always analogical when we speak of God, so "rational" here has a slightly odd meaning: but I agree that philosophy of religion is possible given an appropriate philosophical framework or variety of frameworks.

John Cobb, too, has constructed a theology out of Whitehead's ideas, though concentrating more on the relationship between God's primordial and consequent natures than on God's relationship to other entities. He believes that Whitehead's cosmology could lead to a more unified God than Whitehead himself suggests, for God is one "actual entity," so both poles of God's nature are involved in God's aims, which are eternally unchanging.[90] Pittenger relates the two poles to each other by blurring the distinction between them. He does this by redefining language: "The transcendence of God is his inexhaustibility, not his remoteness";[91] and thus "he is himself," he is "One Thing, the divine Reality himself, working in and energizing

---

85. Whitehead, *Process and Reality*, 532; Whitehead, *Process and Reality: corrected edition*, 351.
86. Hartshorne, *A Natural Theology for our Time*.
87. Hartshorne, *The Divine Relativity*, 26.
88. Hamilton, *The Living God and the Modern World*, 168–69.
89. Hartshorne, *The Divine Relativity*.
90. Whitehead, *Process and Reality*, 27–28; Whitehead, *Process and Reality: corrected edition*, 18; Cobb, *A Christian Natural Theology*, 180–81.
91. Pittenger, *Process Thought and Christian Faith*, 24.

through another thing, the world. . . ."[92] Peter Hamilton takes a different course. He wants to keep the two poles separate from each other because only a God who is separate from the world can be religiously satisfying.[93] God "'prehends' all other entities: he takes them into himself as objects, and in so doing he is affected by them";[94] and God is personal because possessing

> unity and self-identity . . . consciousness or awareness . . . freedom to choose ends, and capacity to act according to aims . . . the deepest way in which [Whitehead's] philosophy can help Christian belief may be its meaningful interpretation of *how* God loves the world.[95]

So Hamilton's God is "immanent in the world and in ourselves," but must also be "sufficiently transcendent for us to be able to pray to him and receive guidance from him."[96]

Process theologians seem to have transferred the church's longstanding difficulty over the relationship between the divine and the human in Jesus Christ into the heart of God: two poles, rather than two natures: and they are making similar attempts to relate them to each other. Somehow both immanence and transcendence need to be maintained: a task that might be made easier by understanding that the requirement is in fact for *otherness* rather than for transcendence. But this does not mean that these theologians are uninterested in Christology. The process theologians, like Pierre Teilhard de Chardin, regard the cosmos and the human race as incomplete, unfulfilled, and coming to be, and Jesus of Nazareth as a focal point in history. Whitehead describes Jesus' life as

> a revelation of the nature of God and of his agency in the world . . . there can be no doubt as to what elements have evoked a response from all that is best in human nature. The Mother, the Child, and the bare manger; the lowly man, homeless and self-forgetful, with his message of peace, love and sympathy: the suffering, the agony, the tender word as life ebbed, the final despair; and the whole with the authority of supreme victory.[97]

Pittenger thinks of Jesus as God's

---

92. Pittenger, *God in Process*, 25.
93. Hamilton, *The Living God and the Modern World*, 155.
94. Hamilton, *The Living God and the Modern World*, 88.
95. Hamilton, *The Living God and the Modern World*, 89.
96. Hamilton, *The Living God and the Modern World*, 183.
97. Whitehead, *Adventures of Ideas*, 214.

pervasive and universal Activity (called in Christian Theology the Eternal Word or the divine Logos, who is Deity in his Self-Expression) given a focus and a point . . . The conviction that Jesus Christ is indeed the definitive Action of God in this world has found its normative expression in the phrase "Incarnation."[98]

Thus the "occasion" of Jesus is "important," and is "definitive for us."[99]

Perhaps the most thorough process Christology is David Ray Griffin's *A Process Christology*, in which he tries to bring together

> the new quest for the historical Jesus, the neo-orthodox emphasis on God's self-revealing activity in history, and the theology based primarily on the process philosophy of Alfred North Whitehead and Charles Hartshorne.[100]

First of all, Jesus *reveals* God:

> The aims given to Jesus and actualized by him during his active ministry were such that the basic vision of reality contained in his message of word and deed was the supreme expression of God's eternal character and purpose,[101]

and also of his agency.[102] So "Jesus was God's supreme act of self-expression, and is therefore appropriately apprehended as God's decisive revelation."[103] Importantly, Jesus is God's *act*. "The prehension of God constituted Jesus' self,"[104] enabling the aims that God had given to him to "directly reflect the general aim of God for his creation."[105] This revelation is the beginning of a process that leads to us receiving from God some aims "that more directly express God's character and purpose."[106]

However, it is not unfair to suggest that Christology has been of less concern to process theologians than God the Creator whom Jesus called "Father." David Pailin's *God and the Processes of Reality* seeks a "coherent, significant and credible faith for people today"[107] by speaking of God as

---

98. Pittenger, *God in Process*, 20, 25.
99. Pittenger, *Christology Reconsidered*, 100.
100. Griffin, *A Process Christology*, 9.
101. Griffin, *A Process Christology*, 218.
102. Griffin, *A Process Christology*, 225.
103. Griffin, *A Process Christology*, 227.
104. Griffin, *A Process Christology*, 229.
105. Griffin, *A Process Christology*, 231.
106. Griffin, *A Process Christology*, 242.
107. Pailin, *God and the Processes of Reality*, 18.

both absolute and relative, as necessary and contingent, as changing and unchanging, as eternal and temporal, and as infinite and finite, by developing Whitehead's "dipolar God," and also Hartshorne's subsequent theological reflections, into a vision of all reality as dipolar, giving to each of God's attributes a necessary and a contingent element.[108] But we are not told how the two poles relate to each other, whether in events, in objects, or in God. If "dipolar" is to express some kind of unity, as Pailin hopes that it does, then that unity needs to be defined. (The ubiquity of action does not face the same problem; and because patterns are all action as well as patterns, they do not pose a problem either). Pailin's God is "essentially perfect" and is "the ultimate in value":[109] two rather Platonic concepts. However, there is "potentiality in the divine . . . [that] is not a mark of imperfection but a necessary implication of the personal aspects of God's reality,"[110] although "potentiality" implies "actuality" and thus some unchanging value or state that is aimed at.

While Pailin allows that there is change in God, this must not threaten God's "goodness,"[111] as if "goodness" is somehow a fixed datum to which God must conform: a position somewhat at odds with God being "the unsurpassable self-surpassing."[112] The connection is of course based on Plato's presuppositions; and when Pailin turns to the change that *we* experience, God becomes the "framework" within which it happens,[113] thus neatly distancing God from the problem of evil. On this, Pailin's position is that "there is a problem to be solved. It is the problem of understanding the nature of divine agency and its relationship to all the other forces that constitute the world. Only when that problem is solved will it be possible to determine whether there is a genuine problem of evil for theists to solve":[114] but this is not true: there is *in any case* a problem to be solved. It might be a problem with many layers, but at its heart it is the problem of evil and of suffering, and any theology must address it.

A *particularly* important issue that Pailin *does* address directly is that of historical events and of God's relationship to them:

> If . . . Lessing's "ugly, broad ditch" between history and theistic belief can be bridged, it can only be through metaphysical

---

108. Pailin, *God and the Processes of Reality*, 37, 65, 75.
109. Pailin, *God and the Processes of Reality*, 96.
110. Pailin, *God and the Processes of Reality*, 105.
111. Pailin, *God and the Processes of Reality*, 107.
112. Pailin, *God and the Processes of Reality*, 108.
113. Pailin, *God and the Processes of Reality*, 133–53.
114. Pailin, *Probing the Foundations*, 141.

insights which show how God is to be discerned as agent in specifiable ways in specifiable events for specifiable purposes.[115]

Elsewhere, Pailin recognises that there is a discussion to be held as to whether it is the events themselves that express truth about God, or whether it is the records of events that do so;[116] but he is clear that the events matter, that God relates to them, and that God is therefore in process; although strangely he still thinks that truth is the same now as it was in the apostolic age.

Pailin's theology is an attempt to work out some of the consequences of Whitehead's dipolar God, so it is not surprising that the resulting theology is thoroughly dipolar, with the relationship between the unchanging and the changing still not defined, and with the changing and the unchanging still not underpinned by a metaphysic that might either reconcile them or show them to be radically different from each other.

The "process theologians" have not in Europe given rise to a process theology school, as they have in the United States, but their insights have found many echoes in others' work: although whether any causality can be attributed is an open question requiring further research. We have already discussed Norman Pittenger's theology. John Robinson, in his *Exploration into God*,[117] speaks of the same "panentheism" as do Pittenger[118] and Jürgen Moltmann; and both Moltmann[119] and the Church of England's Doctrine Commission[120] speak of a God who suffers, Moltmann showing how, according to Isaiah 63:9[121] and other passages, God suffers with Israel; and how, according to Revelation 13:8, "the Lamb was slaughtered from the foundation of the world," there is "already a cross in the heart of God before the world was created and before Christ was crucified on Golgotha."[122]

---

115. Pailin, "The Supposedly Historical Basis of Theological Understanding," 235.

116. Pailin, *God and the Processes of Reality*, 197.

117. Robinson, *Exploration into God*.

118. Pittenger, *God in Process*, 17.

119. Moltmann, *Das Gekreuzigte Gott*, 259–63; Moltmann, *The Crucified God*, 270–74.

120. Church of England, Doctrine Commission, "We Believe in God."

121. "In his love and in his pity he redeemed them; he lifted them up and carried them all the days of old." (New Revised Standard Version)

122. Moltmann, "God's Kenosis in the Creation and Consummation of the World," 147. Moltmann wrongly references the passage as Rev 18:8, and also does not mention a perfectly legitimate alternative translation: "Everyone whose name has not been written from the foundation of the world in the book of life of the Lamb that was slaughtered" (New Revised Standard Version).

There is now a movement in ecclesial and theological circles away from a theology in which "substance" and static categories are more prominent, and towards one in which "process" and generally more dynamic concepts are central, and in which God is affected by the world. The presuppositions of the process theologians are now widely accepted, and are making possible a theological consensus that might lead to a new common metaphysic and to a new common systematic theology, albeit a provisional one. Whitehead would have been pleased.

However, the process theologians,[123] starting with Whitehead, might not have been radical enough; and to the extent that they have mixed "static" categories with "dynamic" categories, they might have made their theological systems over-complex and anachronistic. The relationship between the two poles of Whitehead's God is not sufficiently spelt out. *How* do they affect each other? If the consequent nature is affected and does not affect the primordial nature, then is there a relationship between the two poles in any meaningful sense of the word "relationship"? Teilhard de Chardin's God possesses a similar duality. "God is complete for himself, while for us he is continually being born."[124] God is in the process, but the process is not in God.

John Cobb's God is more unified than is Whitehead's. Along with Whitehead, Cobb terms God an "actual entity," but also a "living person," and believes that "this view makes the doctrine of God more coherent, and . . . no serious new difficulties are raised."[125] Cobb also identifies Christ with

> the creative transformation of theology that has broken our relationship to every established form . . . We find Christ today as the principle of affirmation of the resultant pluralism;[126]

and we find Christ immanent in the "creative transformation discoverable in nature, in history, and in personal experience,"[127] thus relating Jesus to God's consequent pole rather than to God's primordial pole. However, God still has an aim that is "eternally unchanging,"[128] and the relationship

---

123. For discussion of process theologians and their ideas, and of the relationships between their different theologies, see Dorrien, *The Making of American Liberal Theology*, 60–132, 190–268.

124. *Dieu achève pour soi, et cependant, pour nous, jamais finit de naître*: Teilhard de Chardin, *Le Coeur de la Matière*, 70; English translation from Rideau, *Teilhard de Chardin*, 149.

125. Cobb, *A Christian Natural Theology*, 192.

126. Cobb, *Christ in a Pluralistic Age*, 61.

127. Cobb, *Christ in a Pluralistic Age*, 80.

128. Cobb, *A Christian Natural Theology*, 180–81.

of such an unchangeableness to the effects on God of the changing aims of other actual entities—and particularly of the changes that Jesus Christ, the incarnate Word, undergoes—is not clear. The situation is much as we discovered it to be in relation to Hamilton's God: both the immanent changing pole, and the transcendent unchanging pole, are affirmed, but it is not clear how they relate to each other.[129] This is one approach. The other is Pittenger's: here, "transcendence" is dissolved into "inexhaustibility,"[130] but he still retains "Supreme Being" language, and regards God and the world as separate things.[131] In ways similar to the process theologians, Moltmann's "trinitarian" theology leaves us asking whether each "person" suffers, or whether, as in Heschel's "dipolar theology," "God is free in himself and at the same time interested in his covenant relationship and affected by human history,"[132] again retaining the distinction between the transcendent and the immanent. John Robinson, for all his talk of God-language as pointing "to an ultimate relatedness in the very structure of our being,"[133] still insists that "the Creator is not created, God is not evolved."[134] Similarly, Gregory Boyd, in an attempt to reconcile Charles Hartshorne's process thought with a more traditional Christian theology, suggests that

> the relationship between the Trinity and the world process is that the creative process of the self-sufficient God graciously grounds and encompasses the creative process of the world. And the ultimate result is the world's redemptive sharing in the eternal self-delight that characterizes and constitutes the creative self-becoming of the triune God.[135]

God's sociality is as primordial as God's actuality;[136] and the incarnation is the taking of the "dynamic essence" of Jesus into the dynamic essence of God, resulting in the world's redemption:

---

129. Hamilton, *The Living God and the Modern World*, 173.

130. Pittenger, *Process Thought and Christian Faith*, 24; Pittenger, *The Lure of Divine Love*, 94.

131. Pittenger, *God in Process*, 15, 20.

132. Moltmann, *Das Gekreuzigte Gott*, 261; *The Crucified God*, 272.

133. Robinson, *Exploration into God*, 72.

134. Robinson, *Exploration into God*, 100.

135. Boyd, *Trinity and Process*, 404.

136. Boyd, *Trinity and Process*, 341.

> The ceaseless achievement of the expression of God's deity in the Trinity will now eternally include the expression of the beauty of the non-divine order, and all of this through Christ.[137]

For both Robinson and Boyd, God is the source of all that is dynamic, and appears to be unaffected by human action. Here is a God closer to Aquinas's God who is "pure act,"[138] who is not changed by anything or anyone else,[139] but who "moves Himself,"[140] than to Whitehead's God with a consequent pole. In Robinson's and Boyd's theologies the primordial pole remains firmly in charge.

Pittenger contrasts what he calls "classical theism" with his version of "process theism." Table 8.1 expresses the contrasts.

Table 8.1: Norman Pittenger's comparison of classical and process theisms

Classical theism	Process theism
Aseity (self-contained existence).	Love-in-relationship as the root attribute of God.
"being" as inclusive of "becoming."	"becoming" as the more inclusive term.
Transcendence as "unconditionedness."	Transcendence as perfection in love, and hence relational; and as faithfulness to purpose or aim, and to an inexhaustible capacity to bring love to bear on all situations.
The possibility of speaking about God in abstraction from the world.	The necessity of thinking of God always in terms derived from and relative to his creative activity in the world.

Source: Table constructed by the author from Pittenger, *Alfred North Whitehead*, 37.[141]

Pittenger attaches Whitehead's name to "process theism" and not to "classical theism," whereas the left-hand column coheres well with what Whitehead says about God's primordial pole. Whitehead, and all of the writers discussed above, are balanced precariously on the fence between the changing and the

---

137. Boyd, *Trinity and Process*, 400–401.
138. Aquinas, *Summa Theologiae*, I, 9, 1.
139. *intelligere et velle et amare*: Aquinas, *Summa Theologiae*, I, 9, 1.
140. Aquinas, *Contra Gentiles*, I, 9, 1.
141. Charles Hartshorne offers a longer list of such contrasts in Hartshorne, *Man's Vision of God*, 235, usefully tabulated by William Alston in Alston, "Hartshorne and Aquinas," 79–80.

unchanging, between "classical theism" and "process theism" (as defined by Pittenger): when what might be needed, and what Pittenger clearly thinks that Whitehead should have offered, is a decisive shift from "classical theism" to "process theism": or rather, from "being theism" to "action theism." As Paul Weiss puts it: "Neither Whitehead nor Hartshorne has room for a God who is angry, who is not the only finality, or who creates."[142] A God who is compassionate and angry to his core, a God who relates, a God who is changed by those relationships, and a God who is at the same time the source, meaning and end of everything, is the only religiously and ethically satisfying God, and we need a theology that says that.

The whole point of a paradigm is to offer categories within which to understand and to relate to the worlds in which we live, and paradigm shifts are necessary because the data changes,[143] and because paradigms shift in disciplines relating to the ones in which we operate. Revolutions only finally occur when sufficient numbers of people let go of an old paradigm and commit themselves to a new one:[144] an act of faith consistent with the knowledge that no paradigm will ever offer a complete description of the world. As the revolution matures, new value might be found in the (possibly reformulated) older paradigm: but such a new value would not have been discovered had it not been for the paradigm shift. (Would we have got to quantum physics so quickly had the shift from "particles" to "waves" not taken place in so thorough a fashion?) The process theologians, by retaining throughout a balance between the old and the new paradigms, might have stifled a revolution waiting to happen, and we might now help that revolution to occur if we concentrate on the development of a new paradigm, an "action" paradigm, and then come back later to "being"-language, to find it reformed and renewed.

F. TOWARDS A SUFFERING GOD

The time might be ripe for us to abandon the "unchanging" pole for a while, and, at the same time to cease to regard God as a being who is changed and who causes change, and to begin to speak of God as the process of change, as "change," as "process," and as "activity." God must no longer be the object or the subject of change (and thus distanced from change), but must become change itself: the very possibility of change, and at the same time particular patterns of change, patterns of activity immanent within all activity, and yet

---

142. Weiss, "Nature, God and Man," 115.
143. Kuhn, *The Structure of Scientific Revolutions*.
144. Moscovici, "Toward a Theory of Conversion Behavior."

also particular in their chief characteristics: the self-giving generosity that we call "grace," the pattern of "death and resurrection," and countless others. If we take seriously Whitehead's suggestion that "God is not to be treated as an exception to all metaphysical principles involved to save their collapse. He is their chief exemplification,"[145] then to treat God as actions in patterns conforms better to this requirement than Whitehead's own dipolar God.

We can already see hints of this approach in the writers that we have been studying. Moltmann's theology *can* be interpreted as a statement that God is crucified: "God has taken upon himself death on the cross"; and we are taken up into

> the death and resurrection of God . . . The believer really participates in the suffering of God in the world, because he partakes in the suffering of the love of God . . . a trinitarian theology of the cross perceives God in the negative element and therefore the negative element in God, and in this dialectical way is panentheistic. For in the hidden mode of humiliation to the point of the cross, all being and all that annihilates has already been taken up in God and God begins to become "all in all." . . . Even Auschwitz is in God himself.[146]

Robinson admits that "unless we can represent [God] in functional rather than ontological terms, he will rapidly lose all reality. As a Being he has no future."[147] Hartshorne wonders whether we should cease to call God "absolute," for "the absolute is not more, but less than God, in the obvious sense in which the abstract is less than the concrete."[148] Teilhard de Chardin thinks of God's action on the world as "respecting all, 'forced into' many roundabout ways and obliged to tolerate many things which shock us at first . . . but ultimately integrating and transforming all."[149] Were the quotation marks around '*obligée*,' translated here as 'forced into,' a guilty afterthought?

We do not need the language of transcendence or of absoluteness for a religiously adequate God to whom we can pray and whom we can worship; or, if we do need the language of transcendence, then that of "transcendent love" would be nearer to the Christian revelation. There is no need to keep

---

145. Whitehead, *Process and Reality*, 521; Whitehead, *Process and Reality: corrected edition*, 343.

146. Moltmann, *Das Gekreuzigte Gott*, 265–6; Moltmann, *The Crucified God*, 277–8.

147. Robinson, *Exploration into God*, 41.

148. Hartshorne, *The Divine Relativity*, 26, 83.

149. *respectant tout, "obligée" à beaucoup de détours et de tolérances qui nous scandalisent à première vue—mais finalement integrant et transformant tout*: Teilhard de Chardin, *Comment Je Crois*, 45; Teilhard de Chardin, *Christianity and Evolution*, 35.

part of God's nature "unstained by the world":[150] indeed, to do so is to create a distant and ultimately invulnerable God. No, the logic of Christian experience leads us to a God totally vulnerable, to a suffering God, a God suffering to every corner of God's life; and to a God better spoken of in terms of action than in terms of substance or essence, at least for the time being.

Such a paradigm is certainly consistent with the ways in which we now view ourselves and our world. The atom is a universe of moving particles which are themselves more adequately described as wave motions. As individuals we are constantly changing, and no unchanging centre can or should be sought; and our society is in constant flux. The only constant thing about history is its constant change. The cosmos is now expanding, and might eventually collapse in upon itself, only to create a new explosion of activity. In this still new millennium, every aspect of existence can only be understood through the concepts of "action" and "change," so it is inevitable that Christian theology should come to understand itself in such terms. As we have seen in our discussion of process theology, such a new paradigm is going to have colossal implications for our understanding of God, particularly if, for the moment, we abandon Whitehead's "primordial" pole, as I believe that we must.

G. PROCESS THEOLOGY IN PROCESS

Whitehead constantly created space in his metaphysic for the unchanging, and appears not to have wanted to let go of the unchanging God of the church's more platonic heritage: but our increasing need to relate to a fast-changing world, and to a science framed in terms of action, and to relate God and suffering to each other, have forced on us a redefinition of reality as action, and of God as "consequent" as well as transcendent and creative. Whether or not we eventually return to being-language, we now need to leave to one side the "primordial" nature of God, the being-language, the permanent, the unmoved, and the static, and to turn to a definition of God in terms of the dynamic. Are we just playing with words here? No: at least, no more than a "being" narrative does. For in neither narrative is there a secure reference from language about action to action outside language, or from language about being to being outside language: rather, the patterned action that is language tells a story about actions in patterns, thus enabling content and vehicle to cohere: a relationship not possible in the context of being-language. There is no proof, and there is still no secure reference: but there is a story that can be told, and its meaning changes as language

150. Jas 1:27.

changes, and that is as it should be, for we are speaking of a God who is action and a God who is actions in patterns.

I hope that Whitehead would have approved of an attempt to revise his ideas. He believed theological revision to be an essential process:

> Those societies which cannot combine reverence for the symbols with freedom of revision must ultimately decay either from anarchy or from the slow atrophy of a life stifled by useless shadows.[151]

We should expect a theology that is about action never to stand still: for if it did then it would become a state of affairs, and thus without meaning in a language-game focused on action.

But if, as I have suggested, we should regard the "being" and "action" narratives as different stories about reality able to live alongside one another, we experience a dilemma: to operate two paradigms at once offers a balanced position, one that coheres more closely with the way things seem to be than would a single paradigm: but it also gives us a balance bought at the cost of communicability, a balance that can stifle intellectual adventure, a balance that can deny us new religious and other experience, and that can close off avenues that might lead to fruitful revolutions. Those theologies that have had a major impact upon us have often been those that have employed a particular paradigm (whether a new one or an old one) and then left to one side or explicitly rejected other paradigms that might have expressed elements of our experience not represented by the chosen paradigm. Process theology, by defining God as dipolar, has taken the safer route. I choose a different approach: to speak of God wholly in terms of action, while recognising that being-language remains legitimate and often appropriate.

Which is the best basis for apologetics: Whitehead's complex process categories and a dipolar God, or an understanding of reality in terms of action, Action, change, and movement: that is, a wholly dynamic approach? It must be a matter of opinion as to which coheres most closely with the modern world: but as to which retains most contact with the Christian tradition we might be able to make a more objective assessment, at least in one respect. At the heart of the Christian Faith is a God who is both different from this changing world and deeply involved with it: both transcendent and immanent. In order to express this, Whitehead has to divide his God into primordial and consequent poles, so that the primordial pole is not immanent, and the consequent pole is not transcendent. A theology based

---

151. Whitehead, *Symbolism*, 88.

on an Action metaphysic will understand God as Action, that is, as the source of all action, and as the totality of all action, as well as being actions in changing patterns that relate to a universe that is actions in changing patterns. Transcendence here is the transcendence of Action, and not that of Being. Understanding God within a Being metaphysic, and therefore as Being, the source of all being, makes it difficult to understand God as both transcendent and involved in the action, movement, change and diversity of a suffering world. Understanding God within an Action metaphysic, and therefore as Action, the source of all action, encounters no such difficulty, because the changing patterns of actions that constitute God's constant Action can relate to any and every changing pattern of action. The transcendence and the immanence now complement one another, rather than forming a paradox. In this respect at least, a theology based on an Action metaphysic will be more in touch with the Christian tradition than will be Whitehead's process theology, although not necessarily more in touch than Robinson's or Boyd's theologies.

9

Geoffrey Studdert Kennedy's suffering God

A. INTRODUCTION

Teilhard de Chardin appears not to have allowed his experience in the First World War trenches to affect his theology. Geoffrey Studdert Kennedy—a priest in the Church of England, who had served in a poor parish in Worcester and then volunteered as an army chaplain—certainly did.

Studdert Kennedy trained as a priest at Ripon Hall, a Church of England theological college of which Henry Major was Principal. Major was a passibilist, understanding God as suffering and changing, and Studdert Kennedy was clear that Major's lectures in the philosophy of religion had influenced both his life and his theology:[1] an influence at its clearest in the way in which Studdert Kennedy understood God as both active in the world, and as suffering with it. The nature of God is philosophical as well as theological subject-matter, and in this respect it is right to regard Studdert Kennedy as a philosopher as well as a theologian. The philosophy might not have been stated in traditional philosophical terms—it is mixed up with

---

1. Brierley, "Introducing the Early English Passibilists," 228; Mozley, "Studdert Kennedy," 53; Parker, *A Seeker after Truths*, 25.

narrative about Studdert Kennedy's experiences in the trenches, and is often expressed as narrative or poetry—but it is philosophy nevertheless. It is also theology, whatever Studdert Kennedy might have said about it:

> This is not a theological essay... This is a fairly faithful and accurate account of the inner ruminations of an inwardly religious man under battle conditions.[2]

There might be a "lack of balance," but it is still both theology and philosophy,[3] and, as we shall see, Studdert Kennedy is able to justify his doctrinal views. Here lies the reason for different relationships between theology and the experience of the trenches that we find in Teilhard de Chardin and Studdert Kennedy. Teilhard de Chardin's theology took place in a conceptual field that in the end did not challenge the traditional Roman Catholic theological structure within which he had been trained as a priest, and that remained ubiquitous in the church. Studdert Kennedy had been influenced during a formative period of his life by some very different theological currents, based on a very different conceptual structure in relation to the nature of God. This enabled him to integrate the experience of suffering with his theology in ways that might have been impossible for Teilhard de Chardin.

B. BEFORE THE TRENCHES

When he first arrived in France, Studdert Kennedy was stationed behind the lines, and so met soldiers as they were going to the front, as they were returning from it, and in hospital. There, in response to an injured officer's question—"Now can you tell me? What is God like?"—Studdert Kennedy pointed to a crucifix and said, "Yes, I think I can tell you; God is like that. He that hath seen Him hath seen the Father."[4] And he writes:

> The God I worship, the God who leads the army of innocent sorrow... the God upon the cross. If I did not believe that God was suffering now, I could not pray to Him; He would be to me a devil, not a God... on that Cross my God still hangs and calls on all true men to come out and share his sorrow and help to save our world.[5]

---

2. Studdert Kennedy, *The Hardest Part*, 189–90.
3. Studdert Kennedy, *The Hardest Part*, 190.
4. Studdert Kennedy, *Rough Talks by a Padre* (London: Hodder and Stoughton, 1918), 129; G.A. Studdert Kennedy, *The Hardest Part* (London: Hodder and Stoughton, 1919), xi–xiv.
5. Studdert Kennedy, *Rough Talks by a Padre*, 129–30.

Studdert Kennedy is inviting soldiers to understand their suffering in much the same way as Paul understood his: "I am now rejoicing in my sufferings for your sake, and in my flesh I am completing what is lacking in Christ's afflictions for the sake of his body, that is, the church."[6] Studdert Kennedy was not asking of others what he did not ask of himself. In Worcester, his preaching was not only immediate and engaging:[7] it was tinged with suffering. As someone who heard him preach put it, "he was the saddest preacher I heard. There was an undercurrent of pain, sorrow and gloom running through his preaching and his personality."[8] Such suffering—his own, and that of the soldiers whose pastor he was—was redemptive, whether analogously to Jesus' suffering, or—as Paul rather suggests—as alongside it in the history of salvation.[9]

Studdert Kennedy suggested that the "necessary truth" of a "suffering God" first dawned on him in the streets of Worcester's slums[10]—or perhaps as he was listening to Henry Major's lectures: but it is also true that the theology took on a more radical form among the carnage of trench warfare.

C. IN THE TRENCHES

Studdert Kennedy soon found himself in the trenches. He never shied away from being where the greatest suffering was happening, to the detriment of his own already poor health.[11] He suffered a gas attack, which made his health even worse;[12] and he earned a Military Cross for his bravery tending wounded soldiers under fire.[13] As he makes clear in *The Hardest Part*, written during the war,[14] it was this extreme situation, of seeing the worst of human suffering, that gave birth both to a rejection of much traditional theology, and to a theology that might be of some use in the trenches.

> Almighty and Everlasting God, High and Mighty, King of kings and Lord of lords . . . to Whom all things in heaven and earth and under earth do bow and obey, do I know anything at all about Him?[15]

---

6. Col 1:24.
7. Jeffs, *Princes of the Modern Pulpit*, 133–35.
8. Jeffs, *Princes of the Modern Pulpit*, 160.
9. Parker, *A Seeker after Truths*, 50–51.
10. Studdert Kennedy, *The Hardest Part*, 193.
11. Parker, *A Seeker after Truths*, 54–57, 76–77, 85–92.
12. Purcell, *Woodbine Willie*, 121.
13. Carey, "War Padre," 142.
14. Parker, *A Seeker after Truths*, 57.
15. Studdert Kennedy, *The Hardest Part*, 7.

Such statements functioned as "accusations against God":[16]

> It is Christ upon the Cross that comforts; never God upon a throne. One needs a Father, and Father must suffer in his children's suffering. I could not worship the passionless potentate.[17]

D. AFTER THE WAR

Experience of the war turned Studdert Kennedy into a pacifist. Moore Ede, Dean of Worcester at the time, said that Studdert Kennedy

> went to the war as to a holy crusade which by victory would vindicate righteousness, but he returned hating the wickedness and folly of war. He became an apostle for peace and a tireless fighter in the economic war.[18]

At the end of the war, Studdert Kennedy could find little cause for celebration:

> Waste of Muscle, waste of Brain,
> Waste of Patience, waste of Pain, . . .
> Waste of Blood, and waste of Tears, . . .
> Waste of Glory, waste of God,—
> War![19]

In one of his long dialect poems, "The Pensioner,"[20] written in the first person to reflect the language of the trenches, he envisages an old soldier looking back:

> I'm a man who's seen and suffered,
> Not a child to spoil and please;
> I 'ave known the shame of nations,
> And the sorrow of the seas.
> I 'ave seen my best pal lying,
> In a crumpled, bloody 'eap,
> With 'is 'ead all blown to pieces,
> And I've 'eard 'is mother weep.
> I remember—I remember,
> I'm not going to forget,

16. Studdert Kennedy, *The Hardest Part*, 8.
17. Studdert Kennedy, *The Hardest Part*, 10, 12.
18. Quoted in Grundy, *A Fiery Glow in the Darkness*, 59.
19. Studdert Kennedy, "Waste," *The Unutterable Beauty*, 31–32.
20. Studdert Kennedy, *Peace Rhymes of a Padre*, 66–69; Studdert Kennedy, *The Unutterable Beauty*, 173–75.

> Till we've done the job we started,
> Till the flag of peace is set
> On the ramparts of the nations,
> Till it floats abroad unfurled,
> Over every child and mother,
> To the boundaries of the world.[21]

His preaching became even more an expression of a sense of sin and of the pain that sin brings with it.[22] As Ernest Jeffs put it,

> No easy comforting gospel would do. Studdert Kennedy found a reality in the idea of a suffering God; of suffering being somehow a part of God, so that all fruitful suffering—indeed, even suffering which seems at the time to be fruitless and meaningless . . . can be accepted as a part of worship and faith.[23]

Again echoing Paul's theology, the cross was central to the message.[24] In Jeffs' view, there was not enough of Jesus' resurrection in Studdert Kennedy's theology, and perhaps not sufficient connection with parts of the historic creeds:[25] but perhaps this was a small price to pay for the only kind of theology that could respond adequately to the experience of trench warfare and to a suffering world. In a poem "Good Friday falls on Lady Day," there is no joy for Mary at Jesus' birth:

> She claims no crown from Christ apart,
> Who gave God life and limb.
> She only claims a broken heart
> Because of Him.[26]

And there was not much joy for anyone else, either.

E. THE STRUGGLE FOR A NEW SOCIAL ORDER

In his parish, Studdert Kennedy had found deep poverty, and had spent his energies and his money in trying to tackle it.

---

21. Studdert Kennedy, *Peace Rhymes of a Padre*, 66.
22. Jeffs, *Princes of the Modern Pulpit*, 161.
23. Jeffs, *Princes of the Modern Pulpit*, 162.
24. Jeffs, *Princes of the Modern Pulpit*, 162.
25. Jeffs, *Princes of the Modern Pulpit*, 164, 167.
26. Studdert Kennedy, *Songs of Faith and Doubt*, 44; Studdert Kennedy, *The Unutterable Beauty*, 98.

> We must rescue individuals [from poverty] and devote ourselves to the reform of those conditions which force him into this position . . . A dream of a new social order is as much an essential part of the Christian life as prayer, and communion with God[27]

—which meant that the Eucharist must not be divorced from "the dream of a Christian social order."[28]

As an army chaplain, Studdert Kennedy found himself calling on soldiers to look beyond the war and to determine to fight the evils of slavery, jealousy, avarice, and indifference, that had killed Jesus: a fight in which they would suffer.[29] The evils were to be fought, but that did not imply hatred of the individuals who found themselves perpetrating them. God's love extended to German soldiers just as much as to British ones, so British soldiers should extend their love to them, too. What needed to be fought was

> . . . the god the German leaders worship, an idol of the earth . . . a crude and cruel monster who lives on human blood. He is the enemy that God has fought for ages, and at whose hand He has suffered His centuries of pain. . . .[30]

After the war, as an Industrial Christian Fellowship Messenger, Studdert Kennedy continued to campaign for an end to poverty. Bob Holman calls him "the greatest social evangelist of his time."[31] Suffering in this cause was inevitable, because for Studdert Kennedy Christian discipleship was an imitation of Christ that meant an imitation of every significant event of his life:

> The great Acts of His earthly life were but the expression in time of His eternal nature. He always brought to those who saw Him, a New Birth, an agony of Crucifixion, a Resurrection, and an Ascension, and through that fourfold act of the inmost soul, a conviction of touch with ultimate reality, a new vision of the meaning of the world and of God's creation.[32]

One of Studdert Kennedy's most deeply felt poems, which contrasts the violence of Calvary with the indifference that he found around him on his return from the war, is titled simply "Indifference."

> When Jesus came to Golgotha they hanged Him on a tree . . .

---

27. Studdert Kennedy, *The Word and the Work*, 7, 65.
28. Studdert Kennedy, *The Word and the Work*, 65.
29. Studdert Kennedy, *Rough Talks by a Padre*, 134–40.
30. Studdert Kennedy, *Rough Talks by a Padre*, 195.
31. Holman, *Woodbine Willie*, 177.
32. Studdert Kennedy, *The Word and the Work*, 50.

> When Jesus came to Birmingham they simply passed him by...
> Still Jesus cried, "Forgive them, for they know not what they do,"
> And still it rained the winter rain that drenched him through and through.
> The crowds went home and left the streets without a soul to see,
> And Jesus crouched against a wall and cried for Calvary.[33]

It is action that is required: and the essential action is suffering. Indifference—inaction—might prove to be a worse evil than suffering and the violence that causes it.

F. A THEOLOGY OF SUFFERING

At the heart of Studdert Kennedy's theology is the doctrine of the incarnation.

> ... O Christ my God, my only God, so near, so suffering, and so strong.[34]

Here we find a common theological tendency in Studdert Kennedy's writings: God and Jesus or Christ are used interchangeably. Studdert Kennedy's experience had made a distant and passionless God useless—and, as we shall see, immoral—which made it imperative that God had both to suffer and to be unable to change the circumstances of the war. This removed any blockage in the way of understanding the divinity of Jesus as Jesus *being* God, and, for instance, Jesus' cross being "God's cross."[35]

> The true God is naked, bloody, wounded, and crowned with thorns, tortured, but triumphant in His love... with bloody brow and pierced hands, majestic in His nakedness, superb in his simplicity, the King Whose crown is a crown of thorns. He is God.[36]

> They beheld His glory, glory as of the only begotten of the Father. In His suffering manhood they saw God, and learned to love and worship.[37]

---

33. Studdert Kennedy, *Peace Rhymes of a Padre*, 37–38; Studdert Kennedy, *The Unutterable Beauty*, 34–35.
34. Studdert Kennedy, *The Hardest Part*, 10, 12.
35. Studdert Kennedy, *The Hardest Part*, 28.
36. Studdert Kennedy, *The Hardest Part*, 71, 95.
37. Studdert Kennedy, *The Hardest Part*, 131–32.

In the poem "The Comrade God," in which neither "Jesus" nor "Christ" appear, but only "God," we find Studdert Kennedy saying that

> Only in Him can I find home to hide me,
> Who on the cross was slain to rise again;
> Only with Him, my Comrade God, beside me,
> Can I go forth to war with sin and pain.[38]

All around him, Studdert Kennedy saw dead, dying, and injured human bodies:

> Here, broken bodies and pools of blood are the most ordinary things in life . . . is it wrong to see in them His Body and His Blood . . . God's Body, God's Blood? . . . God suffers in man's suffering, and man, if he be man, suffers with God, and the world is saved by the suffering of God in many.[39]

There are two roots to Studdert Kennedy's theology of the suffering God: the pastoral experience that only such a God is of any use, and the theological impossibility of an omnipotent and passionless God.

> God is helpless to prevent war, or else He wills it and approves of it. There is the alternative. . . I hate war, and if God wills it I hate God . . . if God does not suffer agony because of war . . . then I cannot and will not worship Him.[40]

But the God whom we see "suffering, striving, crucified, but conquering" is one whom he can worship: "I want to win the world to the worship of the patient, suffering God revealed in Jesus Christ."[41]

None of this means that there will not be a final victory over death and suffering: there will be—and progress towards it

> is the work of God, but it bears no trace of being the work of an Almighty God. It has been a broken, slow and painful progress marked by many failures, a Via Dolorosa wet with blood and tears.[42]

This is a theology of hope *and* a theology of a suffering God: and for the two to be compatible the suffering has to be the means for achieving the final victory:

38. Studdert Kennedy, *The Unutterable Beauty*, 31.
39. Studdert Kennedy, *The Hardest Part*, 134.
40. Studdert Kennedy, *The Hardest Part*, 34, 36–37.
41. Studdert Kennedy, *The Hardest Part*, 42, 41.
42. Studdert Kennedy, *The Hardest Part*, 42.

> God is Suffering Love, and . . . all real progress is caused by the working of Suffering Love in the world.[43]

No element of Christian doctrine escapes Studdert Kennedy's attention, and every element, and all of the elements together, find their location in a Christian theology focused on Jesus' suffering which is God's suffering. Take for instance the doctrine of creation:

> One sees Nature in Christ, and Christ in Nature . . . I have no fear of Nature's horror chambers; they are just God's Cross, and I know that the Cross is followed by an Empty Tomb and victory. God is limited now, and has been ever since creation began, by the necessities inherent in His task: but those necessities are not eternal, they are only temporary and contingent, and God will overcome them in the end.[44]

But the created order is not simply the location where God's suffering and final victory are played out: creation is one of the two causes for God's suffering:

> Part of God's sorrow is absolutely necessary, and part is only necessary because we will it to be so. It is absolutely necessary that God should create and suffer in creation. We make it necessary that He should also redeem and suffer in redemption.[45]

So the cross is neither the beginning nor the end of God's suffering. It is

> the act in time which reveals to us the eternal activity of suffering and redeeming love all down the ages.[46]

The Bible, too, is understood through the lens of a suffering God who achieves a final victory through the suffering:

> One cannot find God Almighty in the Bible any more than we find Him in nature or history. We see in the Bible, as we see everywhere else, the patient, persistent suffering spirit of love and beauty at war with awful and incomprehensible necessities, and slowly conquering them.[47]

In the books of the prophets—and particularly in Hosea, Isaiah and Job—Studdert Kennedy finds glimpses of God's suffering: but these books fail to

---

43. Studdert Kennedy, *The Hardest Part*, 44.
44. Studdert Kennedy, *The Hardest Part*, 28.
45. Studdert Kennedy, *The Hardest Part*, 61.
46. Studdert Kennedy, *The Hardest Part*, 62.
47. Studdert Kennedy, *The Hardest Part*, 59.

grasp the "bitter sorrow in God's heart."[48] It is Jesus who "carries innocent suffering into the heart of God,"[49] so that now the suffering God "is crucified afresh every day."[50]

Studdert Kennedy's theology was not an existing theology that then related to suffering in an attempt to integrate it into an existing theological scheme. God's suffering was the ground of the theology, and all else was integrated with that. The effect on the doctrine of the incarnation was stark. Not only was Jesus the Word of God come in human flesh: God was human.

> O God ineffable, immense in love,
> How canst Thou be
> The God Thou art?
> And how can we,
> Inhuman, plumb the depths
> Of Thy humanity?[51]

As always, a radical sense of radical sin.

In one of his dialect poems, "The Sorrow of God,"[52] Studdert Kennedy asks about God's reaction to the death of a young soldier:

> I'd rather be dead, wi' a 'ole through my 'ead,
> I would, by a dam long sight,
> Than be livin' wi' you on your 'eavenly throne,
> Lookin' down on yon bloody 'eap.
> That were once a boy full o' life and joy,
> And 'earin' 'is mother weep,
> The sorrow o' God mun be 'ard to bear
> If 'E really 'as love in 'is 'eart.
> And the 'ardest part i' the world to play
> Mun surely be God's part. . . .[53]

This is where the title of the book *The Hardest Part* comes from.[54] As the poem goes on, it envisages Jesus walking in the trench:

> And I guess it would finish 'Im up for good
> When 'E came to this old sap end,

---

48. Studdert Kennedy, *The Hardest Part*, 66.
49. Studdert Kennedy, *The Hardest Part*, 34.
50. Studdert Kennedy, *The Hardest Part*, 153.
51. Studdert Kennedy, *Songs of Faith and Doubt*, 25.
52. Studdert Kennedy, *Rough Rhymes of a Padre*, 17–24. Also in Studdert Kennedy, *The Sorrows of God and Other Poems*, 125–32.
53. Studdert Kennedy, *Rough Rhymes of a Padre*, 19–20.
54. Parker, *A Seeker after Truths*, 58.

> And 'E seed that bundle o' nothin' there,
> For 'E wept at the grave o' 'Is friend.
> And they say 'E were just the image o' God.
> I wonder if God sheds tears,
> I wonder if God can be sorrowin' still
> And 'as been all these years...
> ... What if 'E came to the earth to show
> By the paths 'o pain that 'E trod,
> The blistering flame of eternal shame
> That burns in the heart of God.[55]

The soldier asks why God does not stop the suffering, and speaks of his own wilful son:

> ... maybe that's 'ow it is wi' God,
> 'Is sons 'ave got to be free;
> Their wills are their own, and their lives their own,
> And that's 'ow it 'as to be.
> So the Father God goes sorrowing still...
> ... 'E knows the feel ov a bullet, too...[56]

This is a theology that works, in the sense that the soldier finds a renewed faith. He turns to the dead young soldier:

> I thought as ye'd taught me that God were dead,
> But ye've brought 'Im to life again.
> And ye've taught me more of what God is
> Than I ever thought to know.
> For I never thought 'E could come so close
> Or that I could love 'Im so....[57]

The clearest expression of Studdert Kennedy's faith in a suffering God is to be found in the poem with that title: "The Suffering God":[58]

> How can it be that God can reign in glory,
> Calmly content with what His Love has done,
> Reading unmoved the piteous shameful story,
> All the vile deeds men do beneath the sun?
> Are there no tears in the heart of the Eternal?

---

55. Studdert Kennedy, *Rough Rhymes of a Padre*, 21.
56. Studdert Kennedy, *Rough Rhymes of a Padre*, 23.
57. Studdert Kennedy, *Rough Rhymes of a Padre*, 24.
58. Studdert Kennedy, *The Unutterable Beauty*, 11–14. Also in Studdert Kennedy, *Rough Rhymes of a Padre*, 58–63, and in Studdert Kennedy, *The Sorrows of God and Other Poems*, 2–5.

Is there no pain to pierce the soul of God?
Then must He be a fiend of Hell infernal,
Beating the earth to pieces with His rod . . .
. . . Father, if He, the Christ, were Thy Revealer,
Truly the First Begotten of the Lord,
Then must Thou be a Suff'rer and a Healer,
Pierced to the heart by the sorrow of the sword.
Then must it mean, not only that Thy sorrow
Smote Thee that once upon the lonely tree,
But that to-day, to-night, and on the morrow,
Still it will come, O Gallant God, to Thee.
Swift to its birth in spite of human scorning
Hastens the day, the storm-clouds roll apart;
Rings o'er the earth the message of the morning,
Still on the Cross the Saviour bares His heart. . . .[59]

G. A THEOLOGY OF ACTION

It was no surprise that the Eucharist was at the heart of Studdert Kennedy's preaching and his practice, because the Eucharist is a set of actions that offers a sacramental relationship with the God who suffers.

> Coming to the sacrament is coming to the Cross, and coming to the Cross is coming to God, the only God, Whose body is for ever broken and Whose blood is ever shed, until the task of creative redemption shall at last be all complete.[60]

> When his body was taken away from them they knew Him in the breaking of bread. The sacrament was just Jesus Christ to them, and Jesus Christ was God.[61]

This is an extreme identification of Jesus with God, of the Eucharist with Jesus, and therefore of the Eucharist with God. The actions of the Eucharist are the very actions of God and so *are* God.

> How through this Sacrament of simple things
> The great God burns His way,
> I know not—He is there.
> The silent air

---

59. Studdert Kennedy, *The Unutterable Beauty*, 12–13.
60. Studdert Kennedy, *The Hardest Part*, 129.
61. Studdert Kennedy, *The Hardest Part*, 131–32.

> Is pulsing with the presence of His grace....[62]

Prayer for Studdert Kennedy was always a seeking to know God's will: a seeking to which God responds.[63] It was

> the means of communication by which the suffering and triumphant God meets His band of volunteers and pours His Spirit into them, and sends them out to fight, to suffer, and to conquer in the end.[64]

At the heart of Studdert Kennedy's theology is the suffering of God: and it is always an active God who is suffering. God "leads the army of innocent sorrow";[65] God comes; and God sheds tears.[66] The way in which Studdert Kennedy moves between "Jesus" and "God" in his poems—the clearest example is "The Sorrow of God"[67]—means that the action that constitutes Jesus is the action that constitutes God: so in the crucifixion we must

> ... See the wounded God go walking down the world's eternal way. For his task is never done...[68]

As Robert Slocum sums up Studdert Kennedy's theology:

> The true God is the suffering God, the crucified God who shares our struggles and engages the limitations of our lives and all creation.[69]

To express such a theology within an ontology within which God is changeless, static, unitary, Being, and the source of all being, would be impossible. To express it within an actology within which God changes, is dynamic, is diverse, is Action, and is the source of all action, is possible, and therefore essential.

---

62. Studdert Kennedy, *Peace Rhymes of a Padre*, 47; Studdert Kennedy, *The Unutterable Beauty*, 58.
63. Slocum, "Geoffrey Studdert Kennedy," 234–36.
64. Studdert Kennedy, *The Hardest Part*, 115.
65. Studdert Kennedy, *Rough Talks by a Padre*, 129.
66. Studdert Kennedy, *Rough Rhymes of a Padre*, 21.
67. Studdert Kennedy, *Rough Rhymes of a Padre*, 17–24. Also in Studdert Kennedy, *The Sorrows of God and Other Poems*, 125–32.
68. Studdert Kennedy, *Peace Rhymes of a Padre*, 93.
69. Slocum, "Geoffrey Studdert Kennedy," 241.

10

Ludwig Wittgenstein and John Boys Smith

Changing language in the midst of changing action

A. INTRODUCTION

In this chapter we shall study two twentieth century thinkers who both took a journey from the unchanging and the unitary to change and diversity in relation to language. In the sense that they were writing about language, rather than about the nature of reality more generally, there might be questions to be asked as to whether consideration of these two thinkers belongs in this book. However, for Wittgenstein, language belongs within "forms of life," suggesting that language is as much actions in patterns as is anything else—or rather, as are any other actions in patterns. For Boys Smith, the meaning of "evolution" constantly changes, as do the meanings of language: and as language is our only access to meaning, to understand that "evolution" evolves is to understand that evolution evolves, and that change changes, and that the patterns that we experience in actions constantly change. From these two philosophers we learn that language belongs with the rest of reality, that all of that reality is actions in patterns, and that the patterns are themselves actions in changing patterns.

B. WITTGENSTEIN: LANGUAGE AS DIVERSE AND CHANGING HUMAN ACTION

a. The start of the journey

Wittgenstein's early "Tractatus Logico-Philosophicus" was an attempt to discuss systematically the relationships between the world and our thought and language. In the *Tractatus*,

> The world is everything that is the case . . .
> What is the case, the fact, is the existence of atomic facts[1]

—a concept that is employed throughout as a kind of bedrock, and one of the concepts that Wittgenstein later abandoned.

> We make to ourselves pictures of facts . . .
> The picture is a model of reality . . .
> The picture is a fact . . .
> . . . the picture is linked with reality; it reaches up to it.[2]

Because the pictures are themselves facts, they are in the world, and they relate to what they picture: but the picture cannot itself represent its form of representation—it can only "show" it, thus leaving a gap in the system that was to widen later on:

> 4.121 Propositions can represent the whole reality, but they cannot represent what they must have in common with reality in order to be able to represent it—the logical form . . . The propositions *show* the logical form of reality. They exhibit it.[3]

As we read the *Tractatus* we gain the impression of an unchanging world within which an unchanging language represents the way that the world is: but there are also passages that hint at the way in which Wittgenstein's thought will evolve:

> 4.03 A proposition must communicate a new sense with old words.[4]

And significantly:

---

1. Wittgenstein, *Tractatus Logico-Philosophicus*, §§ 1, 2: 30–31. References give Wittgenstein's paragraph numbers followed by the page numbers after the colon.
2. Wittgenstein, *Tractatus Logico-Philosophicus*, §§ 2.1, 2.12, 2.141, 2.1511: 38–39.
3. Wittgenstein, *Tractatus Logico-Philosophicus*, § 4.121: 78–79.
4. Wittgenstein, *Tractatus Logico-Philosophicus*, § 4.03: 68–69.

> 4.112 ... Philosophy is not a theory but an activity. A philosophical work consists essentially of elucidations ... Philosophy should make clear and delimit sharply the thoughts which otherwise are, as it were, opaque and blurred.[5]

In the *Tractatus*, we find already the recognition that systematisation has its limits:

> 6.3 ... outside logic all is accident.[6]

Wittgenstein's later work, brought together in the *Philosophical Investigations*, discovers just as much complexity as the *Tractatus*. An initial reading might suggest that Wittgenstein changed his mind between the *Tractatus* and the *Investigations*, but a closer reading finds hints in the *Tractatus* of later positions, and also attempts at systematisation in the *Investigations*.[7]

b. The journey continues

At the beginning of the *Investigations*, we find Wittgenstein recognising Frank Ramsey's criticisms of the *Tractatus* as an important contribution to the development of his thought, and straight away we find him discussing the complexity and the interconnectedness of language. In "five red applies" there is no question of discovering the meaning of each word: it is how the words are used together that matters.

> Now think of the following use of language: I send someone shopping. I give him a slip marked "five red apples." He takes the slip to the shopkeeper, who opens the drawer marked "apples"; then he looks up the word "red" in a table and finds a colour sample opposite it; then he says the series of cardinal numbers—I assume that he knows them by heart—up to the word "five," and for each number-word he takes an apple of the same colour as the sample out of the drawer.—It is in this and similar ways that one operates with words.—"But how does he know where and how he is to look up the word 'red' and what he is to do with the word 'five'?"—Well, I assume that he *acts* as I have described. Explanations come to an end somewhere.—But what is the meaning of the word "five"?—No such thing was in question here, only how the word "five" is used.[8]

---

5. Wittgenstein, *Tractatus Logico-Philosophicus*, § 4.112: 76–77.

6. Wittgenstein, *Tractatus Logico-Philosophicus*, § 6.3: 172–73.

7. See Grayling, *Wittgenstein*, vi. Wittgenstein's thought was systematic, although not systematically expressed.

8. Wittgenstein, *Philosophische Untersuchungen/Philosophical Investigations*, § 1: 2.

When we use language, we play "language games." Like other games, language use is inextricably integrated with the rest of life: "The term 'language-*game*' is meant to bring into prominence the fact that the *speaking* of language is part of an activity, or of a life-form."[9] "Life-form" or "form of life" is a crucial idea for Wittgenstein, for it is within forms of life that language is located. Grayling puts it like this: A form of life is "the underlying consensus of linguistic and nonlinguistic behaviour, assumptions, practices, traditions and natural propensities which humans, as social beings, share with one another and which is therefore presupposed in the language they use."[10] I'm not sure that that's quite right. As I read Wittgenstein, I find particularity and change everywhere. "Consensus" suggests some settled configuration, some regularity: and "traditions" certainly suggests that. Surely *any* configuration of actions, any changing pattern of action, can constitute a "form of life." Some forms of life might be fairly stable, at least for a while, and it is certainly true that in order to be able to construct "forms of life" we need to be able to identify different forms of life as belonging together in a category:[11] but change is ubiquitous, so the only question is how fast language and other forms of life are changing, not whether they are. Some forms of life will be fleeting.

One aspect of forms of life that Grayling has got right is the idea that they are "shared." While it is perfectly possible to regard the patterns of activity that constitute an individual human being as a "form of life," the forms of life in which Wittgenstein seems to be most interested are social ones, for it is usually these that possess linguistic elements.

Like other activities, and other games, there are many different language games:

> ... Giving orders, and obeying them—
> Describing the appearance of an object, or giving its measurements—
> Constructing an object from a description (a drawing)—
> Reporting an event—
> Speculating about an event—
> Forming or testing a hypothesis—...[12]

We find Wittgenstein using "language game" terminology to refer both to particular language games in particular contexts, and to a "whole": "I shall

---

Wittgenstein divided the first part of the *Philosophical Investigations* into paragraphs (so both paragraph and page numbers are given), but not the second part (so when the second part is quoted, only page numbers are given.)

9. Wittgenstein, *Philosophische Untersuchungen/Philosophical Investigations*, § 23: 10.
10. Grayling, *Wittgenstein*, 97.
11. Grayling, *Wittgenstein*, 121.
12. Wittgenstein, *Philosophische Untersuchungen/Philosophical Investigations*, § 23: 10.

also call the whole, consisting of language and the actions into which it is woven, the 'language game'."[13] Wittgenstein terms this "whole"—by which he probably means a local language along with all of the actions with which it is bound up—a "system";[14] a "scaffolding";[15] a "frame of reference";[16] a "whole picture."[17] The "whole" is "*unbegründet*," "not founded"[18]—"[philosophy] cannot give it any foundation"[19]—but it "proves its worth"[20] as a vital element in our lives. It is a vast network of interrelated diverse and changing language games with shifting meanings in changing contexts, and within it we explore the meanings of words by referring to a changing diversity of other words.[21] So there are different language games, but no particular language game is closed by a frontier. "For how is the concept of a game bounded? What still counts as a game and what no longer does? Can you give the boundary? No."[22] "Our knowledge forms an enormous system. And only within this system has a particular bit the value we give it"[23]—a value described and appropriated in terms of language and other forms of life.

Always it is language *use* that is the criterion for its meaning:[24] that is, how language is used in a particular context of actions and words—which means that the same word can have different connections with different words and different actions in different contexts, and therefore different meanings in different contexts.

But while language games are not reducible to one another, they are not totally dissimilar from each other, and there will often be what Wittgenstein calls "family resemblances" between them.[25] Similarly, in different contexts the same word will have different meanings—as Patrick Sherry

13. Wittgenstein, *Philosophische Untersuchungen/Philosophical Investigations*, § 7: 5.

14. Wittgenstein, *Über Gewissheit/On Certainty*, § 144. References give Wittgenstein's paragraph numbers.

15. Wittgenstein, *Über Gewissheit/On Certainty*, § 211.

16. Wittgenstein, *Über Gewissheit/On Certainty*, § 83.

17. Wittgenstein, *Über Gewissheit/On Certainty*, § 209.

18. Wittgenstein, *Über Gewissheit/On Certainty*, § 253. See Bambrough, *Reason, Truth and God*, 94. "*Unbegründet*" might be better translated "ungrounded."

19. [Die Philosophie] kann ihn auch nicht begründen: Wittgenstein, *Philosophische Untersuchungen/Philosophical Investigations*, § 124: 42.

20. Wittgenstein, *Über Gewissheit/On Certainty*, § 474.

21. Bambrough, *Reason, Truth and God*, 94.

22. Wittgenstein, *Philosophische Untersuchungen/Philosophical Investigations*, § 68: 28.

23. Wittgenstein, *Über Gewissheit/On Certainty*, § 410.

24. Grayling, *Wittgenstein*, 90.

25. *Familienähnlichkeiten*: Wittgenstein, *Philosophische Untersuchungen/Philosophical Investigations*, § 67: 27.

puts it: "grammatical substantives do not necessarily denote a single thing or essence"[26]—but the different meanings will not be entirely dissimilar, and the word will have "*eine Familie von Bedeutungen,*" "a family of meanings."[27] In order to explore what he means by this, Wittgenstein takes the example of games: board games, card games, and so on. They are all games, and one game will exhibit similarities with other games: but there is nothing identifiable that will be common to all of them. Instead, "we see a complicated network of similarities overlapping and criss-crossing; sometimes overall similarities, sometimes similarities of detail."[28] Because a word's or a sentence's meaning is its use in a variety of interconnected language games, philosophy cannot interfere with that. "A philosophical problem has the form: 'I don't know my way about.' Philosophy may in no way interfere with the actual use of language; it can in the end only describe it. . . . It leaves everything as it is."[29] Knowing what a word means means knowing how to use it. "*This is how these words are used.*" "Now I know how to go on":[30] and throughout the *Philosophical Investigations* we learn "how to go on" and "how . . . words are used" by experiencing examples of the use of words in a wide variety of circumstances. In the end, we exhaust justifications and can only say "This is simply what I do."[31]

> Our mistake is to look for an explanation where we ought to look at what happens as a "proto-phenomenon." That is, where we ought to have said: *this language-game is played.*[32]

Language is what we *do*: and in essence (or rather "in action") it is no different from anything else that we do. "Every sign *by itself* seems dead. *What* gives it life?—In use it is *alive.* Is life breathed into it there?—or is the *use* its life? . . . What has to be accepted, the given, is—so one could say—*forms of life.*"[33]

26. Sherry, *Religion, Truth and Language,* 4.

27. Wittgenstein, *Philosophische Untersuchungen/Philosophical Investigations,* § 77: 31.

28. Wittgenstein, *Philosophische Untersuchungen/Philosophical Investigations,* § 66: 27.

29. Wittgenstein, *Philosophische Untersuchungen/Philosophical Investigations,* §§ 122–23: 42.

30. Wittgenstein, *Philosophische Untersuchungen/Philosophical Investigations,* § 180: 62; § 179: 62. Italics in the original.

31. *So handle ich eben*: Wittgenstein, *Philosophische Untersuchungen/Philosophical Investigations,* § 217: 72.

32. Wittgenstein, *Philosophische Untersuchungen/Philosophical Investigations,* § 654: 141. Italics in the original.

33. Wittgenstein, *Philosophische Untersuchungen/Philosophical Investigations,* § 432: 108; 192.

This is where the journey that started in the *Tractatus* has led Wittgenstein. Some elements of the earlier parts of the journey have fallen away (such as the attempt to relate propositions to facts), but some have now become fully developed as a definition of meaning as use. There is thus a good deal of consistency between the two books. Wittgenstein never wholly changed his mind: he simply looked more closely at how language is actually used, and recognised that it belongs as much in amongst the shifting activity of life as does every other human activity.

c. Wittgenstein's God

What kind of a word *is* "God"? Wittgenstein has suggested that "the meaning of a word is its use in the language,"[34] so how the word "God" is used determines its meaning: or, rather, *is* its meaning. Language is always used in the context of particular "forms of life,"[35] and it is that use that gives it its meaning, so it is through the word "God"'s use in diverse secular and religious contexts that the word "God" has meaning for us. Because there are connections between different language games, religious language can be evaluated in terms of other types of discourse, and can itself be a source of evaluation. We are participants in a process, rather than observers reasoning out meanings: we are engaged in a public activity that is the basis of all meaning—and this is as true of theological language as it is of any other kind.[36] Gordon Graham suggests that we must take care not to press the meanings of either "form of life" or "language game" beyond what Wittgenstein intended: that is, we must understand a "language game" to be something that is done within a particular lived context, and a "form of life" as a particular configuration of activity within a particular human context.[37] Employing "form of life" to describe a religion, and "language game" to describe the language used within a particular religion or religions, might therefore be to stretch Wittgenstein's terminology beyond his intentions: but having said that, Wittgenstein did suggest that it was legitimate to speak of "the whole, consisting of language and the actions into which it is woven";[38]

---

34. *Die Bedeutung eines Wortes ist sein Gebrauch in der Sprache*: Wittgenstein, *Philosophische Untersuchungen/Philosophical Investigations*, § 43: 18.

35. *Lebensformen*: Wittgenstein, *Philosophische Untersuchungen/Philosophical Investigations*, 192.

36. Kerr, *Theology after Wittgenstein*, 28–30 and 145–47.

37. Graham, *Wittgenstein and Natural Religion*, 40, 44–5.

38. Wittgenstein, *Philosophische Untersuchungen/Philosophical Investigations*, § 7: 5.

of "the "language game" in the singular;[39] of a "scaffolding";[40] of a "frame of reference";[41] and of a "whole picture."[42] It would therefore not be entirely illegitimate to employ such terms as "language game" and "form of life" with meanings beyond the highly particular. In this section we shall treat religious language as an extended language game, encompassing multiple language games, with each one embedded in a form of life, and the multiple forms of life together constituting the patterned activity that we call religion or a particular religion.

In both religious and secular contexts, the word "God" is used in a variety of ways in a variety of contexts, and so has a variety of meanings. There is no identifiable and definable element that is consistent throughout the diverse actual or conceivable uses of the word "God," but there will be family resemblances between the uses: or, more accurately, a family of family resemblances, as each religious tradition can be regarded as containing a family of uses (although of course similarities can be discovered between members of different families). All of this is also true of such words as "truth" and "beauty," where again there will be a diversity of meanings relating to diverse uses of the words in a variety of different contexts: so it would be legitimate to suggest an analogy between the meaning of "knowledge of God" and "knowledge of truth," and their equal legitimacy. To know how to use the word "truth" in a variety of contexts can of course never exhaust the possible meanings of the word "truth." Similarly, to know how to use the word "God" in a variety of contexts can never exhaust the meaning of the word "God."

For Wittgenstein, there is no philosophical route to the construction of a conceptual structure within which meaning can be discovered. Philosophy is constituted by diverse methods: not by "*a philosophical method, though there are indeed methods, like different therapies.*"[43] The task is to explicate, not to construct: and so Wittgenstein enjoyed reading William James's *The Varieties of Religious Experience*[44] because there he found an exploration of language use in the context of particular experiences: that

39. Wittgenstein, *Philosophische Untersuchungen/Philosophical Investigations*, § 7: 4.
40. Wittgenstein, *Über Gewissheit/On Certainty*, § 211.
41. Wittgenstein, *Über Gewissheit/On Certainty*, § 83.
42. Wittgenstein, *Über Gewissheit/On Certainty*, § 209.
43. *eine Methode der Philosophie, wohl aber gibt es Methoden, gleichsam verschiedene Therapien*: Wittgenstein, *Philosophische Untersuchungen/Philosophical Investigations*, § 133: 44.
44. James, *The Varieties of Religious Experience*; and see Graham, *Wittgenstein and Natural Religion*, 115–25.

is, of forms of life. Similarly, there is no autonomous self. Fergus Kerr summarizes Wittgenstein's position like this:

> The locus of meanings is not the epistemological solitude of the individual consciousness but the practical exchanges that constitute the public world which we inhabit together . . . The "essence" of human language is the round of collaborative activity that generates the human way of life.[45]

So the locus of the meaning of "God" is "the round of collaborative activity that generates the human way of life": human life both secular and religious, and perhaps particularly the activities that we call sacramental:[46] "Certain things have to be done";[47] that is, actions in patterns. A significant example of religious life and language giving birth to definitions of "God" is, of course, the Trinity. Christian experience and related language games relate Jesus, the Holy Spirit, and the Creator, or Father, to God, giving to "God" a threefold meaning, with each meaning bearing a family resemblance to the others. The interesting thing about such an understanding is that there is no reason to stop at three: and, in general, no longer must various definitions of "God" be fitted into each other: rather, the diverse definitions must be located, related, and validated, on their own merits, and in relation to a variety of language uses and forms of life.[48] Not only that: because there is "the whole, consisting of language and the actions into which it is woven";[49] a "scaffolding";[50] a "frame of reference";[51] a "whole picture"[52] that "proves its worth,"[53] religious language, and specifically language about God, is never in principle isolated from language about anything else. God-language can therefore relate to any form of life and to any particular language game, and any language game and any form of life can relate to God-language.[54] Everything is action, and every action is related to multiple human activities, language uses, and meanings (which are simply yet more language):

45. Kerr, *Theology after Wittgenstein*, 58.
46. Graham, *Wittgenstein and Natural Religion*, 161–76.
47. Pattison, *A Short Course in Christian Doctrine*, 109.
48. Sherry, *Religion, Truth and Language Games*, 68–184.
49. Wittgenstein, *Philosophische Untersuchungen/Philosophical Investigations*, § 7: 5.
50. Wittgenstein, *Über Gewissheit/On Certainty*, § 211.
51. Wittgenstein, *Über Gewissheit/On Certainty*, § 83.
52. Wittgenstein, *Über Gewissheit/On Certainty*, § 209.
53. Wittgenstein, *Über Gewissheit/On Certainty*, §§ 493, 473–74.
54. See Mitchell, *The Justification of Religious Belief*, 34–35, 95, on the possibility that this offers a single rationality characterised by "consistency, coherence, simplicity, elegance, explanatory power, fertility."

and all of it is connected to the action that constitutes the world around us. Theology is a language game that is played; "actions in patterns" language is a language game; and these language games can connect with each other, and with any other language game that is played.

d. The ubiquity of change

As Grayling points out: Wittgenstein's discussion of forms of life, and of language's relationship with them, inexorably leads to the conclusion that there is nothing unchanging or secure about the building blocks of Wittgenstein's philosophy. If the meaning of language is its use, and different uses exhibit family relationships, and never identity, then the meanings of "use," "form of life," and every other word or phrase that Wittgenstein employs to attempt to make his meaning clear, will shift as their contexts change. As David Bloor puts it, a "stream of life pulses through the language game."[55]

Forms of life are constituted by action in changing patterns, words are actions in changing patterns (although the written word is actions in patterns in a way somewhat different from the spoken word), and the uses and therefore meanings of words are constituted by action in changing patterns. There is no fixed point from which we can evaluate all of this. All we can do is join in.

Similarly, the meaning of "God" shifts as its context changes, and the multiple ways in which it relates to other words and to forms of life changes constantly. "God," whether written or spoken, is therefore action in changing patterns, and its relationships with forms of life change constantly in changing patterns. So "God" is in principle as meaningful as anything else, with its meaning constituted in much the same way as anything else; and the forms of life within which it has meaning will bear family resemblances with other forms of life, and all of it will belong to the whole system of action in changing patterns.

To recognise that there need be no absolute grounds for any particular discourse is to set theology free to develop as an autonomous discipline whilst at the same time being related to other dsciplines, in the same way as sociology or history develop their own methodologies and also relate themselves to other disciplines. To argue about the existence of God is a legitimate enterprise (and we do in fact so argue occasionally), and the fact that we argue about the subject suggests that theology has a part to play in the universal public language-game, and that theology has implications for other fields in the same way that those fields have implifications for

---

55. Bloor, *Wittgenstein*, 47.

theology. No longer do we need to be constantly looking over our shoulder at arbitrary means of verification, for to understand the constantly evolving and diverse nature of language is to place theology and the natural sciences alongside each other as discplines seeking internal and external consistency, coherence, elegance, explanatory power, and fertility, and is to know that there are no absolute grounds for theology, and that there is every reason for pursuing a coherent, contemporary, consistent, culture-related, and elegant discourse about God.

C. JOHN BOYS SMITH: AN EVOLUTIONARY THEOLOGIAN[56]

a. The evolution of a theologian

John Boys Smith was eleven years younger than Wittgenstein, and in many ways very different: but there are some significant similarities in their contributions to philosophy and theology.

Boys Smith studied economics and theology at St. John's College, Cambridge, and then theology at Marburg and Munich. By the age of twenty-six he was Chaplain and Director of Studies in Theology at St. John's College, and was elected a Fellow the following year. Thirteen years later he was Ely Professor of Divinity, a position from which he resigned after three years in order to become Senior Bursar of St. John's College. He was subsequently Master of the college and Vice Chancellor of the University of Cambridge. He wrote little: an unpublished fellowship thesis; sermons preached in the college chapel and elsewhere; parts of the introduction to *Religious Thought in the Eighteenth Century*, coedited with J.M. Creed;[57] *Memories of St. John's College: Cambridge, 1919 to 1969*;[58] articles on theological and other subjects;[59] and a booklet, published in 1930: *Christian Doctrine and the Idea of Evolution*, written for the D Society, a society dedicated to the study of the

---

56. For a thorough discussion of John Boys Smith's life and thought see Torry, "Introduction." Torry, "A Neglected Theologian," is an amended and shortened version of the introduction. A longer version of the introduction can be found in the Library of St. John's College, Cambridge, as the introduction to a fully annotated version of John Boys Smith's sermons.

57. Creed and Boys Smith, *Religious Thought in the Eighteenth Century*.

58. Boys Smith, *Memories of St. John's College*.

59. For a list of John Boys Smith's publications see Boys Smith, *The Sermons of John Boys Smith*, 36–49. This list includes an article on the behavior of a hedgehog: Boys Smith, "Behaviour of Hedgehog."

philosophy of religion and located in the Faculty of Divinity.[60] Boys Smith clearly recognised this booklet to be significant—it is the only item that he lodged in the University Library—and it is.

> The new can never be merely added to the old, because the old is always transfigured by the new. To see more is always to see all differently; for experience is always one world, within which each element is conditioned by its context in the whole.[61]

The consequence for Christian doctrine, as for anything else, is that "when taken into a new world . . . [it] must suffer either reinterpretation or atrophy."[62] Even if the words remain the same, "they too have changed, because a new context has given them a new significance . . . The choice is between the old world as a whole and the new as a whole; and it is impossible to transfer an element from the one into the other unchanged."[63] It is not that a continuing and essentially unchanged object has experienced a certain amount of change: "change of form is always change of substance, more or less."[64]

So is there any continuity at all? There is, but not in the sense of something of the old remaining.

> The continuity of a process consists, not in the persistence within it of a certain fixed and unchanging element (a conception which is self-contradictory), but in the maintenance of some general character, in the exemplification of some general principle, or in the subordination of the successive stages of the process to a wider unity of which they are phases.[65]

There are no "survivors," and "the extent of the change may be indefinitely great":[66] which raises the question as to how we are to evaluate change, because every standpoint that we might occupy will be changing as well. Here Boys Smith employs the concept of "the whole":

---

60. Boys Smith, *Christian Doctrine and the Idea of Evolution*; reprinted in Boys Smith, *The Sermons of John Boys Smith*, 304-18. *Christian Doctrine and the Idea of Evolution* was a D Society booklet. For information on the current D Society, see www.divinity.cam.ac.uk/research/confseminars/seminars/d-society.
61. Boys Smith, *Christian Doctrine and the Idea of Evolution*, 3.
62. Boys Smith, *Christian Doctrine and the Idea of Evolution*, 3.
63. Boys Smith, *Christian Doctrine and the Idea of Evolution*, 3-4.
64. Boys Smith, *Christian Doctrine and the Idea of Evolution*, 4.
65. Boys Smith, *Christian Doctrine and the Idea of Evolution*, 5.
66. Boys Smith, *Christian Doctrine and the Idea of Evolution*, 5.

> the standard is always that immanent in the process itself; each element in experience must be tested by the whole of experience. There is no other standard; but that standard is real, and is really possessed.[67]

As Boys Smith points out, we now assume the centrality of the idea of evolution: and an important part of the evidence for it is that we recognise that the idea of evolution has itself evolved, and continues to evolve.[68] We now expect human experience, history, society, philosophy, and everything else, to exhibit "continuous and coherent, but at the same time real, change."[69] In biology, "evolution" first meant the gradual emergence of what was already there: but now it means the emergence of genuine innovation[70]—and the meaning of the word "evolution" has experienced the same change.[71]

Christian doctrine cannot escape this process: "No less inevitably than the plant, the animal, and man himself, Christian theology, like all systems of thought, has a choice before it: the choice between adaptation and destruction."[72] The process is one of "assimilation and new synthesis":[73] a process that Christianity has always undergone, but now it is a process of which we are more conscious, and that we can see to be ubiquitous. Because everything is subject to evolution, and is now recognised to be subject to it, "evolution" binds all experience into a "whole," and in Boys Smith's view this makes such self-enclosed theology as Karl Barth's impossible.[74]

> The attempt, now noticeable in several quarters, to accept a mere disconnection between religious belief and emotion on the one side, and scientific thought and practical life on the other, is foredoomed to certain failure, and, where it is acquiesced in, it is a sign both of the decadence of religion and of the bankruptcy of thought.[75]

The idea of evolution constitutes no minor change in the way in which we view reality. It represents a radical paradigm shift.

---

67. Boys Smith, *Christian Doctrine and the Idea of Evolution*, 6.
68. Boys Smith, *Christian Doctrine and the Idea of Evolution*, 6.
69. Boys Smith, *Christian Doctrine and the Idea of Evolution*, 7.
70. Boys Smith, *Christian Doctrine and the Idea of Evolution*, 9.
71. Boys Smith, *Christian Doctrine and the Idea of Evolution*, 10.
72. Boys Smith, *Christian Doctrine and the Idea of Evolution*, 14.
73. Boys Smith, *Christian Doctrine and the Idea of Evolution*, 15.
74. Boys Smith, *Christian Doctrine and the Idea of Evolution*, 15.
75. Boys Smith, *Christian Doctrine and the Idea of Evolution*, 15.

> Each element is inter-related, directly or indirectly, with every other within the whole system to which all alike belong. . . . The idea of Evolution, therefore, is significant, not merely as standing for the great extension of knowledge, but as representing a change in its form: it tends to make the world of our experience not merely *new*, but also *one*.[76]

The ideas contained in *Christian Doctrine and the Idea of Evolution* were not new. In an article written in 1928 Boys Smith recognised that everything changes: thought-systems, doctrine, and the valuation of events;[77] and he noted that if the temporal order of events is a fundamental characteristic of reality then evolution is a characteristic of the universe as a whole: but he also recognised the connectedness of everything, and so appealed to a "whole" that is not itself subject to change.[78] Without some kind of continuity there is no meaning: "Events in the past can themselves only be established upon the ground of their coherence with what is already accepted, the evidence consisting in the degree of coherent connexion between the accepted world, upon which the inference rests, and the fact inferred."[79]

Boys Smith took as an example the Christian doctrine of the incarnation. This is based not only upon Jesus, the historical figure, but also "upon him in his place within our world, i.e., upon our world with him included."[80] Just as our value is related to our function in the whole, so is Jesus' value: "It is as embodying the whole in the temporary, to an extent perhaps without parallel, that we must understand the greatness of Jesus."[81] The incarnation is thus intelligible today if it does not imply Jesus' isolation from the rest of history, which implies that doctrinal formulae from the past are no longer adequate to the doctrine's expression today. "Our knowledge of truth . . . changes its form. And for just this reason . . . doctrinal forms cannot be immutable or axiomatic, but must move, like all things which

---

76. Boys Smith, *Christian Doctrine and the Idea of Evolution*, 17.

77. Boys Smith, "The Significance of the Historical Element in the Christian Idea of Incarnation."

78. Boys Smith, "The Significance of the Historical Element in the Christian Idea of Incarnation," 379. This reflects the Idealism of Bradley in which an "Absolute" remains unchanged (Bradley, "Ethical Studies").

79. Boys Smith, "The Significance of the Historical Element in the Christian Idea of Incarnation," 384.

80. Boys Smith, "The Significance of the Historical Element in the Christian Idea of Incarnation," 385.

81. Boys Smith, "The Significance of the Historical Element in the Christian Idea of Incarnation," 388.

would remain alive and whole."[82] As Boys Smith suggested in a book review written around the time of the publication of *Christian Doctrine and the Idea of Evolution*, it is not simply our relationship to a few particular historical events that is at stake, but rather that a massive cultural shift has occurred:

> The difficulty is not that Christianity has ascribed great significance to the historical as a whole and to certain events in particular, but that it has interpreted their significance in terms of a scheme of the world, once unquestioned and able to accommodate all knowledge, but now quite certainly one to which we shall never return.[83]

So everything evolves, including whole worldviews and complete conceptual systems; and, in *Christian Doctrine and the Idea of Evolution*, we find the insight that the meaning of the idea of evolution itself evolves. But Boys Smith did not claim too much for this insight. An evolving evolution does not itself constitute a philosophy, but rather is in need of one: for in order to understand it we need a conceptual framework within which to understand "becoming" and "development," and within which we can embrace both diversity and "the whole."[84] As Boys Smith put it in a sermon preached around the same time that he wrote *Christian Doctrine and the Idea of Evolution*: "We have at the moment no scheme of thought which is generally accepted, no framework within which, with any great degree of confidence, our experience can find unity and significance."[85] There was and is some truth in this: but surely it is also true that an understanding that all reality evolves, and that evolution itself evolves, is already a metaphysic: a conceptual framework within which reality can be understood. Perhaps Boys Smith was not as far from attaining his goal as he might have thought.

---

82. Boys Smith, "The Significance of the Historical Element in the Christian Idea of Incarnation," 390.

83. Boys Smith, Review of *The Faith of a Moralist*, 434.

84. Boys Smith, Review of *The Lord of Life*, 208–209, written in 1930, and therefore around the same time as *Christian Doctrine and the Idea of Evolution*. Boys Smith suggests that the authors' proposed Christology's defect is that it is "without a sufficiently coherent and profound philosophy in terms of which the desired interpretation can be effected" (p. 209).

85. J.S. Boys Smith, The University Sermon, 2nd February 1930, preached at Great St. Mary's, Cambridge, published in the *Cambridge Review*, 7th February 1930, 241, and reprinted in Boys Smith, *The Sermons of John Boys Smith*, 59–66.

b. Influences on John Boys Smith's ideas

In Marburg, Boys Smith read Hegel,[86] and, along with biological evolution, and an understanding that history is evolutionary, it is Hegel's understanding of the evolution of all reality, driven by and towards an Absolute, that informed Boys Smith's ideas.[87] *Christian Doctrine and the Idea of Evolution* specifically acknowledges Hegel's "connectedness of everything" as an influence on Boys Smith's understanding of evolution:[88] an evolution characterized by continuity as well as by innovation. Boys Smith recognised that evolution could sometimes result in greater diversity as well as in deeper unity, and that this was particularly true of the evolution of ideas:[89] but he still assumed that there is a unity driving the process of evolution, a unity to which it is drawn, in a very Hegelian sense.

Before Boys Smith wrote his fellowship thesis in 1927, he read Alfred North Whitehead's *Religion in the Making*.[90] And then, in 1929, at the age of 68, Whitehead published his magnum opus, *Process and Reality*. Boys Smith was a lifelong enthusiast for Whitehead's philosophy,[91] and it is highly likely that he would have read the new book before he wrote *Christian Doctrine and the Idea of Evolution*.[92] Whether or not he had read this new book from Whitehead, and whether or not he had read Bergson, or indeed Blondel, Boys Smith's mind would have been influenced by an academic milieu heavily influenced around the late 1920s by a feeling that action and change, and evolution in particular, were important; that they might be the key to understanding the world and ourselves; and that philosophers—and theologians—ought to engage with them.

---

86. Boys Smith's library, now in the custody of St. John's College, Cambridge, contains several volumes of Hegel's writings in German.

87. In a sermon, "Evolution and Christian Belief," dated 22nd October 1967, Boys Smith lists the roots of the modern concept of "evolution" as firstly Hegel, secondly Darwin, and thirdly the historical point of view (Boys Smith, *The Sermons of John Boys Smith*, 264–68).

88. Boys Smith, *Christian Doctrine and the Idea of Evolution*, 17.

89. A sermon preached on the 11th March 1956 (Boys Smith, *The Sermons of John Boys Smith*, 190–93).

90. Boys Smith, "Religious Faith," 177; Whitehead, *Religion in the Making*.

91. Conversation with John Boys Smith in 1990.

92. Whitehead, *Process and Reality*, 317; Whitehead, *Process and Reality: corrected edition*, 208.

c. Boys Smith's theology

In *Christian Doctrine and the Idea of Evolution*, Boys Smith suggests that "the traditional system of Christian Doctrine is in many respects in conflict with [the] implications of Evolution."[93] The system is full of contrasts—for instance, between natural and supernatural—making "unity and continuity" difficult to achieve.[94] Boys Smith suggests how Christian doctrine might now be understood within an evolutionary scheme:

> It is this world process which is found redemptive: redemption is not redemption from that process by means of isolated interventions, but is redemption through it and within it.[95]

Jesus belongs in the world,

> but only because the world itself is such that it has contained him and all that he means . . . He is unique, not because he stands outside the process of the world, or enters it from beyond, but because of the fulness with which he reveals its nature and meaning."[96]

Just like everything else, Jesus "finality" evolves:

> It is because Jesus has been the focus of this experience [of the Absolute], so far as Christianity is concerned, that he has stood at the centre of Christian theology. He will no doubt continue long to stand at its centre; though the sense in which he does so—the meaning of his centrality—has already become different, and will change further.[97]

In a paper written twenty-four years after *Christian Doctrine and the Idea of Evolution*, Boys Smith is still struggling with the same question: "whether, in any scheme of thought which seems to us in its essentials convincing, the uniqueness of the historical person, Jesus, will be preserved in a sense to make his status at all comparable with that which Christian thought, throughout its past, has assigned to him."[98] Boys Smith pursues the idea to its logical conclusion: "The events round which Christian thought has turned, like its theories of them, may prove to be a temporary and local

---

93. Boys Smith, *Christian Doctrine and the Idea of Evolution*, 19.
94. Boys Smith, *Christian Doctrine and the Idea of Evolution*, 19.
95. Boys Smith, *Christian Doctrine and the Idea of Evolution*, 20–21.
96. Boys Smith, *Christian Doctrine and the Idea of Evolution*, 22–23.
97. Boys Smith, *Christian Doctrine and the Idea of Evolution*, 26.
98. Boys Smith, "The Historical Element in Christianity."

vehicle of what, in the course of ages, may find another and a different expression."[99] Boys Smith's theology contains numerous echoes of Rudolf Bultmann's "demythologizing" programme, which he would have learnt when he studied with Bultmann in Marburg:[100] but the more significant influence would appear to be the "evolution" that is at the heart of Boys Smith's booklet.

We have already recognised that any evaluation of evolving realities can only be made from within evolving reality. The same is true of any attempt to evaluate evolving Christian doctrine. The criterion used

> cannot be known fully in advance but is apprehended only progressively. . . . the denial of the finality of Christianity as it now is or has been in the past is . . . not equivalent to the rejection of Christianity, but is compatible with a belief in its vitality, i.e., its capacity for assimilation and for growth.[101]

As we have discovered, in *Process and Reality* Whitehead proposed a God with both "primordial" and "consequent" natures, the "consequent" nature implying "a reaction of the world on God . . . God's conceptual nature is unchanged, by reason of its final completeness. But his derivative nature is consequent upon the creative advance of the world."[102] Norman Pittenger, whom we have already recognised as a significant process theologian, acknowledged debts to Whitehead, to Teilhard de Chardin—and to John Boys Smith.[103] I can only conclude that Boys Smith continued to discuss the possibilities of process theology in philosophical and theological circles in Cambridge, but that unfortunately those discussions have left no written record.[104]

In Boys Smith's extant writings we find numerous pointers to the character of the kind of systematic theology that he might have created: but we do not find such a systematic theology. Maybe he thought that the fact that evolution and everything else evolves would make such an attempt impossible.

---

99. Boys Smith, *Christian Doctrine and the Idea of Evolution*, 27.

100. For a number of Bultmann's papers, see Bultmann, *Kerygma and Myth*.

101. Boys Smith, *Christian Doctrine and the Idea of Evolution*, 28.

102. Whitehead, *Process and Reality*, 523–4; Whitehead, *Process and Reality: corrected edition*, 345.

103. Pittenger, *Process Thought and Christian Faith*, 11.

104. In my one conversation with John Boys Smith, he asked me whether people still discussed process theology. I assured him that some of us do.

d. The Moral Sciences Club

Whether the Cambridge University Moral Sciences Club dates from 1874 or 1878 is a matter for debate,[105] but what we do know is that for much of its history the Club has debated ideas at the forefront of philosophy. Unfortunately, the membership list for 1927 has not survived,[106] and minute-takers never recorded who attended the meetings, so we cannot know whether Boys Smith attended a meeting on the 25th November 1927. If he had, then he would have heard a Miss Klugman read a paper on "facts and events," a paper that noted that *everything* changes, and that an event is not something that happens to something, but is itself the primary fact. The brief minutes do not tell us whether Henri Bergson's *La Perception du Changement*,[107] or Whitehead's "process" ideas, was the source of this insight: but the minutes do record Klugman's debt to Bertrand Russell's view that events are the only existants, and that facts, being non-temporal, are mere abstractions from the concrete situation. In 1912, Russell had written that "physical science, more or less unconsciously, has drifted into the view that all natural phenomena ought to be reduced to motions";[108] and in 1914, in *Our Knowledge of the External World*, he had agreed with Bergson's view that "in the case of change which appears continuous, such as motions, it seems to be impossible to find anything other than change so long as we deal with finite periods of time, however short."[109] Russell was a member of the Moral Sciences Club, and even if Boys Smith did not hear Miss Klugman's paper, and had not read Russell's books, it is likely that by 1930 he was aware of Russell's view that all there is is change.

Wittgenstein's *Tractatus* appeared in 1921. In 1929, he returned to Cambridge,[110] and from then until the 1940s he took an active part in

---

105. For information on the Moral Sciences Club, see www.phil.cam.ac.uk/seminars-phil/seminars-msc-history.

106. Membership lists for the early 1920s do not include Boys Smith's name, although we know that he attended a meeting in 1923 because he made notes on a paper given by F.R. Tennant on the 16th November 1923. There were then no lists until the list of 1936, which does include Boys Smith's name.

107. Bergson, *La Perception du Changement*.

108. Russell, *The Problems of Philosophy*, 13. See Sainsbury, *Russell*, 249, on Russell's identification of objects with their histories, and the necessity of such an ontology for the natural sciences; and see Sainsbury, *Russell*, 258, on Russell's treatment of matter as a series of events.

109. Russell, *Our Knowledge of the External World*, 158. (On pp. 26-28, Russell suggests that Bergson's "evolutionism" was not justified by contemporary knowledge of biology.)

110. Monk, *Ludwig Wittgenstein*, 255.

philosophical debate. We know that in 1939 Boys Smith and Wittgenstein debated the nature of implicit belief at a meeting of the Moral Sciences Club.[111] We do not know whether the two debated philosophical questions prior to the publication of *Christian Doctrine and the Idea of Evolution*, but similarities between the ideas in the booklet and in Wittgenstein's *Philosophical Investigations* provide at least circumstantial evidence that they were aware of each other's ideas. In *Christian Doctrine and the Idea of Evolution* we find the idea that the meaning of language changes in the same way that everything else does,[112] and that at the same time there is connectedness and continuity, expressed by Boys Smith in the phrase "some general character."[113] We have already discussed Wittgenstein's understanding that the meaning of language, constituted by language's use, changes constantly in the context of forms of life, and that continuity and connectedness can be expressed in the phrase "family likeness."

It is possible that Wittgenstein's, as well as Russell's, contributions to discussion at the Moral Sciences Club—the meetings of which Wittgenstein somewhat dominated[114]—provided some of the inspiration for Boys Smith's *Christian Doctrine and the Idea of Evolution*. Another intriguing possibility is that Wittgenstein heard Boys Smith discuss *his* ideas, and thus came to question the ideas contained in the *Tractatus*. More likely is the possibility that both Boys Smith and Wittgenstein were aware of Russell's views, and were influenced by an increasingly widesread philosophical milieu characterized by action, change, and diversity, and that they were led to similar conclusions.

---

111. Attached to a paper entitled "Some Problems about Belief," which Boys Smith read to the Moral Sciences Club on the 2nd March 1939, is a note on the discussion that followed. Wittgenstein raised the question as to whether there is anything "going on" when we believe implicitly, and asked whether any limit can be set to what we believe implicitly: questions entirely consistent with the position of much of the *Philosophical Investigations*. The minutes of the meeting record parts of the same discussion, and particularly Wittgenstein's view that Boys Smith had been misled by the term "belief" into thinking that there must be an attitude that persists rather than just the action of believing. Wittgenstein was concerned to evaluate every particular case of believing—so Boys Smith asked why the same word "belief" is used of all of them. Wittgenstein suggested that the cases "pass into one another," and that the same word is therefore legitimate. This particular discussion occurred in 1939, but similar discussions might have occurred ten years earlier.

112. Boys Smith, *Christian Doctrine and the Idea of Evolution*, 3–4, 10.

113. Boys Smith, *Christian Doctrine and the Idea of Evolution*, 5.

114. Monk, *Ludwig Wittgenstein*, 263.

D. CONCLUSION

Wittgenstein and Boys Smith might appear to function only at the level of language and ideas, rather than at the level of reality as a whole, but because for both of them language belongs within a single field of action, or within a single complex evolutionary process, there is no fundamental distinction to be drawn between language and other kinds of activity. This connection invites us to extend to the whole of reality—however we understand that, and however we understand its relationship with ourselves and our language—the same understanding that meaning is actions in patterns: for what else is language use but a special case of actions in patterns?

The major difference between Boys Smith's ideas and Wittgenstein's—apart from the considerable difference in their manner of expression—is that for Boys Smith the task is ultimately theological, whereas for Wittgenstein it is not. For Wittgenstein, language about God is like any other language: it is a language game, with relationships with other language games, and with relationships with forms of life: but there would appear to be no interest in the question as to whether there are actions in patterns external to the language-user to which the linguistic actions in patterns relate. There is certainly no interest in the kind of vast evolutionary constructions that such scholars as Hegel, Blondel, Bergson, and Teilhard de Chardin were writing about. While John Boys Smith was somewhat reticent about what it might be possible to say about history, the universe, and God, he was clear that theological language is just as legitimate as any other kind, and that all of it evolves, with a changing evolution, so that as far as we are concerned God evolves, with a changing evolution, even if there might be some (inaccessible) sense in which God does not. As Boys Smith puts it:

> The new can never be merely added to the old, because the old is always transfigured by the new. To see more is always to see all differently; for experience is always one world, within which each element is conditioned by its context in the whole.[115]

Everything—or rather, every action, and every bundle of actions in patterns that we experience as a stable reality of some kind—is action, with its source in Action. All of it is action in changing patterns: and the meaning of "actions in patterns," and of "actions in changing patterns," changes along with everything else. There is no still point where we can stand to survey the shifting landscape.

---

115. Boys Smith, *Christian Doctrine and the Idea of Evolution*, 3.

11

Towards an actology

A. SOME TENTATIVE CONCLUSIONS

One of the tasks that I set myself in this book was to scour the Western philosophical tradition for examples of conceptual structures characterized by change, action, Action, and movement, with an eye to diversity as well, in order to provide a basis in the history of Western philosophy for an alternative or complementary metaphysic, or actology, that might be useful to us in our fast-changing world, and in particular might be useful to the church as it constructs theology that might relate to such a world.

In the service of that task, I shall rehearse some of the conclusions that we have reached: but first of all I shall raise a question that we left open at the beginning of this book: that is, when we discuss the paired concepts change/unchanging, movement/rest, action/being, Action/Being, the dynamic/the static, diversity/the unitary, should we speak of spectrums or of distinctions? The question might best be answered in relation to some related questions: Can we envisage midpoints between the two members of a pair? Is one member of the pair defined in relation to the other? Can we envisage a transition from one member of the pair to the other? In relation to change and the unchanging, we can potentially answer all three questions in the affirmative, and the same is true of movement and rest, and of the static and the dynamic. So in relation to these pairs we might legitimately speak of spectrums. The same is not true of action and being, or of Action and Being. "Action" is a distinctive way of viewing reality, and so is "Being"; and if we wish to relate "being" and "action" then we have to find some way of doing that: for instance, "being" or "a being" might be understood as "actions in patterns." So here we have a distinction, not a spectrum. However, where we find that a philosopher is working with a hybrid conceptual structure that could be understood as either an "Action" metaphysic or a "Being" one, and perhaps as both, then we might be able to speak of an "Action/Being spectrum" and/or an "action/being" spectrum, and we might be able to locate philosophers and their various statements at various points along those spectrums. We might find that we can closely relate Being and Action, as Blondel does: but that is to create a particular relationship between two members of a distinction, not a spectrum with the two concepts at its two ends. So in general we might speak of the spectrums defined by change/the unchanging, movement/rest, and the static/the dynamic, and of the distinctions between action and being and between Action and Being. The diversity/unitary pair provides us with something of a conundrum. The number 1 is different from all other numbers, and it is a number, so at one level there is a distinction, and at another there is not. We might therefore regard diversity and the unitary as a clear distinction between opposites, or as members of a spectrum, with the unitary at one end, and diversity across the rest of it.

I now turn to the conclusions that we have reached at the ends of the individual chapters:

We have discovered that, contrary to the way in which Parmenides has generally been read, the logic of his poem is that only a metaphysic constructed at the change end of the change/unchanging spectrum, and on the diversity side of the diversity/unity distinction, can ensure that we can speak of both Action and Being, both actions and beings, both change and the unchanging, both diversity and unity. We have arrived at the same conclusion following our study of Heraclitus's philosophy. Being is fire, beings are constituted by fire, and fire is a unifying factor within the diversity: and fire itself changes, and is active and diverse. Again, we are at the change end of the spectrum, and on the Action and diversity sides of the distinctions. If we wish to be able to converse about both Action and Being, both actions and beings, both change and the unchanging, and both diversity and unity, then we need to start with change, diversity, and action: with Hesiod's chaos as the primary reality, and with order as a secondary one.

As we studied Plato, we recognised that his thought lies in a variety of positions in relation to the spectrums and distinctions, and that if he had added verb-based universals to his noun-based ones then he would have enabled us to understand the whole of reality as participating on both sides of the Action/Being distinction. Aristotle, too, could have added to his idea that there is no motion without things[1] the idea that there are no things without action, without *enérgeia*, just as there is no God without *enérgeia*. A little more recognition that for Aquinas everything is "*in actu*" would lead us in the same direction.

According to Heraclitus, God is as much constituted by fire and by diversity as is anything else. Change and diversity are not only how reality is and how it works: it is also how God works and how God is. For Plato to have pursued the possibility of verb-based Forms, as well as the Forms based on adjectival nouns that he did discuss, would have located his philosophy as much on the "Action" side of our distinction as on the "Being" side of it. This would also have enabled a creator God, also defined in terms of action, constantly to give birth to the Forms, and at the same time to create a universe on the model of the Forms. Aristotle's God might be "unmoved,"[2] but at the same time God has "life most good and eternal,"[3] which implies change; and God has *enérgeia*, which means "action, operation, energy,"[4] as well as "actuality." For Aquinas, God is as "*in actu*" as anything else is. In Aristotle, in Aquinas, and in the English language, we find connections between "action" and "actually," as in "exists actually"—that is, something really does exist, rather than existing potentially, or only in thought. Something has come into existence: an "action" of "becoming," or rather, of "having become." This *energeía* and this *in actu* suggest that every being, including God, must exist "*in actu*" in order to exist at all. Action is prior to being.

We have found in these early philosophers the building-blocks of the kind of metaphysic, or actology, that we shall need.

When we turn to Hegel we find a *Geist*-shaped dialectic, and in Marx we find a social and economic dialectic. Everything here is evolutionary change, and in both cases the action is in dialectical patterns, and is driven by an inner momentum shaped by an end-point that is itself actions in patterns. In both cases the whole of reality is encompassed by the dialectic and

---

1. Aristotle, *Metaphysics*, book XI, 1065b7–8.
2. *akíneton*
3. *zōè aristē kai aídios*
4. Liddell and Scott, *An Intermediate Greek-English Lexicon*.

the trajectory: although we have also recognised that dialectic itself seems not to be subject to a dialectical process.

Hegel's God is "no doubt undisturbed identity and oneness with itself":[5] but this description plays no part in the argument. God enters the picture to the extent that God contributes to the self-realisation of *Geist* in the Absolute. *Geist* is a religious word: and it is *Geist* that Hegel's philosophy is all about. We are at liberty to interpret *Geist* as "God," but, as we have seen, Hegel might not have done so.

In both Hegel and Marx we have discovered an understanding of history that is informed by an "actions in patterns" metaphysic. However, there remains a rigidity in the action: a pattern that does not change. It will be in John Boys Smith's brief philosophical works that we shall find an understanding of this dilemma and something of a resolution of it in the evolution of evolution.

In Blondel's "Action" we have found a true universal, a Platonic Form, constituting and naming a category in which every particular action belongs: and, as we have recognised, this Form is itself constituted by action, so it changes constantly, forever taking on new patterns or configurations. "To be is to act,"[6] and Being, because it encompasses the total becoming across time and space, and so all action across time and space, is Action. Action is ubiquitous, so there is nothing fixed about Being, and every action remains independent and with multiple causes, and so continues to influence the totality of action and thus of Being. There is no suggestion that there might be an end-point to Action or action. We came to the important conclusion that Being is Action; that Action, understood in its totality, is Being; and that "Being . . . the same as God."[7] Because "to be is to act"[8] applies as much to God as to us, to God belongs an "incessant creativity,"[9] characterized by the particular configuration or pattern of action that we call "love," creating communion between God and all becoming,[10] and bonding a trinity of persons into a unity. In Blondel we have discovered an action-based conceptual structure that is unique in its consistency and breadth. There will still be

---

5. *wohl die ungetrübte Gleichheit und Einheit mit sich selbst*: Hegel, *Phänomenologie des Geistes*, Vorrede; Hegel, *Hegel's Phenomenology of Spirit*, §§18–19.

6. *Être, c'est agir*: Blondel, *L'Être et les Êtres*, 341.

7. *l'Être . . . Dieu même*: Blondel, *L'Être et les Êtres*, 333.

8. *Être, c'est agir*: Blondel, *L'Être et les Êtres*, 341.

9. *incessante fécondité*: Blondel, *L'Être et les Êtres*, 333.

10. Blondel, *L'Être et les Êtres*, 442.

new things to learn about an actology constructed on the basis of actions in patterns, but all of that will be commentary, and a discovery of implications.

When we studied Bergson's philosophy, we concluded that he was attempting to create an overall vision of reality, a metaphysic, but that he did not achieve that, and that Blondel's "action" would have helped him to amend and to connect the various disconnected and inconsistent parts of his metaphysic. If they had worked together then they might have developed understandings of both space and time as action in layered and changing patterns, thus creating the kind of framework required for a coherent understanding of reality.

It is when we came to Teilhard de Chardin that we had to desist from writing separate paragraphs about philosophy and theology, because here the two were intimately tied together: or rather, they constantly related to each other in the most intimate way. We have recognised that Teilhard could have constructed a metaphysic, a theology, and a cosmology—a theocosmology—that could have encompassed everything (or rather, every action) within a single conception. To have understood God and everything else as actions in patterns would have offered to Teilhard the possibility of an evolution constituted by ubiquitous chaotic action (understood initially as abstracted from all being, beings, things, and stabilities) in constantly changing patterns. Then the Omega Point could have been defined as constantly changing patterns of action, drawing all reality towards itself, and propelling it onwards as action in yet more changing patterns. Understanding God as Action, as the source of all action, and as the source of all of the patterns that we and the cosmos experience, is a task that we must now take over from Teilhard de Chardin. As Heraclitus suggested, "fire" might be the best way to envisage such a theocosmology.

We have found in Whitehead's process philosophy a conceptual structure that retains complicating undynamic elements, and we have found equally undynamic and nonrelational elements in his God. If we are to create a relevant theology for today, then for the time being we shall need to abandon the "primordial" nature of God, the being-language, the permanent, the unmoved, and the unconnected, and begin on the "action" side of the distinction before finding ways to talk about the stabilities and similarities that we experience: otherwise we shall deny ourselves the paradigm shift that we need. We need to speak of reality and of God wholly in terms of action, and then of actions in patterns, and in this way, and not otherwise, to discover that being-language can continue to be legitimate and often appropriate.

In Geoffrey Studdert Kennedy's theology, Jesus "carries innocent suffering into the heart of God,"[11] so that the suffering God "is crucified afresh every day."[12] The action that constitutes Jesus is the action that constitutes God, so God *is* "Suffering Love."[13] This is an extreme identification of Jesus with God; and, as we discovered, there is an equally extreme identification of the Eucharist with Jesus, and therefore of the Eucharist with God.[14] There is nothing passive here. God, Jesus, and the Eucharist, are defined by action. God "leads the army of innocent sorrow";[15] God comes; and God sheds tears;[16] and in the crucifixion:

> . . . See the wounded God go walking down the world's eternal way.
> For his task is never done . . .[17]

Our final two scholars might appear to function at the level of language rather than at the level of reality as a whole, but in fact they do not do so. By locating language in forms of life, Wittgenstein binds language to the rest of reality. This invites us to extend to the whole of reality—however we understand that, and however we understand its relationship with ourselves and our language—the same understanding that meaning is actions in patterns: for what else is language use but a special case of actions in patterns? The same can be said of Boys Smith's understanding of the evolution of language, including theological language. The meaning of "evolution" evolves, so, as far as we are concerned, evolution evolves, even if there might be some (inaccessible) sense in which it does not. The meaning of religious language evolves, so as far as we are concerned God evolves—with a changing evolution—even if there might be some (inaccessible) sense in which God does not.

As John Boys Smith puts it:

> The new can never be merely added to the old, because the old is always transfigured by the new. To see more is always to see

---

11. Studdert Kennedy, *The Hardest Part*, 34.
12. Studdert Kennedy, *The Hardest Part*, 153.
13. Studdert Kennedy, *The Hardest Part*, 44.
14. Studdert Kennedy, *Peace Rhymes of a Padre*, 47; Studdert Kennedy, *The Unutterable Beauty*, 58.
15. Studdert Kennedy, *Rough Talks by a Padre*, 129.
16. Studdert Kennedy, *Rough Rhymes of a Padre*, 21.
17. Studdert Kennedy, *Peace Rhymes of a Padre*, 93.

all differently; for experience is always one world, within which each element is conditioned by its context in the whole.[18]

Everything—or rather, every action, and every bundle of actions in patterns that we experience as a stable reality of some kind—is action, with its source in Action. All of it is action in changing patterns: and the meaning of "actions in patterns," and of "action in changing patterns," changes along with everything else. There is no still point where we can stand to survey the shifting landscape.

To draw together the wide variety of different conclusions to which we have come: We have found among the writings of early Greek philosophers and Aquinas the building blocks for an action-in-patterns metaphysic; in Hegel and Marx we have found an understanding of history as actions in patterns (especially if we go on to understand dialectic as itself a changing pattern); in Blondel, we have found that reality—including being—is understood in terms of action; we have found that if we remove his remaining rigidities, then Bergson can offer us an understanding of space and time as actions in patterns; we have found that although he did not get this far himself, Teilhard de Chardin invites us to contemplate God, the cosmos, and everything else, in terms of actions in patterns; we have found that Whitehead and the other process theologians invite a more consistent treatment of reality than they achieved, and also invite an understanding of God in terms of Action; in Studdert Kennedy we have found a suffering God active in the midst of the world's suffering; in Wittgenstein we have found an understanding of language in terms of actions in patterns connected to other actions in patterns; and we have found that John Boys Smith invites an understanding of changing patterns of changing language, and changing patterns of other actions in patterns too.

To return to a question raised but not tackled at the beginning of this book: We have fashioned our explorations around a variety of spectrums, and particularly the change/unchanging spectrum and the movement/rest spectrum; and around some distinctions: Action/Being, action/being, diversity/unity. We have recognised that there are connections between the different sides of the distinctions, and that various thinkers' thought can be located at a variety of points along the spectrums. I shall continue to leave somewhat unresolved the question as to whether the different spectrums and distinctions can be related in a particular way. There is of course a sense in which change is action and movement is action, and there are clearly relationships

18. Boys Smith, *Christian Doctrine and the Idea of Evolution*, 3.

between rest, the unchanging, and being. There are also connections between unity, Being, and being, and between diversity, Action, and action: although these connections are not necessarily easy to compare with each other. As loose categorisations we might understand action, Action, change and movement on the "dynamic" end of a spectrum or on one side of a single distinction, and being, Being, the unchanging, and rest on the "static" end of the spectrum or on the other side of the overall distinction: but we have already discovered how connected being and action can be, and therefore how connected Being and Action might be. As loose generalisations, "the dynamic" and "the static" might be helpful in some circumstances, but we should not employ them to suggest that these categorisations in any way reduce the extent of the diversities within them. We do not in fact need to make definitive decisions about the relationships between the different distinctions and spectrums, and it might be best to leave the diversity as it is: but for the purposes of what is to follow I shall characterize an "Action" metaphysic as one characterized by change rather than by the unchanging, by movement rather than by rest, by action rather than by being, and by the dynamic rather than by the static.

There has been a certain circularity about the argument of this book. I have justified an "actions in patterns" framework in relation to the tradition, and I have described that tradition largely in terms of its actual or potential relationship with the new suggested framework. But when it comes to fundamental axioms, inductive argument rather than deductive argument is all that we have, and the reader will need to judge whether I have built any kind of cumulative case, in relation to the kind of world that we now live in, and in relation to our philosophical survey, for a conceptual pattern defined by actions in patterns.

The Western philosophical tradition has given to us a wealth of material on which to ponder as we have constructed our actology: and the tradition will continue to provide us with material as we reconstruct the actology as the context and the meaning of everything continues to change. Perhaps the most important lesson that we can take away from our detailed study is the importance of not looking back, at least for a while: of not hankering after Being, beings, being-language, the static, the unchanging, the unmoving, and the unitary. We shall find plenty of ways within an "actions in patterns" conceptual framework within which to understand the stabilities that we experience. And then, when we have ceased to look back, and have thoroughly acquainted ourselves with a wholly new actions in patterns narrative, and have come to understand the cosmos, ourselves, language, God, and everything else, in those terms, we shall understand this narrative as just one particular narrative, we shall be able to revisit a narrative of Being, beings, the unchanging, the static, and the unitary—and, even more importantly, we shall be able to explore yet more options. Until that time comes, we shall concentrate on building and making use of an actology: a conceptual framework about Action, actions, the dynamic, change, movement, and diversity—and all of it changing: the building blocks of which we have discovered in the Western philosophical tradition—or perhaps it might be more appropriate to say that we have discovered sufficient patterns of action to enable us to create a symphony of ideas that will shape the changing metaphysics and theology that we now need.

But we are still only at the beginning of the process of developing a new paradigm. Such paradigms are not easy to formulate because our language and questions always relate to existing frameworks and not to emerging new ones.[19] The current contortions of the Western philosophical tradition are symptomatic of a paradigm that needs a rest. If "actions in patterns" has explanatory economy, then it will, for a while at least, replace the traditional paradigm, and it will explain reality to us, and thus reality to Christian faith and Christian faith to reality. The paradigm shift is long overdue, although we ought to be under no illusions: any new paradigm will pose its own problems, which should prepare us continually to test and amend our ideas. So we shall need to test the actology that we have constructed in the context of a wide variety of aspects of reality, and in the context of society, ourselves, the sciences, theology, and much else. Only a conceptual framework which relates positively to these areas of interest will be of any use to us in expressing the world that we are part of, and only a conceptual framework that relates positively to these areas of interest will help us to express our deepest questions, convictions, and hopes. And then, once we have tested and lived with the new paradigm for a while, we shall need to prepare ourselves for the next paradigm shift.

---

19. On the development of new paradigms in the sciences (and thus in theology), see Kuhn, *The Structure of Scientific Revolutions*.

Bibliography

Ackrill, J.L. "Aristotle's Distinction between *Energeia* and *Kinesis*." In *New Essays on Plato and Aristotle*, edited by Renford Bambrough, 121–42. London: Routledge and Kegan Paul, 1965.

Ackrill, John L. "Aristotle on Action." *Mind* 87 (4) (1978) 595–601.

Adams, Nicholas. *Eclipse of Grace: Divine and Human Action in Hegel*. Chichester: Wiley-Blackwell, 2013.

Adluri, Vishwa. *Parmenides, Plato and Moral Philosophy: Return from Transcendence*. London: Continuum, 2011.

Alston, William. "Hartshorne and Aquinas: A Via Media." In *Existence and Actuality: Conversations with Charles Hartshorne*, edited by John B. Cobb and Franklin I. Gamwell, 78–98. Chicago: University of Chicago Press, 1984.

Anderson, John. *Parmenides and Presocratic Philosophy*. Oxford: Oxford University Press, 2009.

Année, Magali. *Énoncer le Verbe Être*. Paris: Librairie Philosophique J. Vrin, 2012: an essay to accompany a text and French translation of Parmenides' *Fragments*.

Ansell-Pearson, Keith. *Philosophy and the Adventure of the Virtual*. London and New York: Routledge, 2002.

Ansell-Pearson, Keith, and Jim Urpeth. "Bergson and Nietzsche on Religion." In *Bergson, Politics, and Religion*, edited by Alexandre Lefebvre and Melanie White, 246–64. Durham and London: Duke University Press, 2012.

Anselm. *Proslogion*. "Prooemium" and "2, Quod vere sit Deus." www.thelatinlibrary.com/anselmproslogion.html.

———. *Proslogium*. Preface, and chapter II. https://legacy.fordham.edu/halsall/basis/anselm-proslogium.asp.

Aquinas, Thomas. *Commentaria in Octo Libros Physicorum*. https://isidore.co/aquinas/Physics.htm.

———. *Commentary on Aristotle's Metaphysics*. Translated by John P. Rowan from *Sententia super Metaphysicam*. https://isidore.co/aquinas/english/Metaphysics.htm.

———. *Commentary on Aristotle's Physics*. Translated by Pierre H. Conway from *Commentaria in Octo Libros Physicorum*. https://isidore.co/aquinas/Physics.htm.

———. *Commentary on the* Book of Causes. Translated by V.A Guagliardo, C.R. Hess and R.C. Taylor from *Super Librum De Causis Expositio*. Washington, DC: Catholic University of America Press, 1996.
———. *Contra Gentiles*. https://isidore.co/aquinas/ContraGentiles.htm.
———. *Contra Gentiles*. Translated into English by Pierre H. Conway, OP. https://isidore.co/aquinas/ContraGentiles.htm.
———. *De Ente et Essentia*. https://isidore.co/aquinas/DeEnte&Essentia.htm.
———. *On Being and* Essence. Translated by Joseph Kenny, O.P. from *De Ente et Essentia*, 1965. https://isidore.co/aquinas/DeEnte&Essentia.htm.
———. *On Being and Essence*. Translated by Robert T. Miller from *De Ente et Essentia*, 1997, http://legacy.fordham.edu/halsall/basis/aquinas-esse.asp.
———. *On the Power of God*. Translated by the English Dominican Fathers, Westminster, Maryland, from *Questiones Disputatae de Potentia Dei*, 1952. https://isidore.co/aquinas/QDdePotentia.htm.
———. *Questiones Disputatae de Potentia Dei*. https://isidore.co/aquinas/QDdePotentia.htm.
———. *Scriptum super Sententiis*. http://www.corpusthomisticum.org/snp1004.html.
———. *Sententia super Metaphysicam*. https://isidore.co/aquinas/english/Metaphysics.htm.
———. *Summa Theologiae*. https://isidore.co/aquinas/summa/index.html.
———. *Summa Theologiae*. Translated into English by Fathers of the English Dominican Province. https://isidore.co/aquinas/summa/index.html.
———. *Super Librum De Causis Expositio*. Edited by Roberto Busa S.J.. Corpus Thomisticum, 1954. http://www.corpusthomisticum.org/cdc01.html.
Aratus. *Phaenomena*, I. In *Callimachus, Hymns and Epigrams. Lycophron. Aratus*. Translated by A.W. and G.R. Mair, Loeb Classical Library, volume 129. London: William Heinemann, 1921.
Archbishop of Canterbury's Commission on Urban Priority Areas. *Faith in the City: A Call for Action by Church and Nation*. London: Church House, 1985.
Aristotle. *Aristotle in 23 Volumes*, Vol. 19. Translated by H. Rackham. Cambridge, MA and London: Harvard University Press and William Heinemann, 1934. www.perseus.tufts.edu/Texts/chunk_TOC.grk.html.
———. *Categories*. Translated by E. Edghill. www.ellopos.net/elpenor/greek-texts/ancient-greece/aristotle/categories.asp?pg=4.
———. *Ethica Nicomachea*. Edited by J. Bywater. Oxford: Clarendon, 1894. www.perseus.tufts.edu/Texts/chunk_TOC.grk.html.
———. *Metaphysics*. Edited by W.D. Ross. Oxford: Clarendon, 1924. With an English translation from *Aristotle in 23 Volumes*, vols. 17 and 18. Translated by Hugh Tredennick. Cambridge, MA: Harvard University Press, and London: William Heinemann, 1933, 1989, www.perseus.tufts.edu/Texts/chunk_TOC.grk.html.
———. *Nicomachean Ethics*. Translated by H. Rackham from *Ethica Nicomachea*. Cambridge, MA: Harvard University Press, and London: William Heinemann, 1934. www.perseus.tufts.edu/Texts/chunk_TOC.grk.html.
———. *Physics*. With an English translation from the *Commentary on Aristotle's Physics by St. Thomas Aquinas*. Translated by Richard J. Blackwell et al.. London: Routledge and Kegan Paul, 1963. https://isidore.co/aquinas/Physics.htm.
———. *Rhetoric*. In *Ars Rhetorica*, I. Edited by W. D. Ross. Oxford: Clarendon, 1959. With an English translation, *Rhetoric*, from *Aristotle in 23 Volumes*, vol. 22.

Translated by J. H. Freese. Cambridge MA: Harvard University Press, and London: William Heinemann, 1926. www.perseus.tufts.edu/Texts/chunk_TOC.grk.html.
Ashraf, S.E. *A Critical Exposition of Iqbal's Philosophy*. Patna: Associated Book Agency, 1978.
Bambrough, Renford. *Reason, Truth and God*. London: Methuen, 1969.
Barnes, Jonathan. "Metaphysics." In *The Cambridge Companion to Aristotle*, edited by Jonathan Barnes, 66–108. Cambridge: Cambridge University Press, 1995.
———. "Aristotle." In *Greek Philosophers*, edited by C.C.W. Taylor et al., 191–302. Oxford: Oxford University Press, 1999.
———. *Early Greek Philosophy*. London: Penguin, 1987.
Barthélémy-Madaule, Madeleine. *Bergson et Teilhard de Chardin*. Paris: Éditions du Seuil, 1963.
Beets, M.G.I.. *The Coherence of Reality: Experiments in Philosophical Interpretation: Heraclitus, Parmenides, Plato*. Delft: Eburon, 1986.
Beiser, Frederick. "Introduction: Hegel and the Problem of Metaphysics." In *The Cambridge Companion to Hegel*, edited by Frederick Beiser, 1–24. Cambridge: Cambridge University Press, 1993.
———. "Hegel's Historicism." In *The Cambridge Companion to Hegel*, edited by Frederick C. Beiser, 270–300. Cambridge: Cambridge University Press, 1993.
Benda, Julien. *Le Bergsonisme ou Une Philosophie de la Mobilité*. Third edition. Paris: Mercure de France, 1912.
Bergson, Henri. *Cours sur la Philosophie Grecque*. Lectures delivered 1884–85. Paris: Presses Universitaires de France, 2000. The translation is by the author, who could not find a published English translation.
———. *Creative Evolution*. Translated by Arthur Mitchell from *L'Évolution Créatrice*. Paris: Presses Universitaires de France, 1911.
———. *The Creative Mind: An Introduction to Metaphysics*. Translated by M.L. Andison from *La Pensée et le Mouvant: Articles et Conférences Datant de 1903 à 1923*. Westport: Greenwood, 1946.
———. *Les Deux Sources de la Morale et de la Religion*. Paris: Presses Universitaires de France, 1932. http://classiques.uqac.ca/classiques/bergson_henri/deux_sources_morale/deux_sources_morale.html.
———. *Duration and Simultaneity*. Translated by Robin Durie from *Durée et Simultanéité: À Propos de la Théorie d'Einstein*. Manchester: Clinamen, 1999.
———. *Durée et Simultanéité: À Propos de la Théorie d'Einstein*. Paris: Les Presses Universitaires de France, 1968. First published in 1922. http://classiques.uqac.ca/classiques/bergson_henri/duree_simultaneite/duree.html.
———. *Essai sur les Données Immédiates de la Conscience*. Paris: Presses Universitaires de France, 1970. First published in 1888. http://classiques.uqac.ca/classiques/bergson_henri/essai_conscience_immediate/conscience_imm.html.
———. *L'Évolution Créatrice*. Paris: Les Presses Universitaires de France, 1959. First published in 1907. http://classiques.uqac.ca/classiques/bergson_henri/evolution_creatrice/evolution_creatrice.html.
———. *Matière et Mémoire: Essai sur la Relation du Corps à l'Esprit*. Seventh edition. Paris: Les Presses Universitaires de France, 1939. First published in 1896. http://classiques.uqac.ca/classiques/bergson_henri/matiere_et_memoire/matiere_et_memoire.html.

———. *Matter and Memory*. Translated by Nancy Margaret Paul and W. Scott Palmer from *Matière et Mémoire*. London: George Allen and Unwin, 1911.

———. *Mélanges*. Edited by André Robinet. Paris: Presses Universitaires de France, 1972.

———. *La Pensée et le Mouvant: Articles et Conférences Datant de 1903 à 1923*. Paris: Les Presses Universitaires de France, 1969. First published in 1934. http://classiques.uqac.ca/classiques/bergson_henri/pensee_mouvant/pensee_mouvant.html.

———. *La Perception du Changement*. Oxford: Clarendon, 1911.

———. "La Perception du Changement." In Henri Bergson, *La Pensée et le Mouvant: Articles et Conférences Datant de 1903 à 1923*, 80–97. Paris: Les Presses Universitaires de France, 1969. First published in 1934. http://classiques.uqac.ca/classiques/bergson_henri/pensee_mouvant/pensee_mouvant.html. "La Perception du Changement" was first published as *La Perception du Changement*, Oxford: Clarendon, 1911.

———. *Time and Free Will: An Essay on the Immediate Data of Consciousness*. Translated by F.L. Pogson from *Essai sur les Données Immédiates de la Conscience*. London: George Allen and Unwin, 1910.

———. *The Two Sources of Morality and Religion*. Translated by R. Ashley Andra and Cloudesley Brereton with W. Horsfall Carter, from *Les Deux Sources de la Morale et de la Religion*. Notre Dame: University of Notre Dame Press, 1977.

Bernstein, Richard J. *Praxis and Action*. London: Duckworth, 1972.

Bjelland, Andrew. "Durational Succession and Proto-mental Agency." In *Bergson and Modern Thought: Towards a Unified Science*, edited by Andrew C. Papanicolaou and Peter A.Y. Gunter, 19–28. Chur: Harwood Academic, 1987.

Blanchette, Oliva. "Maurice Blondel's Philosophy of Action: Translator's Preface." In Maurice Blondel, *Action*, translated by Oliva Blanchette, xi–xxx. Notre Dame: University of Notre Dame Press, 1984.

Blondel, Maurice. *Action*. Translated by Oliva Blanchette from *L'Action*. Notre Dame: University of Notre Dame Press, 1984.

———. *L'Action*. Paris: Quadrige/Presses Universitaires de France, 1993. First published in 1893.

———. *L'Être et les Êtres*. Paris: Librairie Felix Alcan, 1935. http://classiques.uqac.ca/classiques/blondel_maurice/etre_et_les_etres/etre_et_les_etres.html.

———. *L'Illusion Idéaliste*. In Maurice Blondel, *Les Premiers Écrits de Maurice Blondel*, 97–122. Paris: Presses Universitaires de France, 1956. First published in 1898.

———. *L'Itinéraire Philosophique de Maurice Blondel: Propos Recueillis par Frédéric Lefebvre*. Paris: Éditions Spes, 1928. http://classiques.uqac.ca/classiques/blondel_maurice/itineraire_philosophique/itineraire_philosophique.html.

———. *La Philosophie et l'Esprit Chrétien*, volume 1, second edition. Paris: Presses Universitaires de France, 1950. First published in 1944. http://classiques.uqac.ca/classiques/blondel_maurice/philo_esprit_chretien_t2/philo_esprit_chretien_t2.html.

Bloor, David. *Wittgenstein: A Social Theory of Knowledge*. London and Basingstoke: Macmillan, 1983.

Bostock, David. "Plato on Change and Time in the Parmenides." *Phronesis* 23 (3) (1978) 220–42.

———. "Plato on understanding language." In *Language*, Companions to Ancient Thought, 3, edited by Stephen Everson, 10–27. Cambridge: Cambridge University Press, 1994.

Bowin, John. "Aristotle on the Unity of Change: Five Reduction Arguments in *Physics*, viii, 8." *Ancient Philosophy* 30 (2) (2010) 319–46.

Boyd, Gregory A. *Trinity and Process: A Critical Evaluation of Hartshorne's Di-Polar Theism Towards a Trinitarian Metaphysics*. New York: Peter Lang, 1992.

Boys Smith, J.S. "Behaviour of Hedgehog, *Erinceus europaeus*." *Journal of Zoology* 153 (4) (1967) 564–66.

———. *Christian Doctrine and the Idea of Evolution*. D Society Pamphlets III. Cambridge: Bowes and Bowes, 1930.

———. "The Historical Element in Christianity." Unpublished paper read to Eranus, Trinity College, Cambridge, 11th May 1954.

———. *Memories of St. John's College: Cambridge, 1919 to 1969*. Cambridge: St. John's College, 1983.

———. "Religious Faith: A Discussion of Certain of its Characteristics." Unpublished fellowship thesis, 1927.

———. Review of *The Faith of a Moralist*, by A.E. Taylor. *Journal of Theological Studies* 32 (1931) 434.

———. Review of *The Lord of Life*, by H.T. Andrews et al.. *The Journal of Theological Studies* 31 (1930) 208–209.

———. *The Sermons of John Boys Smith: A theologian of integrity*. Edited and with an introduction by Malcolm Torry. Cambridge: Aquila, for St. John's College, Cambridge, 2003.

———. "The Significance of the Historical Element in the Christian Idea of Incarnation." *Modern Churchman* 18 (7) (1928) 372–90.

Bracken, Joseph A. *The One and the Many: A Contemporary Reconstruction of the God-World Relationship*. Grand Rapids, Michigan: Eerdmans, 2001.

Bradley, F.H. *Ethical Studies*. London: Henry S. King, 1876.

Braun, Eva. *The Logos of Heraclitus: The First Philosopher of the West on its Most Interesting Term*. Philadelphia: Paul Dry, 2011.

Bredlow, Luis Andrés. "Parmenides and the Grammar of Being," *Classical Philology* 106 (4) (2011) 283–98.

Brierley, Michael. "Introducing the Early English Passibilists." *Journal of the History of Modern Theology* 8 (2001) 218–33.

Broadie, Alexander. "Aristotle on Rational Action." *Phronesis* 19 (1) (1974) 70–80.

Brouillard, Henri. *Blondel and Christianity*. Translated by James M. Somerville. Washington DC: Corpus, 1969.

Brown, Lesley. "The Verb 'To Be' in Greek Philosophy: Some Remarks," in *Language*: Companions to ancient thought, 3, edited by Stephen Everson, 212–36. Cambridge: Cambridge University Press, 1994.

Bultmann, Rudolf. *Kerygma and Myth*. Edited by Hans-Werner Bartsch. Translated by Reginald H. Fuller. London: SPCK, 1972.

Burbidge, John W. "Hegel's Conception of Logic." In *The Cambridge Companion to Hegel*, edited by Frederick C. Beiser, 86–101. Cambridge: Cambridge University Press, 1993.

———. *Real Process: How Logic and Chemistry Combine in Hegel's Philosophy of Nature*. Toronto: University of Toronto Press, 1996.

Burrell, David. *Aquinas: God and Action*. London: Routledge and Kegan Paul, 1979.
Calton, Patricia Marie. *Hegel's Metaphysics of God: The Ontological Proof as the Development of a Trinitarian Divine Ontology*. Aldershot: Ashgate, 2001.
Carey, D.F. "War Padre." In *G.A. Studdert Kennedy by his Friends*, edited by J.K. Mozley, 115–61. London: Hodder and Stoughton, 1929.
Carr, H. Wilden. *The Philosophy of Change*. London: Macmillan, 1914.
Chahine, Osman E. *La Durée chez Bergson*. Paris: Huguette, 1970.
Charles, David. *Aristotle's Philosophy of Action*. London: Duckworth, 1984.
Chen, Chung-Hwan. "Aristotle's Analysis of Change and Plato's Theory of Transcendent Ideas." *Phronesis* 20 (2) (1975) 129–45.
Cherubin, Rose. Review of *Parménide: Fragments Poème*, by M. Année. *The Classical Review* 65 (1) (2015) 45–47.
Chevalier, Jacques. *Henri Bergson*. Translated by Lilian A. Clare. London: Rider, 1928.
Church of England, Archbishop's Commission on Christian Doctrine. *Doctrine in the Church of England: The Report of the Commission on Christian Doctrine Appointed by the Archbishops of Canterbury and York in 1922*. London: Society for Promoting Christian Knowledge, 1938.
Church of England, Doctrine Commission of the General Synod of the Church of England. "We Believe in God." In *Contemporary Doctrine Classics from the Church of England*, by the Doctrine Commission, 1–127: London: Church House, 2005. First published in 1987.
Cobb, John. *Christ in a Pluralistic Age*. Philadelphia: Westminster, 1975.
———. *A Christian Natural Theology*. London: Lutterworth, 1966.
Conway, Michael A. *The Science of Life: Maurice Blondel's Philosophy of Action and the Scientific Method*. Frankfurt: Peter Lang, 2000.
Coope, Ursula. "Aristotle." In *A Companion to the Philosophy of Action*, edited by Timothy O"Connor and Constantine Sandis, 439–45. Oxford: Wiley-Blackwell, 2013.
———. *Time for Aristotle: Physics IV. 10–14*. Oxford: Clarendon, 2005.
Coope, Ursula, and Christopher Shields. "Aristotle on Action." *Proceedings of the Aristotelian Society*, supplementary volumes, 81 (2007) 109–38.
Creed, J.M., and J.S. Boys Smith, eds. *Religious Thought in the Eighteenth Century*. Cambridge: Cambridge University Press, 1934.
Cuénot, Claude. *Teilhard de Chardin*. Monaco: Le Rocher, 1986. First published in 1958. (The short form reference will be Cuénot, *Teilhard de Chardin*.)
———. *Teilhard de Chardin*. Translated by Vincent Colimore. London: Burns and Oates, 1965. (The short form reference will be Cuénot, *Teilhard de Chardin* (Eng.).)
Curd, Patricia. *The Legacy of Parmenides: Eleatic Monism and Late Presocratic Thought*. Princeton NJ: Princeton University Press, 1998.
Dar, B.A. *A Study in Iqbal's Philosophy*. Lahore: Sheikh Muhammad Ashraf, 1944.
D'Armagnac, Christian. "La Pensée de Pierre Teilhard de Chardin comme Apologétique Moderne." In *Études Teilhardiennes: Sciences et Foi*, by Claude Cuénot, 61–90. Brussels: L'Association des Amis de Pierre Teilhard de Chardin Centre Bruges, 1968.
De Lubac, Henri. *Blondel et Teilhard de Chardin*. Paris: Beauchesne, 1965.
———. *La Pensée du Père Teilhard de Chardin*. Paris: Aubier, 1962.
———. *The Religion of Teilhard de Chardin*. Translated by René Hague from *La Pensée du Père Teilhard de Chardin*. London: Collins, 1967.

Diels, Hermann, and Walther Kranz. *Die Fragmente der Vorsokratiker*. Tenth edition. Berlin: Weidmann, 1952.

Dilcher, Roman. "How Not to Conceive Heraclitean Harmony." In *Doctrine and Doxography: Studies on Heraclitus and Pythagoras*, edited by David Sider and Dirk Obbink, 263–80. Berlin: De Gruyter, 2013.

Dorrien, Gary. *The Making of American Liberal Theology: Crisis, Irony and Postmodernity, 1950-2005*. Louisville: Westminster John Knox, 2006.

Drewer, Matthew. "Dorner's Critique of Divine Immutability." *Process Studies* 31 (1) (2002) 77–92.

Dupont, Christian. *Phenomenology in French Philosophy: Early Encounters*. Dordrecht: Springer, 2014.

Elliger, Karl, and Wilhelm Rudolph. *Biblia Hebraica Stuttgartensia: A Reader's Edition*. Peabody: Henrickson.

Ellis, George F.R. "Kenosis as a Unifying Theme for Life and Cosmology." In *The Work of Love: Creation as Kenosis*, edited by John Polkinghorne, 107–26. Grand Rapids: William B. Eerdmans, 2001.

Fabre, Jacques. "Les Niveaux du Réel et les Mécanismes de l'Évolution." In *Teilhard de Chardin, son Apport, son Actualité*, edited by Henri Madelin et al., 47–65. Paris: Éditions du Centurion, 1982.

Farraux, Paul. *Une Philosophie du Médiateur: Maurice Blondel*. Paris: Éditions Lethielleux, 1986.

Floridi, Luciano. *The Fourth Revolution: How the Infosphere is Reshaping Human Reality*. Oxford: Oxford University Press, 2014.

Forster, Michael. "Hegel's Dialectical Method." In *The Cambridge Companion to Hegel*, edited by Frederick C. Beiser, 130–70. Cambridge: Cambridge University Press, 1993.

Gallop, David. *Parmenides of Elea: Fragments: A Text and Translation*. Toronto: University of Toronto Press, 1984.

Gatliffe, David. "Jung and Teilhard de Chardin: Individualising the Collective Conscious." Unpublished essay, 2002.

Gill, Mary Louise. *Aristotle on Substance: The Paradox of Unity*. Princeton: Princeton University Press, 1989.

———. "Aristotle's Distinction between Change and Activity." *Axiomathes* 14 (1) (2004) 3–22.

Gouhier, Henri. *Bergson dans l'Histoire de la Pensée Occidentale*. Paris: Librairie Philosophique J. Vrin, 1989.

Graham, Daniel W. "Once More into the Stream." In *Doctrine and Doxography: Studies on Heraclitus and Pythagoras*, edited by David Sider and Dirk Obbink, 303–20. Berlin: De Gruyter, 2013.

Graham, Gordon. *Wittgenstein and Natural Religion*. Oxford: Oxford University Press, 2014.

Granger, Herbert. "Early Natural Theology: The Purification of the Divine Nature." In *Doctrine and Doxography: Studies on Heraclitus and Pythagoras*, edited by David Sider and Dirk Obbink, 163–200. Berlin: De Gruyter, 2013.

Gray, Donald. *The One and the Many: Teilhard de Chardin's Vision of Unity*. London: Burns and Oates, 1969.

Grayling, A.C.. *Wittgenstein*. Oxford: Oxford University Press, 1988.

———. "Metaphysics: Introduction." In *Philosophy: A Guide Through the Subject*, edited by A.C. Grayling, 183-48. Oxford: Oxford University Press, 1995.
Grenet, Paul. *Teilhard de Chardin: The Man and his Theories*. Translated by R.A. Rudorff. London: Souvenir, 1961.
Griffin, David Ray. *A Process Christology*. Philadelphia: Westminster, 1973.
Grundy, Michael. *A Fiery Glow in the Darkness: Woodbine Willie, Padre and Poet*. Worcester: Osborne, 1997.
Guyer, Paul. "Thought and Being: Hegel's Critique of Kant's Theoretical Philosophy." In *The Cambridge Companion to Hegel*, edited by Frederick Beiser, 171-210. Cambridge: Cambridge University Press, 1993.
Haarscher, Guy. *L'Ontologie de Marx*. Brussels: L'Édition le l'Université de Bruxelles, 1980.
Hamilton, Peter. *The Living God and the Modern World*. London: Hodder and Stoughton, 1967.
Hamlyn, D.W. *A History of Western Philosophy*. London: Penguin, 1987.
Hankinson, R.J. "Philosophy of Science." In *The Cambridge Companion to Aristotle*, edited by Jonathan Barnes, 109-39. Cambridge: Cambridge University Press, 1995.
Hanson, Anthony. "Ecclesia Quaerens: The Future of Christian Doctrine." In *Teilhard Reassessed*, edited by Anthony Hanson, 157-78. London: Darton, Longman and Todd, 1970.
Hare, R.M. "Plato." In *Greek Philosophers*, by C.C.W. Taylor et al., 103-90. Oxford: Oxford University Press, 1999.
Harris, H.A. "Hegel's Intellectual Development to 1807." In *The Cambridge Companion to Hegel*, edited by Frederick Beiser, 25-51. Cambridge: Cambridge University Press.
Hartshorne, Charles. *The Divine Relativity*. New Haven: Yale University Press, 1948.
———. *Man's Vision of God*. Hamden: Archon, 1964.
———. *A Natural Theology for our Time*. La Salle: Open Court, 1967.
Hegel, G.W.F. *Encyclopedia of Philosophical Sciences: The Logic*. www.marxists.org/reference/archive/hegel/works/sl/slbeing.htm#SL85.
———. *Enzyklopädie der Philosophischen Wissenschaften im Grundrisse*. www.hegel.de/werke_frei/startfree.html.
———. *Hegel's Phenomenology of Spirit*. Translated by A.V. Miller from *Phänomenologie des Geistes*. Oxford: Oxford University Press, 1977.
———. *Hegels Science of Logic*. Translated by A.V. Miller from *Wissenschaft der Logik*. London: George Allen and Unwin, 1969.
———. *Lectures on the History of Philosophy*. Translated by S. Haldane. https://www.marxists.org/reference/archive/hegel/works/hp/hpintroa.htm.
———. *Lectures on the Philosophy of Religion*. www.marxists.org/reference/archive/hegel/works/re/parta.htm.
———. *Phänomenologie des Geistes*, 1807. www.gwfhegel.org/PhenText/compare.html.
———. *Phenomenology of Mind*. Translated by J.B. Baillie from *Phänomenologie des Geistes*. www.gwfhegel.org/PhenText/compare.html.
———. *Vorlesungen über die Geschichte der Philosophie*, Werke in Zwanzig Bänden, Band 18, Frankfurt am Main, 1979. www.zeno.org/nid/20009182055.

———. *Vorlesungen über die Philosophie der Religion.* http://texte.phil-splitter.com/html/_religionsphilosophie_1.html.

———. *Wer Denkt Abstrakt?*, www.iim.uni-flensburg.de/soziologie/uploads/pdf/Downloads_Tamm/Hegel_Wer_denkt_abstrakt.pdf.

———. *Who Thinks Abstractly?* In *Hegel: Texts and Commentary*, edited by Walter Kaufman, 113–18. Garden City: Anchor, 1966. www.marxists.org/reference/archive/hegel/works/se/abstract.htm.

———. *Wissenschaft der Logik.* Project Gutenberg. http://projekt.gutenberg.de/buch/wissenschaft-der-logik-1653/1.

Heinaman, Robert. "Alteration and Aristotle's Activity-Change Distinction." *Oxford Studies in Ancient Philosophy* 16 (1998) 227–57.

———. "Is Aristotle's Definition of Change Circular?" *Apeiron* 27 (1) (1994) 25–37.

Heraclitus. *The Art and Thought of Heraclitus: An Edition of the Fragments with Translation and Commentary.* Translated by Charles H. Kahn from *Die Fragmente der Vorsokratiker*, edited by Hermann Diels and Walther Kranz. Cambridge: Cambridge University Press, 1979. (Fragments are numbered as in Hermann Diels and Walther Kranz, *Die Fragmente der Vorsokratiker*, tenth edition. Berlin: Weidmann, 1952.)

———. *Fragments.* Diels text. http://philoctetes.free.fr/uniheraclite.htm. (Fragments are numbered as in Hermann Diels and Walther Kranz, *Die Fragmente der Vorsokratiker*, tenth edition. Berlin: Weidmann, 1952.)

Hesiod. *The Theogony.* Translated by Hugh G. Evelyn-White, 1914. www.sacred-texts.com/cla/hesiod/theogony.htm.

Holman, Bob. *Woodbine Willie: An Unsung Hero of World War One.* Oxford: Lion, 2013.

Holt, Justin. *Karl Marx's Philosophy of Nature: A New Analysis.* Cambridge: Cambridge Scholars, 2009.

Hook, Sidney. *From Hegel to Marx.* Ann Arbor: University of Michigan Press, 1962.

Houlgate, Stephen. *Freedom, Truth and History: An Introduction to Hegel's Philosophy.* London and New York: Routledge, 1991.

Hülsz, Enrique. "Heraclitus on *Logos*: Language, Rationality, and the Real." In *Doctrine and Doxography: Studies on Heraclitus and Pythagoras*, edited by David Sider and Dirk Obbink, 281–301. Berlin: De Gruyter, 2013.

Hussey, Edward. "Heraclitus." In *The Cambridge Companion to Early Greek Philosophy*, edited by A.A. Long, 88–112. Cambridge: Cambridge University Press, 1999.

Hyppolite, John. *Studies on Marx and Hegel.* London: Heinemann, 1969.

Iqbal, Muhammad. "Bāl-i Jibrīl," Lahore: 1936. Translated by B.A. Dar, and quoted in "Inspiration from the West," by B.A. Dar, in *Iqbal: Poet-Philosopher of Pakistan*, edited by Hafeez Malik, 187–202. New York: Colombia University Press, 202.

———. "The Quest," July 1920. Translated by R.A. Nicholson, and quoted in *The Secrets of the Self: A Muslim Poet's Interpretation of Vitalism*, by R.A. Nicholson, Lahore: 1961, 23–24; requoted in "Inspiration from the West," by B.A. Dar, in *Iqbal: Poet-philosopher of Pakistan*, edited by Hafeez Malik, 187–202. New York: Colombia University Press, 199.

———. *Six Lectures on the Reconstruction of Religious Thought in Islam.* Lahore: Kapur Art Printing Works, 1930.

Irwin, Terence. *Classical Thought.* Oxford: Oxford University Press, 1989.

James, William. *The Varieties of Religious Experience.* New York: Longmans, Green, 1902.

Jankélévitch, Vladimir. "Bergson and Judaism." In *Bergson, Politics, and Religion*, edited by Alexandre Lefebvre and Melanie White, 217–45. Durham and London: Duke University Press, 2012.

Jeffs, Ernest H. *Princes of the Modern Pulpit: Religious Leaders of a Generation*. London: Sampson, Low, Marston, 1931.

Johansen, Thomas Keller. *Plato's Natural Philosophy: A Study of the* Timaeus-Critias. Cambridge: Cambridge University Press, 2004.

Jordan, L. "Heraclitus' Discursive Authority." *Akroteron* 49 (0) (2004) 57–64. http://akroterion.journals.ac.za/pub/article/view/87.

Justin Martyr. "First and Second Apologies." In *The Apostolic Fathers with Justin Martyr and Irenaeus*, in *The Ante-Nicene Fathers*, edited by Cleveland Cox. Grand Rapids: Eerdmans, 1977.

Kahn, Charles H. *The Art and Thought of Heraclitus: An Edition of the Fragments with Translation and Commentary*. Cambridge: Cambridge University Press, 1979.

Kant, Immanuel. *The Critique of Pure Reason*. Translated by J.M.D. Meiklejohn from *Kritik der Reinen Vernunft*. Project Gutenberg, http://onlinebooks.library.upenn.edu/webbin/gutbook/lookup?num=4280.

———. *Kritik der Reinen Vernunft*. Project Gutenberg. First published in 1781. www.gutenberg.org/cache/epub/6342/pg6342.html.

Kedourie, Elie. *Hegel and Marx: Introductory Lectures*. Oxford: Blackwell, 1995.

Kenny, Anthony. *Aquinas on Being*. Oxford: Clarendon, 2002.

Kerr, Fergus. *Theology after Wittgenstein*. Oxford: Basic Blackwell, 1986.

Kleinbach, Russell L. *Marx via Process: Whitehead's Potential Contribution to Marxist Social Theory*. Washington DC: University Press of America, 1982.

Kolakowski, Leszek. *Bergson*. Oxford: Oxford University Press, 1985.

Kosman, L.A. "Aristotle"s Definition of Motion." *Phronesis* 14 (1) (1969) 40–62.

Kostman, James. "Aristotle's Definition of Change." *History of Philosophy Quarterly* 4 (1) (1987) 3–16.

Kraus, Elizabeth. *The Metaphysics of Experience: A Companion to Whitehead's* Process and Reality. New York: Fordham University Press, 1979.

Kreps, David. *Bergson, Complexity and Creative Emergence*. Basingstoke: Palgrave Macmillan, 2015.

Kretzmann, Norman. "Philosophy of Mind." In *The Cambridge Companion to Aquinas*, edited by Norman Kretzmann and Eleonore Stump, 128–59. Cambridge: Cambridge University Press, 1993.

Krizan, Mary. "Substantial Change and the Limiting Case of Aristotelian Matter." *History of Philosophy Quarterly* 30 (4) (2013) 293–310.

Kuhn, Thomas S. *The Structure of Scientific Revolutions*. Chicago: Chicago University Press, 1962.

Laitinen, Arto, and Constantine Sandis, eds. *Hegel and Action*. Basingstoke: Palgrave Macmillan, 2010

Lawson-Tancred, Hugh. "Ancient Greek Philosophy II: Aristotle." In *Philosophy: A Guide Through the Subject*, edited by A.C. Grayling, 398–439. Oxford: Oxford University Press, 1995.

Lear, Jonathan. *Aristotle: The Desire to Understand*. New York: Cambridge University Press, 1988.

Le Grys, James. "The Christianization of Modern Philosophy according to Maurice Blondel." *Theological Studies* 54 (3) (1993) 455–84.

Leibniz, Gottfried. "Monadology." In *Classics of Western Philosophy*, edited by Steven M. Cahn, 662–69. Indianapolis: Hackett, 1977.
Levinas, Emmanuel. *Éthique Comme Philosophie Première*. Paris: Payot et Rivages, 1998.
———. *Le Temps et L'Autre*. Paris: Quadrige/Presses Universitaires de Paris, 1991.
———. *Time and the Other*. Translated by Richard A. Cohen. Pittsburgh: Duquesne University Press, 1987.
———. *Totalité et Infini: Essai sur l'Extériorité*. La Haye: Martinus Nijhoff, 1961.
———. *Totality and Infinity: An Essay on Exteriority*. Translated by Alphonso Lingis. The Hague: Mijhoff, 1969.
Liddell, Henry George, and Robert Scott. *An Intermediate Greek-English Lexicon*. Oxford: Clarendon, 1889.
Lindsay, A.D. *The Philosophy of Bergson*. London: J.M. Dent and Sons, 1911.
Long, Anthony A. "Heraclitus on Measure and the Explicit Emergence of Rationality." In *Doctrine and Doxography: Studies on Heraclitus and Pythagoras*, edited by David Sider and Dirk Obbink, 201–23. Berlin: De Gruyter, 2013.
Longuenesse, Béatrice. *Hegel's Critique of Metaphysics*. Translated by Nicole J. Simek. Cambridge: Cambridge University Press, 2007.
Longton, Ryan A. "A Reconsideration of Maurice Blondel and the 'Natural' Desire." *The Heythrop Journal* 56 (6) (2015) 919–30.
Lyons, J.A. *The Cosmic Christ in Origen and Teilhard de Chardin*. Oxford: Oxford University Press, 1982.
Marx, Karl. *Capital*, volume 1. Translated by Samuel Moore and Edward Aveling from *Das Kapital*. Edited by Frederick Engels. Moscow: Progress Publishers, 1887. https://www.marxists.org/archive/marx/works/1867-c1/.
———. *A Contribution to the Critique of Political Economy*. Translated by S.W. Ryazanskaya from *Zur Kritik der Politischen Ökonomie*. Moscow: Progress Publishers, 1977. https://www.marxists.org/archive/marx/works/1859/critique-pol-economy.
———. *Economic and Philosophic Manuscripts*. Translated by Martin Mulligan from *Ökonomisch-philosophische Manuskripte*. Moscow: Progress Publishers, 1959. https://www.marxists.org/archive/marx/works/1844/manuscripts/labour.htm.
———. *Das Kapital*. Berlin: Dietz Verlag, 1968. First published in 1867.
———. *Ökonomisch-Philosophische Manuskripte*. Berlin: Dietz Verlag, 1968. First published in 1844. http://www.mlwerke.de/me/me40/me40_510.htm.
———. *Zur Kritik der Politischen Ökonomie*. Berlin: Franz Duncker, 1859. http://www.mlwerke.de/me/me13/me13_007.htm.
Marx, Karl and Friedrich Engels. *Die Deutsche Ideologie: Kritik der Neuesten Deutschen Philosophie in Ihren Repräsentanten: Feuerbach, B. Bauer und Stirner und des Deutschen Sozialismus in Seinen Verschiedenen Propheten*. Moscow: Marx-Engels-Lenin Institut, 1932. Originally written in 1845. http://www.mlwerke.de/me/me03/me03_017.htm#I_I_A.
———. *The German Ideology*. Translated from *Die Deutsche Ideologie*. Moscow: Progress Publishers, 1968. https://www.marxists.org/archive/marx/works/1845/german-ideology/ch01a.htm.
Melling, David J. *Understanding Plato*. Oxford: Oxford University Press, 1987.
Mitchell, Arthur. *Studies in Bergson's Philosophy*. Volume 1, no. 2, of the Bulletin of the University of Kansas Humanities Studies. Lawrence: University of Kansas, 1914.

Mitchell, Basil. *The Justification of Religious Belief.* London and Basingstoke: Macmillan, 1973.
Moltmann, Jürgen. *The Crucified God.* Translated by R.A. Wilson and John Bowden from *Das Gekreuzigte Gott.* London: SCM, 1974.
———. *Das Gekreuzigte Gott.* Munich: Chr. Kaiser, 1973.
———. "God's kenosis in the creation and consummation of the world." In *The Work of Love: Creation as Kenosis,* edited by John Polkinghorne, 137–51. Grand Rapids: William B. Eerdmans, 2001.
Monk, Ray. *Ludwig Wittgenstein.* London: Jonathan Cape, 1990.
Mooney, Christopher F. *Teilhard de Chardin and the Mystery of Christ.* London: Collins, 1966.
Moscovici, Serge. "Toward a Theory of Conversion Behavior." In *Advances in Experimental Social Psychology,* vol. 13, edited by Leonard Berkowitz, 209–39. New York: Academic, 1980.
Mourelatos, Alexander P.D. *The Route of Parmenides.* New Haven and London: Yale University Press, 1970.
Mozley, J.K.. "Studdert Kennedy: Home Life and Early Years of his Ministry." In *G.A. Studdert Kennedy by his Friends,* edited by J.K. Mozley, 13–83. London: Hodder and Stoughton, 1929.
Muers, Rachel, and Mike Higton, *Modern Theology: A Critical Introduction.* London: Routledge, 2012.
Mullarkey, John. *Bergson and Philosophy.* Edinburgh: Edinburgh University Press, 1999.
Oliver, Simon. *Philosophy, God and Motion.* Abingdon: Routledge, 2005.
Opsomer, Jan. "Proclus on Demiurgy and Procession: A Neoplatonic Reading of the *Timaeus*." In *Reason and Necessity: Essays on Plato's* Timaeus, edited by M.R. Wright, 113–43. London: Duckworth, 2000.
Owen, G.E.L. Review of *Heraclitus* by Philip Wheelwright. *Analytical Philosophy* 1 (3) (1960) 19.
Pailin, David. *God and the Processes of Reality.* London: Routledge, 1989.
———. *Probing the Foundations: A Study in Theistic Reconstruction.* Pharos: Kampen, 1994.
———. "The Supposedly Historical Basis of Theological Understanding." In *The Making and Remaking of Christian Doctrine: Essays in Honour of Maurice Wiles,* edited by David Pailin and Sarah Coakley, 213–38. Oxford: Clarendon, 1993.
Panayides, Christos Y. "Heraclitus and the Theory of Flux." *Skepsis* 19 (1–2) (2008) 251–70.
Papanicolaou, Andrew, and Peter A. Y. Gunter, eds. *Bergson and Modern Thought: Towards a Unified Science.* Chur: Harwood Academic Publications, 1987.
Parker, Linda. *A Seeker after Truths: The Life and Times of G.A. Studdert Kennedy ("Woodbine Willie") 1883–1929.* Solihull: Helion, 2018.
Parmenides. *Fragments.* http://philoctetes.free.fr/parmenidesunicode.htm. Diels text with John Burnet's 1892 translation. Fragments are numbered as in Hermann Diels and Walther Kranz, *Die Fragmente der Vorsokratiker,* 10th edition, Berlin, 1952. http://philoctetes.free.fr/parmenidesunicode.htm
Pattison, George *A Short Course in Christian Doctrine.* London: SCM, 2005.
Peirce, C.S. *Collected Papers,* volumes 5 and 6. Cambridge, Massachusetts: The Bellknap Press of the Harvard University Press, 1935.

Pellikan-Engel, Maja E. *Hesiod and Parmenides: A New View on their Cosmologies and on Parmenides' Proem*. Amsterdam: Verlag Adolf M. Hakkert, 1978.

Perl, Eric D. *Thinking Being: Introduction to Metaphysics in the Classical Tradition*. Leiden: Brill, 2014.

Pippin, Robert B. "You Can't Get There from Here: Transition Problems in Hegel's *Phenomenology of Spirit*." In *The Cambridge Companion to Hegel*, edited by Frederick Beiser, 52–85. Cambridge: Cambridge University Press, 1993.

Pittenger, Norman. *Alfred North Whitehead*. London: Lutterworth, 1969.

———. *Christology Reconsidered*. London: SCM, 1970.

———. *Cosmic Love and Human Wrong: The Meaning of Sin in the Light of Process Thinking*. New York: Paulist, 1978.

———. *The Divine Trinity*. Philadelphia: United Church, 1977.

———. *God in Process*. London: SCM, 1967.

———. *Loving Says It All*. New York: Pilgrim, 1978.

———. *The Lure of Divine Love: Human Experience and Christian Faith in a Process Perspective*. Edinburgh: T and T Clark, 1979.

———. *Process Thought and Christian Faith*. Welwyn: Nisbet, 1968.

Plato. *Cratylus*. In *Platonis Opera*, edited by John Burnet. Oxford: Oxford University Press, 1903. English translation from *Plato in Twelve Volumes*, vol. 12, translated by Harold N. Fowler, Cambridge, Massachusetts: Harvard University Press, and London: William Heinemann, 1921. www.perseus.tufts.edu/Texts/chunk_TOC.grk.html.

———. *Euthyphro*. In *Platonis Opera*, edited by John Burnet. Oxford: Oxford University Press, 1903, English translation from *Plato in Twelve Volumes*, vol. 1, translated by Harold North Fowler. Cambridge, Massachusetts: Harvard University Press, and London: William Heinemann, 1967. www.perseus.tufts.edu/Texts/chunk_TOC.grk.html.

———. *Meno*. In *Platonis Opera*, edited by John Burne. Oxford: Oxford University Press, 1903. English translation from *Plato in Twelve Volumes*, vol. 3, translated by W.R.M. Lamb. Cambridge, MA: Harvard University Press, and London: William Heinemann, 1967. www.perseus.tufts.edu/Texts/chunk_TOC.grk.html.

———. *Parmenides*. In *Platonis Opera*, edited by John Burnet. Oxford: Oxford University Press, 1903. English translation from *Plato in Twelve Volumes*, vol. 9, translated by Harold N. Fowler. Cambridge, Massachusetts: Harvard University Press, and London: William Heinemann, 1925. www.perseus.tufts.edu/Texts/chunk_TOC.grk.html.

———. *Phaedo*. In *Platonis Opera*, edited by John Burnet. Oxford: Oxford University Press, 1903. English translation from *Plato in Twelve Volumes*, vol. 1, translated by Harold North Fowler. Introduction by W.R.M. Lamb. Cambridge, Massachusetts: Harvard University Press, and London: William Heinemann, 1966. www.perseus.tufts.edu/Texts/chunk_TOC.grk.html.

———. *Republic*. In *Platonis Opera*, edited by John Burnet. Oxford: Oxford University Press, 1903. English translation from *Plato in Twelve Volumes*, vols. 5 and 6, translated by Paul Shorey. Cambridge, Massachusetts: Harvard University Press, and London: William Heinemann, 1969. www.perseus.tufts.edu/Texts/chunk_TOC.grk.html.

———. *Sophist*. In *Platonis Opera*, edited by John Burnet. Oxford: Oxford University Press, 1903. English translation from *Plato in Twelve Volumes*, vol. 12, translated by Harold N. Fowler. Cambridge, Massachusetts: Harvard University Press, and London: William Heinemann, 1921. www.perseus.tufts.edu/Texts/chunk_TOC.grk.html.

———. *Timaeus*. In *Platonis Opera*, edited by John Burnet. Oxford: Oxford University Press, 1903. English translation from *Plato in Twelve Volumes*, vol. 9, translated by W.R.M. Lamb. Cambridge, Massachusetts: Harvard University Press, and London: William Heinemann, 1925. www.perseus.tufts.edu/Texts/chunk_TOC.grk.html.

Plotinus. *The Six Enneads*, Greek text, http://remacle.org/bloodwolf/philosophes/plotin/enneade55gr.htm; English translation by Stephen McKenna and B.S. Page, http://www.sacred-texts.com/cla/plotenn/index.htm.

Polkinghorne, John. *Science and Creation: The Search for Understanding*. Boston: New Science Library, 1989.

Prince, Brian David. "Physical Change in Plato's *Timaeus*." *Apeiron* 47 (2) (2014) 211–29.

Prior, Arthur N. "Changes in Events and Changes in Things." In *The Philosophy of Time*, edited by Robin Le Poidevin and Murray MacBeath, 35–46. Oxford: Oxford University Press, 1993.

Purcell, William. *Woodbine Willie: A Study of Geoffrey Studdert Kennedy*, second edition. London: Mowbray, 1982.

Raven, Charles E. *Teilhard de Chardin: Scientist and Seer*. London: Collins, 1962.

Reames, Robin. "Heraclitus, Material Language, and Rhetoric." *Philosophy and Rhetoric* 46 (3) (2013) 328–50.

Rescher, Nicholas. *Process Metaphysics: An Introduction to Process Philosophy*. Albany: State University of New York, 1996.

———. *Process Philosophy: A Survey of Basic Issues*. Pittsburgh: University of Pittsburgh Press, 2000.

Rideau, Emile. *La Pensée du Père Teilhard de Chardin*. Paris: Éditions du Seuil, 1965.

———. *Teilhard de Chardin: A Guide to his Thought*. Translated by René Hague from *La Pensée du Père Teilhard de Chardin*. London: Collins, 1967.

Robinson, John. *Exploration into God*. London: SCM Press, 1967.

Robinson, Thomas M.. "Heraclitus and *Logos*—Again." *Schole* 7 (2) (2013) 318–26.

Robjant, David. "Nauseating Flux: Iris Murdoch on Sartre and Heraclitus." *European Journal of Philosophy* 22 (4) (2014) 633–52.

Rocine, B.M. *Learning Biblical Hebrew: A New Approach Using Discourse Analysis*. Macon: Smyth and Helwys, 2000.

Romero, Gustavo E. "Parmenides Reloaded." *Foundations of Science* 17 (3) (2012) 291–99.

Russell, Bertrand. *Our Knowledge of the External World*. London: George Allen and Unwin, 1922. First published in 1914.

———. *The Problems of Philosophy*. Oxford and New York: Oxford University Press, 1967. First published in 1912.

Sainsbury, R.M. *Russell*. London, Boston and Henley: Routledge and Kegan Paul, 1979.

Saint-Sernin, Bertrand. *Blondel: Un Univers Chrétien*. Paris: Librairie Philosophique J. Vrin, 2009.

Saunders, Trevor J. "Introduction." In Plato, *Early Socratic Dialogues*, London: Penguin, 1987.

Scharfstein, Ben-Ami. *Roots of Bergson's Philosophy*. New York: Columbia University Press, 1987.

Schindler, D. C. "The Community of the One and the Many: Heraclitus on Reason." *Inquiry: An Interdisciplinary Journal of Philosophy* 46 (4) (2003) 413–48.

Schmidt am Busch, Hans-Christoph. "What Does it Mean to 'Make Oneself Into an Object'? In Defense of a Key Notion of Hegel's Theory of Action." In *Hegel and Action*, edited by Arto Laitinen and Constantine Sandis,189–211. Basingstoke: Palgrave Macmillan, 2010.

Sedley, David. "Parmenides and Melissus." In *The Cambridge Companion to Early Greek Philosophy*, edited by A.A. Long, 113–33. Cambridge: Cambridge University Press, 1999.

Segvic, Heda. "Aristotle's Metaphysics of Action." *Philosophiegeschichte und Logische Analyse/Logical Analysis and History of Philosophy* 5 (2002) 23–55.

Sherry, Patrick. *Religion, Truth and Language Games*. London and Basingstoke: Macmillan, 1977.

Singer, Peter. *Hegel: A Very Short Introduction*. Oxford: Oxford University Press, 1983.

———. *Marx: A Very Short Introduction*. Oxford: Oxford University Press, 1980.

Slocum, Robert B. "Geoffrey Studdert Kennedy ('Woodbine Willie'): The Crucified God." *Modern Believing* 58 (3) (2017) 217–42.

Soll, Ivan. *An Introduction to Hegel's Metaphysics*. Chicago: University of Chicago Press, 1969.

Somerville, James M. *Total Commitment: Blondel's L'Action*. Washington, Cleveland: Corpus, 1968.

Speight, Allen. *The Philosophy of Hegel*. Montreal and Kingston: McGill-Queen's University Press, 2008.

Speaight, Robert. *Teilhard de Chardin: A Biography*. London: Collins, 1967.

Studdert Kennedy, G.A. *The Hardest Part*. London: Hodder and Stoughton, 1919.

———. *Peace Rhymes of a Padre*. London: Hodder and Stoughton, 1920.

———. *Rough Rhymes of a Padre*. London: Hodder and Stoughton, 1918.

———. *Rough Talks by a Padre*. London: Hodder and Stoughton, 1918.

———. *Songs of Faith and Doubt*. London: Hodder and Stoughton, 1922.

———. *The Sorrows of God and Other Poems*. London: Hodder and Stoughton, 1921.

———. *The Unutterable Beauty*. London: Hodder and Stoughton, fourteenth edition, 1941.

———. *The Word and the Work*. London: Longmans, Green, 1925.

Tarán, Leonardo. *Parmenides: A Text with Translation, Commentary, and Critical Essays*. Princeton: Princeton University Press, 1965.

Teilhard de Chardin, Pierre. *L'Avenir de l'Homme*. Paris: Éditions du Seuil, 1959.

———. *Christianity and Evolution*. London: Collins, 1971.

———. *Le Coeur de la Matière*. Paris: Éditions du Seuil, 1976. First published in 1950.

———. *Comment Je Crois*. Paris: Éditions du Seuil, 1969.

———. *L'Énergie Humaine*. Paris: Éditions du Seuil, 1962.

———. *The Future of Man*. Translated by Norman Denny from *L'Avenir de l'Homme*. London: Collins, 1969.

———. *The Human Energy*. Translated by J.M. Cohen from *L'Énergie Humaine*. London: Collins, 1969.

———. *Hymn of the Universe*. Translated by Gerald Vann from parts of *Le Coeur de la Matière*. London: Fontana/Collins, 1965.

———. *The Making of a Mind*. Translated by René Hague. London: Collins, 1965.

———. "La Masse sur le Monde." In *Le Coeur de la Matière*, 139–56. Paris: Éditions du Seuil, 1976.

———. *Le Milieu Divin*. Paris: Éditions du Seuil, 1957. (The short form reference of the original French *Le Milieu Divin* will be Teilhard de Chardin, *Le Milieu Divin*.)

———. *Le Milieu Divin*. Translated by Bernard Wall from *Le Milieu Divin*. London: Fontana/Collins, 1964. This English translation retained the original French title. Some other translations have employed the title *The Divine Milieu*. (The short form reference for the English translation will be Teilhard de Chardin, *Le Milieu Divin* (Eng.).)

———. *Le Phénomène Humain*. Paris: Éditions du Seuil, 1955.

———. *The Phenomenon of Man*. Translated by Bernard Wall from *Le Phénomène Humain*. London: Fontana/Collins, 1970. Subsequent editions were published under the title *The Human Phenomenon*.

———. *Writings in Time of War*. Translated by René Hague. London: Collins, 1968.

Teilhard de Chardin, Pierre and Maurice Blondel. *Correspondence*. Translated by William Whitman. New York: Herder and Herder, 1967.

Thompson, Melvyn R.. *A Critical Analysis of the Problem of Action in the Writings of Teilhard de Chardin*. Unpublished Ph.D. thesis, King's College, London, 1979.

Torry, Malcolm. "Action, Patterns and Religious Pluralism." *Theology* 106 (830) (2003) 107–18.

———. "Being and Doing: The Priest in the Parish." In *The Parish: People, Place and Ministry: A Theological and Practical Exploration*, edited by Malcolm Torry, 160–71. Norwich: Canterbury, 2004.

———. "Introduction." In J.S. Boys Smith, *The Sermons of John Boys Smith: A Theologian of Integrity*, edited and with an introduction by Malcolm Torry, 1–35. Cambridge: Aquila, for St. John's College, Cambridge, 2003.

———. "'Logic' and 'Action': Two New Readings of the New Testament." *Theology* 111 (860) (2008) 93–101.

———. "A Neglected Theologian: John Sandwith Boys Smith." *Theology* 107 (836) (2004) 89–104.

———. "On Completing the Apologetic Spectrum." *Theology* 103 (812) (2000) 108–15.

———. "Testing Torry's model." *Theology* 109 (851) (2006) 343–52.

———. "'Universal' and 'Unconditional': Definitions and applications." A paper prepared for the Federation for International Social Security Studies at Sigtuna, Sweden, in June 2017.

Towers, Bernard. *Concerning Teilhard, and Other Writings on Science and Religion*. London: Collins, 1969.

Tredennick, Hugh. "Introduction." In Plato, *The Last Days of Socrates*, translated and with an introduction by Hugh Tredennick, second edition. Harmondsworth: Penguin, 1959.

Trivasse, Keith M. "May the Prophet Muhammad Be a Prophet to Christianity?" *Theology* 107 (840) (2004) 418–26.

Van Parys, SJ, Jean-Marie. *La Vocation de la Liberté*. Louvain: Béatrice-Nauwelaerts, 1968.

Virgoulay, René. *L'Action de Maurice Blondel, 1893: Relecture pour un Centenaire*. Paris: Beauchesne, 1992.

Walker, Michael. "Romantic Love, Covenantal Love, Kenotic Love." In *The Work of Love: Creation as Kenosis*, edited by John Polkinghorne, 127–36. Grand Rapids: William B. Eerdmans, 2001.
Wartenberg, Thomas E. "Hegel's Idealism: The Logic of Conceptuality." In *The Cambridge Companion to Hegel*, edited by Frederick C. Beiser, 102–29. Cambridge: Cambridge University Press, 1993.
Waterlow, Sarah. *Nature, Change, and Agency in Aristotle's Physics*. Oxford: Clarendon, 1982.
Wedin, Michael V. *Parmenides' Grand Deduction: A Logical Reconstruction of the Way of Truth*. Oxford: Oxford University Press, 2014.
Weiss, Paul. "Nature, God and Man." In *Existence and Actuality: Conversations with Charles Hartshorne*, edited by John B. Cobb and Franklin I. Gamwell, 113–21. Chicago: University of Chicago Press, 1984.
Weyl, Hermann. *Philosophy of Mathematics and Natural Science*. New York: Atheneum, 1963.
Whitehead, Alfred North. *Adventures of Ideas*. Cambridge: Cambridge University Press, 1933.
———. *The Concept of Nature*. Cambridge: Cambridge University Press, 1964. First published in 1920.
———. *Process and Reality*. New York: Macmillan, 1929.
———. *Process and Reality: Corrected Edition*. Edited by Ray Griffin and Donald W. Sherburne. New York: The Free Press, 1978.
———. *Religion in the Making*. New York: Macmillan, 1926.
———. *Symbolism*. Cambridge: Cambridge University Press, 1927.
Whyte, Lancelot Law. *Accent on Form: An Anticipation of the Science of Tomorrow*. London: Routledge and Kegan Paul, 1955.
———. *The Unitary Principle in Physics and Biology*. London: The Cresset Press, 1949.
Wildiers, N.M. *An Introduction to Teilhard de Chardin*. Translated by H. Hoskins. London: Fontana/Collins, 1968.
Williams, Howard. *Hegel, Heraclitus and Marx's Dialectic*. Hemel Hempstead: Harvester Wheatsheaf, 1989.
Williams, Rowan. *The Edge of Words: God and the Habits of Language*. London: Bloomsbury, 2014.
Wippel, John F. "Being." In *The Oxford Handbook of Aquinas*, edited by Brian Davies. Oxford: Oxford University Press, 2012. www.oxfordhandbooks.com/view/10.1093/oxfordhb/9780195326093.001.0001/oxfordhb-9780195326093.
———. "Metaphysics." In *The Cambridge Companion to Aquinas*, edited by Norman Kretzmann and Eleonore Stump, 85–127. Cambridge: Cambridge University Press, 1993.
———. "Thomas Aquinas and the Axiom That Unreceived Act Is Unlimited." *The Review of Metaphysics* 51 (3) (1998) 533–64.
Wittgenstein, Ludwig. *Philosophische Untersuchungen / Philosophical Investigations*. The German text with a revised English translation, third edition. Translated by G.E.M. Anscombe. Oxford: Basil Blackwell, 2001. The first edition was published in 1953. Wittgenstein divided the first part of the *Philosophical Investigations* into paragraphs (so both paragraph and page numbers are given), but not the second part (so when the second part is quoted, only page numbers are given.)

———. *Tractatus Logico-Philosophicus*. German text, with English translation by C.K. Ogden. London: Routledge, 1990. First published in German in 1921, and in English in 1922. References give Wittgenstein's paragraph numbers followed by the page numbers after the colon.

———. *Über Gewissheit / On Certainty*. The German text with an English translation. Edited by G.E.M. Anscombe and G.H. von Wright. English translation by Denis Paul and G.E.M. Anscombe. Oxford: Basil Blackwell, 1969. References give Wittgensteins paragraph numbers.

Wood, Allen W. "Hegel and Marxism." In *The Cambridge Companion to Hegel*, edited by Frederick C. Beiser, 414–44. Cambridge: Cambridge University Press, 1993.

Xenophanes. *Elegy and Iambus*. Greek text, with an English translation by J. M. Edmonds (amended). Cambridge, Massachusetts: Harvard University Press, and London: William Heinemann, 1931. www.perseus.tufts.edu/Texts/chunk_TOC.grk.html.

Yeomans, Christopher. *The Expansion of Autonomy: Hegel's Pluralistic Philosophy of action*. Oxford: Oxford University Press, 2015.

Žižek, Slavoj. *Less than Nothing: Hegel and the Shadow of Dialectical Materialism*. London: Verso, 2012.

Index

Absolute, the, 80–84, 87, 89–93, 95, 99, 101, 108–9, 172, 205, 213
abstraction, 4–6, 10–11, 13–16, 79, 84, 123, 128, 149, 152, 154, 160, 170, 207, 214
accident, 61–63, 78, 191
act (verb), 3–4, 10–13, 16, 101, 104–5, 110, 112–13, 144, 164, 213
action, viii, xi–xii, 1–18, 20–21, 26, 29–32, 34–36, 37–38, 46–49, 58–59, 62–63, 66–70, 73–79, 81–83, 87–88, 90–91, 100–101, 102–7, 109–113, 115, 118, 122–23, 126–29, 131–33, 137, 139–40, 142–44, 147, 149, 157–59, 162, 166, 171–75, 182, 187–88, 189, 193–98, 204, 208–18
    human, 66–67, 75, 87–88, 100–101, 104, 106, 109, 112, 117, 131, 143–44, 170, 190, 195
Action, viii, 6–7, 12–16, 19, 20–21, 28–29, 34–36, 45, 69, 76, 78–79, 103, 106, 110–13, 149, 159, 161–62, 165, 174–75, 188, 209–14, 216–18
action(s) in changing patterns, xii, 1–2, 18–19, 29, 127, 133–34, 149, 157, 159, 162, 175, 189, 192, 198, 209, 214, 216
action(s) in patterns, viii, ix, xi–xii, 1, 4, 13–19, 21, 36, 41, 43–44, 48–49, 52, 66, 69, 79, 81–82, 87–88, 90–92, 100–101, 109, 111, 113, 126–29, 134, 140, 149, 156–59, 161, 166, 171–75, 189, 192, 196–98, 209, 211–18
activity, 14, 16, 48, 58–59, 62–63, 66, 68, 76, 81–82, 91, 96–97, 100–101, 104, 106, 138, 151–52, 157–58, 161, 165, 170–71, 173, 184, 191–92, 195–97, 209
actology, 16, 20–21, 70, 76, 79, 101, 103, 112–13, 124, 157–58, 188, 210, 212, 214, 217–18
actual, actuality, 16, 56–59, 63–68, 70–71, 73–77, 82, 88, 93–94, 138, 155–56, 160, 166, 169, 212
actual entity, 153–56, 160–61, 163, 168–69
actual occasion, 153, 161
actus (actuality), 74–76
adjective, 4, 7, 43
air, 30–31, 33, 52, 55
alienation, 96–97, 100
ambiguity, 25, 31, 67, 90
analogy, 41–42, 71–73, 75–79, 120, 122, 141, 147, 163, 178, 196
Anaximenes, 30
animals, 5, 52–55, 201
Anselm, 94

238 INDEX

apologetics, viii–ix, 135, 141, 148–49, 174
appearances, 86, 107–8, 145, 151,
Aquinas, Thomas, 19, 37, 70–79, 109, 170, 212, 216
argument, 22, 28, 33–34, 38, 40, 51–52, 71, 75–85, 89, 94–95, 106, 108, 118, 134, 213, 217
Aristotle, 16, 19, 25, 28, 30, 36, 37, 49–71, 76–79, 103, 127, 151, 153, 156–57, 212
assimilation, 201, 206
atom, 33, 53, 123, 146, 173, 190
Atomists, 33
Auschwitz, 172
authority (recognised), 9–10, 29
autonomy, 9, 29, 104, 112, 138, 197–98
    See also heteronomy
axiom, 18, 101, 202, 217

Barth, Karl, 201
beauty, 39, 170, 184, 196
Beauty, Form of, 39–40, 48, 78
becoming, 16–17, 32, 39, 46–48, 57, 60–61, 65, 70, 72–77, 82–87, 90–91, 107=13, 118–19, 147–48, 152, 154–55, 157, 169–72, 203, 212–13
being, viii, 6–7, 12–19, 21–22, 24–29, 32–38, 41, 45–51, 53–54, 58–60, 62–63, 65–70, 72–76, 78–79, 83–87, 91, 94–100, 102–3, 106–12, 115, 124, 126, 129–34, 136, 140, 143, 146, 149, 151–52, 156, 162–63, 169–75, 182, 188, 192, 210–12, 214, 216–18
    human, vii, 28, 54, 65, 72, 91, 96–100, 103, 105, 133, 192. See also humanity
    See also ón, tò (being)
Being, viii, 7, 12–15, 17, 19, 21–23, 28–29, 34–36, 45, 48, 50, 59–60, 65, 68–69, 76, 78, 83, 90, 92, 106–7, 109–13, 124, 169, 172, 175, 188, 210, 213, 216–18
    supreme, 134, 165, 169
belief, 39, 42, 164, 166, 201, 206, 208

Bergson, Henri, 18, 36, 107, 112, 114–30, 132–33, 136, 139, 143, 152, 156, 204, 207, 209, 214, 216
Bible, 160, 184
biology, 67, 115, 124, 132–33, 148, 201, 204
biosphere, 133–3, 140, 142
Blondel, Maurice, 12, 70, 102–13, 128–29, 132, 143–44, 147, 204, 209, 211, 213–14, 216
body, 5, 27, 40, 48, 52, 54–55, 60, 71, 75, 77, 100, 105, 118, 120, 138, 142, 151, 178, 183, 187, 202
Body of Christ, 142
Boys Smith, John, viii, 101, 161, 189, 199–209, 213, 215–16
Bultmann, Rudolf, 206

capitalism, 96–100
Carr, H. Wilden, 123–24
categories, 7–12, 18–19, 50, 52, 54, 59, 61, 68, 70, 76–78, 86, 89, 91–92, 103, 112, 125, 151, 154, 156–57, 168, 171, 174, 192, 213, 217
cause, 6, 32, 41, 44, 49–50, 55–58, 65–67, 70–73, 75, 100, 107, 109, 112, 124, 134, 139, 147, 151, 171, 182, 184, 213
cave analogy, 42
certainty, 86–91
change, vii–xii, 1, 4–22, 25–30, 32–39, 42, 45–49, 54–72, 77–79, 82, 84, 96–98, 100–103, 107–8, 110–19, 121–23, 125–30, 133–34, 140, 151–53, 156–59, 161, 166, 169–71, 173–75, 182, 188–89, 191–92, 195, 197–98, 200–202, 204–13, 216–18
changeless, 34, 46–47, 78, 159, 188
    See also unchanging
chaos/chaotic, xi–xii, 9, 14, 21, 35, 66, 100, 149, 156, 159, 211, 214
characteristics, 8–10, 14, 17–18, 23–25, 27, 30, 38–40, 43, 50–51, 58, 82, 133, 153, 172, 202

Christian doctrine, viii, 92–93, 115, 131, 167–68, 182, 184–85, 197, 200–206
Christian faith, viii–ix, 93–94, 103, 136, 138, 145, 147–48, 165, 174, 180, 186, 218
Christian phenomenon, 132, 134
Christian tradition, 127, 131, 141, 162, 169, 174–75, 177–78, 196, 205
Christogenesis, 137, 143, 147
Christology, 127, 164–65, 203
church, viii, 93, 134, 164, 173, 178, 210
See also Church of England; Roman Catholic Church
Church of England, vii, ix, 167, 176
coaction, 105
communion, 103, 111, 113, 136–37, 139, 145, 148, 181, 213
community, 26, 66, 73, 90–91, 93, 105
complexity, xii, 11, 13, 21, 28, 42, 68–69, 74, 122, 127, 133–34, 136–37, 147, 156–59, 163, 168, 174, 191, 209
concept, 15, 19, 26, 33, 41, 43, 48, 53, 63, 66–69, 79, 83–84, 87, 91, 118, 120, 128, 130, 143, 150, 152–56, 166, 168, 173, 190, 193, 200, 210–11
conception, 16–17, 19, 21, 62, 79, 82–83, 85–86, 94, 100, 124, 136, 149, 200, 214
conceptual framework/structure/system, viii–ix, 13–15, 17, 19–20, 26, 33, 53, 62–64, 67–70, 76, 79, 84–85, 88–89, 91–92, 110–15, 121, 129, 134, 140, 145, 149, 157, 163, 166, 173, 177, 190, 193, 196, 201, 203, 210–11, 213–14, 217–18
See also frame of reference
concrescence, 155–56
configuration, xii, 14, 109–113, 128, 192, 195, 213
See also action in patterns
consciousness, 27, 80–82, 86–88, 90–92, 94–99, 104–5, 120, 122, 133–38, 142–43, 164, 197
Christic/cosmic, 137

consistency, 13, 19, 28, 49, 52, 66, 68, 84, 87, 107–8, 112–13, 171, 173, 196, 199, 213, 216
contemplation, 65–66, 76, 127, 147, 158, 216
context, viii, 2, 8, 11, 17, 21, 60, 64, 67, 72, 75, 88, 90–91, 93, 104, 109–10, 119, 137, 144, 163, 173, 192–93, 195–96, 198, 200, 208–9, 216–18
contingency, 83, 89, 93, 109, 166, 184
continuity, viii, xi, 6, 11, 15, 18, 20, 23, 25–27, 31–32, 43, 49, 61, 65–66, 68, 71, 73, 76, 86, 90, 93, 105, 108, 112, 115–19, 121–22, 124, 126, 128–30, 132, 143, 157–59, 161, 168, 200–202, 205–8, 213–14, 217
cosmology, 35, 44, 131–32, 135, 139, 141, 143, 145, 148–49, 163, 214
cosmos. *See kósmos*
creation, 114, 121, 124, 127, 137, 142, 165, 181, 184, 188
creativity, 108, 110, 113, 118, 124, 129, 137, 155, 161, 213
creator, 47–49, 71, 165, 169, 197, 212
criticism, 90, 100–101, 111, 140–41, 191
cross, the, 141–42, 167, 172, 179–80, 182–87
culture, 61, 87–88, 90–93, 199, 203

dēmiourgós, Demiurge (craftsman), 43, 47–48
definition, 1–13, 23, 27, 40, 49–51, 53, 56, 63–66, 68, 83, 92, 106, 108–9, 116–17, 127–28, 133, 140, 149–50, 158, 161, 163, 165–67, 171, 173–74, 195–97, 200, 210–12, 214–15, 217
democracy, 38
Democritus, 33
demythologizing, 206
determinism, 104–5, 124
Dewey, John, 152
dialectic, 36, 39, 42, 80–101, 104, 109, 172, 212–13, 216
dialogue, 38–40, 46–47, 112

dictionary, 2–5, 10–11, 17
dimensions, 13, 26, 121, 153
Diogenes, 33
disposition, 157–58
distinction, 7, 12–13, 15, 21–22, 29, 34, 46, 48–49, 57–58, 62, 64, 78, 83, 114, 151, 163, 169, 209–212, 214, 216–17
diversity, vii–ix, 1, 6–8, 10–13, 18–23, 25–38, 41, 45, 49–50, 53–54, 59, 61–63, 66–69, 78, 83, 88–89, 100, 108, 110, 124–26, 128, 130, 133, 175, 188, 189–90, 193, 195–97, 199, 203–4, 208, 210–12, 216–18
divinity, 29, 32, 65–66, 72–73, 77–79, 92, 103, 110–11, 127, 131, 135–37, 139, 142, 145, 153, 163–66, 169, 182
    See also God
divisibility, 33, 46, 78, 85, 90, 108, 116–17, 120
drama, 4, 91
dualism, 40, 77, 119
duality, 7, 45, 92, 132, 168
dúnāmis (potentiality), 58–59, 62, 67
    See also potency/potentiality
durée (duration), 116–28, 133
dynamic, the, viii, 1, 7–8, 11–13, 18–19, 32, 35, 72, 77, 82, 85, 93, 114, 118–19, 127, 129, 152, 160–61, 168–70, 173–74, 188, 210–11, 214, 217–18

earth, 30–31, 52, 55, 137, 139, 142, 181
Earth, the, 2, 6, 35, 98, 137, 139, 142, 145–47, 178, 181, 186–87
eîdos (form), 41, 51–54, 67
    See also form (Aristotelian); Form (Platonic)
Einstein, Albert, 18, 119–21, 125–26, 128
élan vital, 36, 121–22, 124, 127–29, 136
electricity, 123
elements, 30–31, 45, 60, 114, 116–19, 133, 137–38, 146–47
empirical, 69, 87, 99, 108, 147

enérgeia (activity, actualization), 16, 57–59, 62, 65–70, 76–77, 212
energy, 3, 18, 59, 66, 76, 97, 105, 119, 121, 125, 131, 133, 142, 146–47, 153, 156, 180, 212
English (language), 2, 17, 58, 76, 212
entelékheia, entelechy (actuality), 55–57, 59, 151
entity, 8, 24, 26–29, 43–44, 62, 113, 121, 153–58, 160–61, 163–64, 168–69
epi-phenomenon, 134
equality, 8, 28, 33, 35, 37, 39, 65, 83, 118, 120, 152–53, 196
eros (love), 35
esse (essence), essence, *essentia* (essence), 16, 24, 39, 41–43, 45, 51–54, 56, 61–63, 65–67, 72–76, 78, 87, 89–92, 94, 96, 99, 101, 106, 134, 152, 156, 166, 169, 173–74, 181, 182, 188, 191, 194, 197, 100, 205
estin (it is), 21–26, 28, 57, 69, 78, 137
eternity, 24, 32, 44–48, 64–66, 73, 77, 88, 111, 115, 126, 160, 163, 165–66, 168–70, 181, 184, 186, 188, 212, 215
ethics, 87, 118, 124, 162, 171
Eucharist, the, 132, 136, 147, 181, 187, 215
event, 1–2, 14, 26–27, 33, 43, 56, 61, 64, 117, 120–21, 130, 152–53, 155, 157–58, 160–61, 163, 166–67, 181, 192, 202–3, 205, 207
evil, 141, 146, 166, 177, 181–82
evolution, 97–98, 102, 111, 115, 118–19, 121–22, 125, 129, 132–38, 140, 142–44, 147, 149, 152, 159, 161, 189, 199, 201–9, 212–15
existence, existent, 14, 16, 22–29, 39–42, 44–46, 48, 50–51, 53, 55–56, 58–60, 62–63, 65, 67–69, 72–78, 83, 88–89, 92–94, 96–99, 103, 107, 109–110, 113–19, 124, 133, 135, 138, 142, 144, 151–53, 155–57, 159,

INDEX   241

162, 170, 173, 190, 198, 207, 212, 218
experience, vii–viii, xii, 14, 17–18, 21, 25, 28, 30–33, 36, 38–39, 41, 43, 45–46, 48, 54, 61, 64, 66–69, 71, 76, 79–80, 82, 84–86, 89, 93–95, 103, 106, 108–109, 116–17, 120–23, 125–29, 132–35, 140–42, 149, 152–55, 161, 166, 168, 173–74, 176=77, 179–80, 182–83, 189, 194, 196–97, 200–203, 205, 205, 209, 214, 216–17
extensity, 75, 111, 117, 119–20, 138, 142, 202

facts, 15–17, 24, 39, 41, 45, 54, 61–62, 66, 76, 90, 103–4, 106, 112, 145, 153–55, 190, 192, 195, 198, 202, 206–7
family likeness/resemblance, 2, 8–13, 193–94, 196–98, 208
family of occurrences, 158
fire, 24, 29, 31–32, 34–35, 42, 52, 55, 84, 114–15, 145–49, 156, 178, 211–12, 214
    See also pûr (fire)
First World War. *See* war
flow, 26, 29–30, 61, 84, 115, 118, 120, 129–30, 133, 138, 143, 145, 158, 160–61, 173
flux. *See* flow
force, 3, 7, 10–11, 59, 86, 98, 121, 129, 132, 152, 166, 172–73, 181
foreknowledge, 161
form (Aristotelian), 51–56, 59–61, 63–67, 69–70, 74, 88, 92, 124, 156–57, 200, 202
    See also eîdos (form)
Form (Platonic), 40–45, 47, 49, 69, 78–79, 103, 112, 213
    See also eîdos (form)
forms of life, 40, 192, 195–98
frame of reference, 193, 196–97
    See also conceptual framework/structure/system
framework, conceptual. *See* conceptual framework/structure/system

freedom, 104–5, 118, 121, 124–25, 127–29, 164, 174
future, the, 14, 23, 25, 36, 108, 118, 121, 124, 127, 133, 135, 138–39, 144, 156

Geist (Mind, Spirit), 36, 80–82, 84, 87–91, 93, 95, 97, 99–100, 212–13
    See also Mind; Spirit
geology, 131, 140
God, vii, 19, 32–33, 35, 43–44, 47–49, 64–67, 70–73, 75–77, 79, 92–95, 106, 109–13, 127, 129, 131–32, 135–40, 142, 145–49, 150–53, 157, 159–75, 176–88, 195–99, 206, 209, 212–17
    suffering of, vii, 142, 159, 162, 167, 169, 172–73, 176–88, 215–16
    See also divinity
god, 29, 33, 35, 38, 44, 47, 106, 181
Good (Platonic Form), vii, 39–40, 42–43, 45, 48–49, 54, 65, 69, 76–78
grace, 163, 172, 188
Grayling, A.C., 192, 198
Greek (language), 16–17, 23–24, 38, 42–43, 50, 52, 78, 133
Griffin, David Ray, 165

Hamilton, Peter, 164, 169
Hanson, Anthony, 148
happiness, 65–66
harmony, 6, 44, 48, 100–101, 114, 135, 151
Hartshorne, Charles, 156, 161, 163, 165–66, 169, 171–72
Hebrew (language), 17
Hegel, Georg Wilhelm, 36, 80–101, 104, 112–13, 152, 204, 209, 212–13, 216
Heraclitus, 16, 21, 29–36, 37, 59, 61, 68, 78–79, 84, 92, 114–15, 147, 149, 151, 156, 211–12, 214
Heschel, Abraham, 169
Hesiod, 35–36, 78–79, 211
heteronomy, 104
    See also autonomy

history, 18, 49, 58, 80, 85, 88–93, 97–101, 107, 111, 124, 132, 139, 152, 156, 163–69, 173, 178, 180, 184, 198, 201–205, 207, 209–10, 213, 216
Holy Spirit, 72, 197
hominization, 134–35, 143
homogeneity, 118, 124, 126, 133
húlē (matter), 51, 67
human being. *See* being, human
humanity, 62, 96, 105, 127, 129, 137, 142, 185

idea (Form, Idea), 41, 82, 93, 151
idealism, 82, 98–100, 111
ideology, 98–99
immanence, 94, 108, 161, 164, 168–69, 171, 174–75, 201
immobility, 116, 123, 129–30
in actu, 37, 70, 73, 75–77, 212
  See also actual, actuality; *actus* (actuality)
incarnation, 93, 136–38, 147, 165, 169, 182, 185, 202
incommensurability, 7, 12, 109, 125
individual, ix–x, 9, 50, 52–54, 74, 87–88, 90–91, 94–95, 97–99, 103, 105, 108, 118, 122–23, 133, 139, 146, 154, 158, 173, 181, 192, 197, 211
Industrial Christian Fellowship, 181
infinity, vii, 2, 33, 43, 71, 109, 162, 166
innovation, 121, 131, 156–57, 201, 204
intellect, 7, 40, 42, 44, 69, 89, 98, 119, 123, 128, 143–45, 174
  See also mind
intelligibility, 14, 25, 31–32, 41–42, 67, 74, 111, 114, 202
interdependence, 109, 153
intuition, 10–11, 82–83, 85, 115, 130
invisible. *See* visible/invisible
Iqbal, Muhammad, 129, 130

James, William, 152, 196
Jesuits. *See* Society of Jesus
Jesus, 127, 142, 160, 162, 164–65, 168–69, 178, 180–85, 187–88, 197, 202, 205, 215

Justice (Platonic Form), 40, 43, 54, 76–77
Justin Martyr, vii, 20

Kant, Immanuel, 85–86, 92, 115, 118, 122
kenosis (emptying), 162
kínēsis (motion), 16, 43–48, 54–62, 64–65, 68, 70, 77, 212
  See also motion
Kingdom of God, 89, 149
knowledge, 16, 29, 36, 38–40, 42, 50, 73, 76, 80–82, 85–86, 88–90, 92, 94, 99, 107, 109, 115, 125, 145, 158, 161, 171, 193, 196, 202–3, 207
koinōnía (community), 26
kósmos (ordering, world), 29, 31, 33–34

labor, 96, 104
language, 2, 15, 17, 20, 36, 53–54, 63, 67–68, 72–73, 76, 91, 111–12, 136, 146, 157, 163, 169, 171–74, 179, 189–99, 208–9, 212, 214–18
language game, 174, 192–98, 209
layers, xi–xii, 106, 126, 166, 214
Leibniz, Gottfried Wilhelm, 151–52
Lessing, Gotthold, 166
Leucippus, 33
Levinas, Emmanuel, 124
liberty. *See* freedom
life, 27, 38, 44, 65–66, 72, 77–78, 86, 96–99, 103–6, 111–12, 117, 120–24, 127, 129–30, 132–35, 137, 140, 142, 144, 156, 164, 173–74, 176, 180–81, 183, 185–86, 189, 192–99, 201, 212
  See also forms of life
light, xii, 31, 120, 126, 128
locomotion. *See* motion
logic, ix, 22, 34, 48, 67, 71, 82–85, 87, 89, 92, 173, 190–91, 197, 205, 211
logos (word, argument, reason, account), 29, 31–34, 36, 84, 165
Lorentz equations, 120

love, 4, 35, 48, 71–72, 111, 113, 138, 162, 164, 167, 170, 172, 181, 184–86, 213, 215

Major, Henry, 176, 178
Malebranche, 151
many, the, 12, 23, 25, 30, 32, 39, 45, 89, 110, 145, 155, 159
  See also one/One, the
Marx, Karl, 18, 36, 81, 95–101, 212–13, 216
Mass on the World, the, 136, 138, 145, 147–48
Mass, the. *See* Eucharist
materialism, 33, 99–100
matter, 33, 51–54, 56, 59–61, 63–65, 67, 70, 73–74, 116, 119–20, 123–24, 132–36, 138, 142–43, 147, 156
means of production, 96–97, 99
memory, 30, 118, 120
metaphor, 7, 30–31, 41, 75–76, 79
metaphysic/metaphysics, viii–x, 6–7, 12–13, 15–16, 20, 28–29, 33–34, 36, 39, 49, 52, 57, 59, 64–70, 78–79, 82, 91–93, 99–100, 102, 108–9, 111–112, 115, 122–23, 127, 129, 135, 139–40, 143, 145, 147–52, 155, 157, 159, 162, 166–68, 172–73, 175, 203, 210–14, 216–18
Michelson-Morley experiment, 120
milieu, 131, 135–36, 139, 142, 204, 208
Mind, 80, 87, 90, 97, 100–101
  See also Geist; Spirit
mind, viii, xi, xii, 9, 13–14, 22, 33, 35, 41, 80, 83, 85, 90, 97, 101, 116, 118–19, 121, 131, 133, 145, 156, 204
  See also psukhḗ (mind, soul)
mobilities, 116
Moltmann, Jürgen, 167, 169, 172
moment (dialectical), 84, 86, 89–90, 92–93
moment (time), 25, 27, 30, 105, 107–8, 118, 120, 133, 137–38, 153
monad/monadology, 138, 151–53
monism, 28

Moral Sciences Club, 207–8
morality, 9, 99, 105, 122, 182
motion, xi, 6–8, 11, 16, 28, 30, 33, 38, 43–48, 54–64, 66, 68–73, 77–79, 82, 119–21, 126, 129, 156, 173, 207, 212
  See also movement
movement, viii, 1, 5–8, 10–13, 15–16, 18–19, 28, 37, 48, 54–55, 57–59, 61, 65, 69, 71–73, 79, 83–84, 86, 100, 105, 110, 115–19, 122–28, 135, 137, 159, 174–75, 210–11, 216–18
  See also motion
mover, first/unmoved, 65–66, 71–72, 138
mystery, 127, 129, 133
mysticism, 125, 127, 139, 142

name, 8–10, 16, 24, 26, 32, 39, 41, 50, 77, 132, 152, 156
narrative, 18–19, 98, 112, 173–74, 177, 217–18
nature (natural world), 32–33, 47, 55, 96, 99, 100–101, 105, 124, 130, 144, 152, 157, 168, 184
  See also phúsis (nature)
negation, 50, 86–87, 94–99, 172
neo-orthodoxy, 165
neoplatonism, 45
New Testament, ix, 137, 146–47
Newton, Isaac, 119
nexus, 154–58
noogenesis, 138
noosphere, 133–34, 140
noumenon, 85, 115
noun, 1, 3–6, 15–17, 28, 43, 48–49, 76–77, 79, 95, 157, 212
novelty, 119, 125, 155–57, 161

object, xi, 14–15, 17–18, 26, 30, 33, 40–46, 52, 65, 76–77, 85–88, 91, 93–94, 96–97, 109, 120, 122, 138, 151, 153, 155, 162–64, 166, 171, 192, 200, 207
objectification, 88, 95–96
objectivity, 27, 81–83, 85–86, 91–92, 147, 174

occasionalism, 151
omega point, 132–35, 137–38, 140, 142, 145, 147, 149, 214
omnipotence, 162, 183
ón, tò (*tò ón*, being), 28, 49–50, 69, 78
   See also being
one/One, the, vii, 12, 23, 32, 49, 69, 145
   See also many, the
ontology, 16–17, 20, 26, 34, 76, 91, 94, 96, 101, 103, 107–8, 112, 143, 157–58, 172, 188, 207
operation, 3, 4, 66, 71–72, 105, 212
opinion, 24, 26, 36, 40, 42, 78, 174
opposite, opposition, 6–8, 11–13, 29, 32, 34, 36, 39–40, 56, 61, 83–84, 86–87, 89, 91, 93, 95–96, 98, 100, 115, 135, 191
organic, organism, 105, 134, 151, 156
organization, 9, 89, 104, 122, 152, 158
Origen, vii
Other, the, 124
ousía (substance), 42, 46, 50–54, 59, 62, 67
   See also substance

pacifism, 179
Pailin, David, 165–67
pain, 90, 141, 149, 178, 179–81, 183, 186–87
palaeontology, 131
pan-Christism, 132
panentheism, 167, 172
pantheism, 124, 161
paradeígma (pattern), 41, 43, 52, 79
   See also action in patterns
paradigm, 43, 63, 171, 173–74, 201, 214, 218
Parmenides, 21–29, 32–37, 68, 78–79, 84, 88, 92, 211
participation, 9, 12, 39, 41–43, 45–46, 48–49, 69, 73, 76–78, 84, 103, 120, 160, 162, 172, 195, 212
particle, xi, 116, 129, 152–53, 156–57, 171, 173
particularity, particulars, 40, 52–53, 63, 81, 87, 93, 123, 158, 160, 192
passibilism, 176
past, the, 23, 25, 88, 116–19, 127, 153, 202, 206
pattern. See action in patterns
pattern, changing. See action in changing patterns
patterns of action. See action in patterns
Paul, St., 127, 178, 180
Peirce, Charles, 152, 158
perception, 43, 86–87, 112, 116, 121–23, 128–29, 139, 151, 207
persistence, 157, 200, 208
person, personal, 5–6, 13, 23, 30, 32, 38–39, 54, 63, 87–88, 103, 113, 116, 120, 124, 126, 128, 133, 135, 142, 147, 155, 157, 160, 164, 166, 168–69, 178–79, 205, 213
perturbations, 119, 126
phenomenology, 87, 89–90, 103, 107, 143
phenomenon, 85–86, 105–7, 115, 125, 132, 134–35, 141, 143–44, 152, 159, 194, 207
philosophy (Western), vii–ix, 12–13, 18–21, 24, 27, 29–30, 33–34, 36–37, 40, 42, 45, 47, 49–50, 58, 67–70, 76–77, 79–80, 85, 88, 90–93, 95, 98, 101–2, 104, 109, 111–15, 121, 124–25, 127, 129–31, 133, 139, 143, 145, 147–48, 150, 163, 176–77, 189–91, 193–94, 196, 198–204, 206–8, 210–14, 216–18
   See also process philosophy
phúsis (nature), 33, 69
   See also nature (natural world)
physical, the, 72, 105, 136, 143, 151
Pittenger, Norman, 153, 160–64
plants, 52, 55, 201
Plato, vii–viii, 13, 16, 29, 34, 36–49, 52–54, 62, 68–70, 76–79, 88, 103, 112, 127, 136, 145, 149, 151, 159, 161, 166, 173, 212–13
Plotinus, 69
pluralism, religious, viii, 168
plurality, 11, 27, 50, 86, 133, 139
polarity, 126, 160, 166–67, 169, 172, 174

potency/potentiality, 5, 7, 43, 55–60, 63, 65–66, 71–73, 75–77, 142, 157, 166, 212, 217
  See also dúnāmis (potentiality)
pragmatism, 152
praxis, 100
prayer, 164, 172, 177, 181, 188
predicate, 24, 40, 43, 50–51, 78
prehension, 153–55, 161, 163, 165
present, the, 23, 25, 27, 44, 107, 117, 119, 124
priest, 131, 139–40, 176–77
prime mover. *See* mover, first/unmoved
principle, 30, 49–50, 55–56, 58–60, 69, 72–75, 84, 114, 122, 136–37, 150, 155–58, 160, 162, 168, 172, 176, 197–98, 200
process, 3–6, 10, 14, 18, 23, 30, 39–40, 42, 44, 49, 55–58, 61, 80–82, 84–87, 89–91, 95, 98–101, 117–19, 121, 132–35, 139, 142–44, 195, 200–201, 204–7, 209, 213, 218
  philosophy, 130, 150–75, 214
  See also philosophy
  theism, 170–71
  See also theism
  theology, viii–ix, 159–75, 206, 216
  See also theology
progress, 5, 90, 105, 122, 141–44, 156, 183–84, 206
prototype, 8–9
psukhḗ (mind, soul), 41, 48, 54
  See also mind; soul
psychic, the, 122, 138, 143–44, 152
psychism, 137–38
psychology, 14, 90, 105, 115, 118–20, 122, 128
psychophysics, 124
pūr (fire), 29, 31–32, 34–35, 40, 84
  See also fire
purpose, 29, 31, 40, 56, 62, 64, 73, 82, 85, 87, 90, 110, 118, 129–30, 133–34, 143–44, 149, 165, 167, 170, 217

quality, 4, 8, 49, 55, 58–59, 61, 70–71, 100, 117, 135, 153
quantity, 55, 59, 61, 70–71, 117–18
quantum physics, 158, 171
Quran, the, 129

Ramsey, Frank, 191
reason, 22, 29, 31, 33–34, 40, 42, 44, 48, 56, 66, 72, 76, 82, 84, 87–88, 104, 106, 108, 110, 130, 151, 195
reconciliation, 33–34, 86, 94–95, 102, 111, 118–21, 125, 131, 136–39, 141, 144–45, 148–49, 157, 167, 169
redemption, 169, 178, 184, 187, 205
reinterpretation, 200
relativity, 18, 119–21, 125–26, 160
religion, vii–ix, 80, 87–88, 92–95, 98–99, 102–3, 106, 110, 127, 131, 139, 141, 144–45, 163–64, 171–72, 174, 176–77, 195–97, 200–201, 213, 215
Rescher, Nicholas, 150–52, 154, 156–60
rest, viii, 1, 7, 11–13, 18–19, 28, 30, 37, 43, 58–59, 62, 69, 78, 91, 129, 210–11, 216–17
resurrection, 142, 172, 180–81
revelation, 132, 139, 164, 167, 172
revolution, 44, 48, 98–101, 171, 174
rhetoric, 67
river, 29–30, 34, 61
Robinson, John, 167, 169–70, 172, 175
Roman Catholic Church, 102, 104, 111, 131, 140, 177
Rosch, Eleanor, 8
Russell, Bertrand, 207–8

Saint-Serin, Bernard, 104
scepticism, 28, 112
science, 16, 33, 43, 50, 67, 77, 79, 89, 91, 98, 102–3, 105–6, 112, 115, 122–23, 131, 140–41, 145, 148, 150, 161, 173, 199, 207–8, 218
self-consciousness. *See* consciousness
senses, 22, 43, 46, 49, 85–87, 89, 114
sign, 31, 194, 201

simultaneity, 14, 117–18, 120, 128
social order, 98, 180–81
society, vii, 4, 35, 96, 98, 100, 122, 142, 173, 201, 218
Society of Jesus, the, 140
Socrates, 39–40, 53–54, 67
soul, 38–42, 44, 47–48, 54, 144, 147, 151, 181–82, 187
  See also psukhḗ (mind, soul); world soul
space, 15, 23, 27, 48, 77, 86, 108, 112, 117–23, 125–28, 130, 144, 158, 173, 213–14, 216
space-time, 26–27, 34, 121, 128
species, 52–54, 60, 62, 66–67, 73–74
spectrum, viii, 5–6, 13, 15, 21, 23–24, 27–29, 34–35, 45–50, 55, 63–66, 68–71, 76, 78, 96, 153, 157, 159, 210–12, 216–18
speech, 40, 46
Spinoza, 28
Spirit, 36, 80, 88–90, 92, 94, 97, 100, 138–39, 188
  See also Geist; Holy Spirit; Mind
spirit, spiritual, 88–90, 94, 97, 105, 129, 139–41, 184
St. John's College, Cambridge, viii, x, 199
stability, 14, 21, 36, 64, 77, 116, 140, 149, 214, 217
static, the, viii, 1, 6–7, 11–13, 18–19, 57–59, 63, 86, 91, 116, 118, 125, 129, 149, 153, 156, 161, 168, 173, 210–11, 217–18
structure, 12, 76, 80, 84, 97, 130, 144, 156, 158, 169
  See also conceptual framework/structure/system; superstructure
Studdert Kennedy, Geoffrey, 142, 176–88, 215–16
subject, 17, 23–24, 26, 30, 32, 50–51, 55, 82, 155, 162–63, 171
subjectivity, 83, 104, 119, 124
sublation, 84, 86–87, 93, 95
substance, 25, 29, 49–55, 59–67, 78, 103, 106, 115, 117, 150–52, 156–57, 168, 173, 200
  See also ousía (substance)
substrate, substratum, 26, 51–52, 56, 117
succession, 6, 14, 110, 117, 120, 200
suffering, vii, 141–42, 146, 162–64, 166, 172, 175–88, 215–16
  See also God, suffering of
supernatural, 106, 205
superstructure, 98
synthesis, 48, 105, 119, 131–32, 135, 140, 154–55, 201
system, systematic, 33, 40, 50, 53, 66–67, 69, 84, 88–89, 97, 114–16, 119, 133, 140, 149, 157–58, 168, 190–91, 193, 198, 202, 205–6
  See also conceptual framework/structure/system

Teilhard de Chardin, Pierre, 129, 131–49, 161, 164, 168, 172, 176–77, 206, 209, 214, 216
telos (final cause), 56–57, 59, 63, 78
temporal, temporary. *See* time
tension, 32, 65, 101, 119
theism, 109, 161, 166, 170–71
  See also process theism
theocosmology, 148–49, 214
theology, vii–x, 14, 19–20, 49, 65, 69–73, 75, 92–93, 102, 108, 110–13, 126–27, 131–32, 135–37, 139–45, 148–49, 176–78, 180, 182–88, 195, 198–99, 201, 204–6, 209–10, 214–16, 218
  See also process theology
theorem, 134
theory, 16–18, 30, 33, 40, 42–43, 49, 52, 62–64, 70, 88–89, 94, 99–100, 109, 111, 119–21, 125–26, 147, 171, 191, 205
things, xi–xii, 4–6, 10–11, 13–16, 18, 21, 23–34, 36, 39–43, 45–46, 49–51, 54–60, 62–69, 72, 75–77, 79, 85–86, 93, 110, 113–118, 123, 128, 136, 139, 146, 149–51, 153, 156–60, 169, 172, 174, 178, 183, 187, 197, 202, 212, 214

third man argument, 43
time, 1, 8, 10, 22, 24–28, 30, 32, 34, 39, 43–46, 48–49, 53, 57–58, 63–64, 75, 84, 86, 88, 90, 103, 107–8, 112, 115–23, 125–28, 130, 132, 137, 152, 156, 158, 160–61, 163, 166, 181, 184, 202, 205, 207, 212–14, 216
  See also space-time
totality, totalization, 14, 19, 27, 62, 69, 84, 89, 95, 103, 107–8, 112–13, 124, 136–37, 139, 162, 173, 175, 193, 213
trajectory, 36, 101, 213
transcendence, vii, 42, 45, 54, 66, 69, 85, 93, 108, 138, 151, 163–64, 169–70, 172–75
transformation, 4, 95, 98, 114–15, 133, 154, 168, 172
transition, 6, 38, 62, 119, 152, 155, 210
Trinity, the, 94, 113, 153, 160, 169–70, 197, 213
True, the, 43, 69, 88, 95
truth, 22, 26, 32, 36, 46, 69, 82–84, 86, 89, 108, 167, 178, 196, 202–3

unchanging, the, vii–viii, xii, 1, 7, 11–13, 15, 18–25, 27–29, 32–38, 45–49, 62–65, 67–69, 71, 78, 103, 116, 126, 145, 151, 153, 157, 159, 163, 166–69, 171, 173, 189–90, 198, 200, 202, 206, 210–11, 216–18
  See also changeless
uncreated, 23, 35–36
understanding, xii, 4, 7, 11, 15, 18, 21, 23–26, 28, 36, 42–43, 64, 66, 68, 70–71, 77, 79–81, 85–87, 89, 91–94, 100–101, 106–8, 120–21, 127–29, 131, 133, 136, 140, 145, 148–49, 152, 156, 159, 164, 166, 173–76, 182, 197, 203–4, 208–9, 213–16
uniformity, 46
unitary, the, viii, 12, 19, 21, 23, 154, 156, 188–89, 210–11, 217–18
unity, 12–13, 24, 26, 29, 31–38, 41, 45, 49–50, 54, 62–63, 67–69, 77–78, 84, 86–88, 90, 93, 95, 103, 105, 108, 113, 122, 133, 137, 143, 146, 164, 166, 200, 203–5, 211, 213, 216–17
universals, 2, 34, 52, 54, 70, 76, 81–82, 87, 93–94, 103–4, 112, 114–15, 120–21, 128, 135, 137–38, 142, 146, 155–56, 165, 198, 212–13
universe, 1, 14, 19, 26, 30–31, 33, 44, 48–49, 52, 67, 69, 95, 105–6, 108, 110, 118, 120–21, 125–30, 135–38, 142–45, 147–49, 151, 156, 159, 161, 173, 175, 202, 209, 212
unmoved mover. *See* mover, first/unmoved
usage, definition by. *See* definition

verb, 1, 3–5, 7, 15–17, 23–24, 26, 28, 34, 42, 48–49, 54, 76–79, 95, 157, 212
visible/invisible, 40, 42–44, 90, 108, 146

war, 32, 38, 114, 141–42, 148, 176, 178–79, 181–84
water, waterfall, 1, 15, 24, 29–31, 52, 55, 60–61
Whitehead, Alfred North, 13, 130, 150–75, 204, 206–7, 214, 216
whole, the, 53, 82, 193, 195, 197, 200, 202–3, 209, 216
Whyte, Lancelot Law, 156–57
will, the, 104
Williams, Rowan, 18
within, the (of matter), 143
Wittgenstein, Ludwig, 2, 189–99, 207–9, 216
word, 2, 6–8, 10–14, 16, 25–26, 31, 33–34, 39, 43, 50, 52–53, 56, 59, 61–62, 69, 72–73, 75, 77, 95, 109, 117, 154, 164–65, 168, 173, 190–96, 198, 200–201, 208, 213
Word, incarnate, 169
Word of God, 72, 95, 165, 185
worker, 96–97
working class, 97, 99

world, xi–xii, 8, 18, 27, 31–35, 38–39, 41–44, 46–48, 54, 62–63, 66–69, 72–73, 85–86, 92–93, 95, 97, 100, 103, 106, 108, 117–18, 122, 127, 131–36, 138–39, 141, 145–48, 151–56, 159–77, 180–81, 183–85, 188, 190, 197–98, 200, 202–7, 209–10, 215–18

world soul, 16, 44
worldview, 136, 203

Xenophanes, 22, 29–30

Zeno, 28

www.ingramcontent.com/pod-product-compliance
Lightning Source LLC
Chambersburg PA
CBHW051634230426
43669CB00013B/2294